# THE CYBER LEADERSHIP IMPERATIVE

POWERFUL STRATEGIES TO UNLOCK
YOUR POTENTIAL AND BECOME
AN EXCEPTIONAL CYBERSECURITY
EXECUTIVE

Phillimon Zongo
Darren Argyle
Jan Schreuder

First published in 2024 by Cyber Resilience Pty Ltd T/A Cyber Leadership Institute
Copyright © 2024 Cyber Leadership Institute
The moral rights of the authors have been asserted.

ISBN: 978-1-7635999-9-4 (Paperback)
ISBN: 978-1-7636564-0-6 (Ebook)

Produced by Cyber Leadership Institute
Layout, typesetting and cover design by WorkingType Studio
A catalogue record for this book is available from the National Library of Australia

A catalogue record for this book is available from the National Library of Australia

*This book is dedicated to our rapidly growing and closely bonded community of cyber leaders, without whose trust and support we would not have built the Cyber Leadership Institute.*

# Contents

# Prologue – Crisis Creates Exceptional Leaders

History is an excellent guide. Throughout the ages, whenever the future of humanity has been at stake, exceptional leaders have risen to defeat evil and pull humanity out of great despair.

Here, the remarkable story of Nzinga, the queen of Ndongo and Matamba, present-day Angola, stands out supreme. Few leaders have had as profound an effect on their time as Queen Nzinga. She was born around 1583 to Ngola Kilombo Kia Kasenda, the king of Ndongo, and one of his concubines. Her name reflected the difficulty her mother endured during labour, in which Nzinga was born with the umbilical cord wrapped around her neck.

Nzinga was born at a time of incredible change, anguish and upheaval when the Portuguese Empire was fast encroaching deeper into her kingdom, having almost depleted the southwest African population whom they shipped to the Americas as enslaved people. During the governorship of Luís Mendes de Vasconcellos, an estimated 50,000 Angolans were enslaved and shipped across the Atlantic. All in all, approximately 12 million Africans were forcibly captured from their land and transported to the Americas as human property.

Showing extraordinary leadership potential and physical prowess from a young age, Nzinga was trained as a warrior and fought many battles alongside her father. She was also allowed to sit in court sessions alongside him to nurture her leadership potential.

Nzinga's brother, Ngola Mbandi, took over the throne when

King Ndongo died around 1617. But Mbandi's reign would prove tumultuous. His ineptitude was severely exposed by the relentless Portuguese attacks, which forced him to move his kingdom further west to the Kindonga Islands. Finally, Mbandi had no option but to dispatch the young Nzinga to the capital to negotiate a peace treaty with the Portuguese.

When Nzinga entered the Portuguese courtyard, she was instructed to sit on the floor while the Portuguese delegation sat on elevated chairs. Nzinga refused to bow, instructing one of her many servants to bend over and serve as a chair, sending an unequivocal message that she wasn't beneath the colonisers, her culture wasn't inferior, and she would only negotiate on equal footing.

Nzinga would tactfully deploy her diplomatic skills over the next six months. She agreed to be baptised and took on a Christian name (Ana de Sousa) in exchange for a peace treaty in which the Portuguese agreed to withdraw their forces and help her kingdom fend off a myriad of mercenary groups. She returned from the capital to Ndongo to a hero's welcome.

When her brother died in 1624, Nzinga quickly took reign as the queen of Ndongo. She would soon distinguish herself as a political and military genius, using her outstanding skills in diplomacy, warfare, espionage and commerce to forge numerous strategic alliances. She kept Ndongo's enemies at bay for more than four decades despite inferior weaponry, becoming one of the most enduring symbols of African resistance against colonisation.

By 1626, however, the Portuguese had violated the peace treaty and attacked Ndongo. This forced Nzinga to flee further inland, where she founded the new state of Matamba and offered a sanctuary to thousands of runaway enslaved people. To reclaim Ndongo, she negotiated an alliance with the Dutch, as well as other militia groups, notably the fierce Imbangala warriors. Even in her sixties, Nzinga still fearlessly led her forces into battle. The Dutch seized Luanda for its own commercial purposes in 1641, but the combined forces were insufficient to dislodge the Portuguese out of Angola completely. When the Portuguese recaptured Luanda, Nzinga was again forced to retreat to Matamba. She would spend the rest of her reign developing Matamba into a commercial powerhouse and a key gateway into Central Africa. By the time Nzinga passed away in 1663, she had transformed Matamba into a formidable commercial state on equal footing with the Portuguese.

Nzinga's story gained international fame with the publication in Paris in 1769 of Jean-Louis Castilhon's biography, *Zingha, Reine d'Angola*. Her life of fierce resistance to human oppression, disregard for engendered norms and unwavering commitment to her people continues to inspire people around the world today. It illustrates the prime importance of decisive leadership as an antidote to chaos and profound hopelessness.

But Nzinga's leadership legend is not unique. From Chief Rāwiri Puhirake (1850s) in New Zealand to Sitting Bull (1830s) in South Dakota, from Martin Luther King Jr. (1960s) in the US to Nelson Mandela (1970s) in South Africa – these remarkable stories demonstrate the power of firm conviction and decisive leadership to overcome unthinkable obstacles, defeat evil and fundamentally alter the course of history. The same stories also illustrate an important point – leadership is defined by teachable principles that can be mastered and applied across many domains.

These enduring narratives also serve as a reminder that with the right mindset, great leaders emerge out of global crises. In the words of **Joshua Rothman**, 'For great leadership to exist, a leader must cross paths with a crisis; an exemplary person must meet her 'sinister mate.' Without an answering crisis, a would-be leader remains just a promising custodian of potential.'[1]

Today, we stand at the precipice of the digital space. The future is at stake. The internet represents the epitome of human ingenuity.

Generative AI is responding to emails, preparing tax returns, recording metal songs, writing pitch decks, debugging code, sketching architectural blueprints and providing health advice. **Cities around the world** are creating ecosystems of IoT (Internet of Things) and OT (operational technology) to increase operational efficiencies, enhance safety and optimise resources.[2]

IoT devices are also radically shaping the future of warfare. For instance, the **Electro-Optical Targeting System** (EOTS) enhances F-35 pilots' situational awareness and allows aircrews to identify areas of interest, perform reconnaissance and precisely deliver laser and GPS-guided weapons.[3]

UBS Asset Management is one of the largest global investment managers. By **representing rights** to the money market fund in a digital contract, it is set to improve processes for fund issuance, distribution, subscriptions and redemptions.[4] From the remotest villages to the most sophisticated global cities, technology promises to improve democracy, prolong life, boost financial inclusion and improve quality of life. The possibilities are endless.

But the rapid pace of digital transformation also keeps exposing the duality of innovation. As digital transformation gains pace, so the internet's evil forces raise their ugly heads higher and higher. Simmering geopolitical tensions, the proliferation of offensive cyber warfare and its associated slipover risks, the weaponisation of artificial intelligence, fragmented regulations, the perennial shortage in skilled cybersecurity professionals, the explosion of high-impact and low-cost cyberattack tools, and a myriad of other factors continue to threaten the future of the internet. Predictably, cyber insecurity continues to feature prominently among the top ten risks in the World Economic Forum's 2024 **Global Risks Report**, with 81% of business leaders saying they feel more or as exposed to cybercrime than last year.[5]

At the Cyber Leadership Institute, we firmly believe that while technology will continue to play a pivotal role, the rising menace of cybercrime can only be meaningfully defeated by building highly skilled and courageous cyber leaders who lead their organisations towards cyber resilience with firm conviction. In this quest, the remarkable stories of Nzinga and other luminaries matter a great deal. As **Winston Churchill once remarked**, 'The future is unknowable, but the past should give us hope' – the hope that human ingenuity, reason and character can combine to save us from the abyss and keep us on a path.[6] In another phrase of Churchill's: to broad, sunlit uplands.

# Welcome Note from the Cyber Leadership Institute

From the CEO, Phil Zongo

### From the Server Room to the Boardroom

Thank you for reading our book, *The Cyber Leadership Imperative. Before we get deep into the how,* I would like to share my personal story and how that links to the overriding mission of the Cyber Leadership Institute. My 20-plus-year journey in technology risk and cybersecurity has been fascinating. However, my most defining leadership moment came in the winter of 2017 when I was appointed to build and lead a cybersecurity function for a reputable Australian wealth management firm.

My ascension into the cyber leadership space defied convention in many ways. I was 36 years old and relatively young compared to the average Australian chief information security officer (CISO). I also wasn't aware of any fellow African Australians working in that space. Predictably, imposter syndrome kept lifting its ugly head. It's very difficult, but not impossible, to become what you cannot see. I was stepping in to deal with scenarios that I had never seen before, as well as presenting to directors who also sat on multiple boards for iconic companies listed on the Australian Stock Exchange. In the ensuing years, I took up additional roles as a virtual CISO – helping companies uncover their critical blind spots and accelerate their cyber transformation programs.

But my sudden elevation from the server room to the boardroom quickly exposed my Achilles heel. I realised that surviving in this high-pressure position had almost nothing to do with my technical competencies. But rather, my ability to inspire high performance, influence decision makers and, most importantly, communicate a bold vision with clarity, persuasion and impact. Further compounding my pain, the cyber leadership world was still heavily siloed, and my executive networks were skinny.

I decided to push all these challenges aside because I knew that the stakes were too high for me to revert to my comfort zone. I thrust myself on an accelerated learning curve – dismantling my fixed mindset, peg by peg, before building myself up again. My new challenges forced me to figure out what it meant to forge relationships that never existed before, and to master leadership skills that were never taught in university.

## The Obstacle Was the Way

As Viktor Frankl once said, 'What is to give light must endure burning.'[7] My life has taught me that behind every significant obstacle lies untapped opportunities. Like oxygen to fire, the challenges and fears I faced during my formative leadership years inspired me and my two amazing business partners to co-found the Cyber Leadership Institute (CLI) back in 2018.

Jan Schreuder is a veteran cyber strategy consultant and board advisor. Jan spent more than 37 years at a Big Four consulting firm, where I had the privilege to meet and work with him. Darren Argyle FCIIS is a chief information security risk officer at a global bank, a former CISO at Qantas and winner of multiple CISO awards. I am privileged to write this important book with these two esteemed cyber leaders.

We determined to set bold rather than timid goals from the start. Our entrepreneurship journey started by asking four important questions.

1. What if we created a global community of cyber leaders who think critically and actively collaborate to drive positive change within their enterprises and accelerate the creation of a resilient digital ecosystem?

2. What if we helped organisations avoid hefty consulting fees by unlocking hundreds of carefully curated and actionable toolkits – helping them achieve cyber resilience at a fraction of the cost?

3. What if we equipped aspiring CISOs with proven strategies to beat the competition during interviews as well as quickly establish credibility with their executives and boards once they landed CISO roles?

4. What if we unlocked cyber leadership pathways alternative to the traditional CISO role, helping cybersecurity professionals realise their full leadership potential?

When Darren, Jan and I first met at a cafe in downtown Sydney back in 2018, we had no idea that what started with only five participants in our Cyber Leadership Program (CLP) would reach global impact.

From the charming coastal region of Cape Town to the stunning Fijian archipelagos, from the vibrant city of Mumbai to the majestic metropolis of New York City – at the time of writing CLI has equipped leaders from more than 70 countries with practical skills to accelerate transformation, influence decision makers and lead through a crisis. Some of our members are charged with protecting critical infrastructure and large multinational companies. CLI, in short, exists to build highly effective cyber leaders.

## Letting a Thousand Flowers Bloom

We built the institute around the enduring African concept of *ubuntu – a deep*-rooted belief that as individuals, our impacts are inconsequential. But together, we can rise above the threats and create a safer digital space for the next generation. Like Queen Nzinga, Chief Rāwiri Puhirake, Sitting Bull, Martin Luther King Jr., and Nelson Mandela, we are living at a pivotal time, one where we are faced with the fate of the digital space. We are staunch believers in the transformative power of leadership to avert evil and create a safer internet space for the next generation.

Ubuntu, the philosophy that underpins our mission, speaks of our interconnectedness, selflessness and respect. Nothing exemplifies the spirit of ubuntu better than CLI's quarterly community calls. It's from these gatherings that we listen to the inspirational stories of CLP alumni who have successfully deployed lessons from our CLP program to land CISO roles and shatter technical ceilings. At the Cyber Leadership Institute, community is everything. What unites our members is their extraordinary determination to defeat the malevolent actors.

Our **Cyber Leaders on the Move series** continues to spotlight some of our distinguished alumni using their voices to drive policy change, champion diversity and inspire possibility.[8] From partners at leading consultancy firms to CISOs at major global brands, our CLP graduates keep defying the odds. As always, credit goes to them, the doers of the deeds, but we are honoured to have been part of their success stories. We have created a platform that pushes our members to unlock their full leadership potential – a field where a thousand flowers can bloom without diminishing each other's glory.

Our work has connected us with some distinguished cyber leaders from all over the world. We continue to be amazed by the depth of talent in our community, and many wonderful stories of cyber professionals who, once they overcome their fears and self-doubt, find their voice and step up to lead, influence make an impact. We have included five of these remarkable stories within the book as follows:

- In the introductory chapter you will meet Saira Hassan, a UK based CISO who successfully utilised the CLI First 100-day plan to breakthrough the technical ceiling and land her first executive role.

- In Chapter 4 we will introduce Georges De Moura, one of the most decorated global CISOs who has held executive and advisory roles at major global brands like the World Economic Forum, Etihad Airways, Thales, IBM, and Airbus.

- In Chapter 6 you will read the awe-inspiring journey of Noureen Njoroge – Director of Global Cyber Threat Intelligence at Nike and winner of multiple global awards for exemplary leadership.

- In Chapter 8 we will introduce Vandana Verma, global chair of the OWASP Foundation and the founder of InfoSec Kids.

- We then conclude the series with the incredible journey of Ashwin Ram in Chapter 13. Ashwin is a Cybersecurity Evangelist (Office of the Chief Technology Officer) at Checkpoint and an acclaimed global keynote speaker.

These cyber leaders embody the spirit of CLI and the reason we exist – to inspire cyber security professionals to push beyond limits and realise their full leadership potential. In this book we have tried to capture the essence of what differentiates the exceptional cyber leaders from the ordinary. Through interacting with hundreds of cyber leaders globally, we have observed what works and what doesn't – learning from their successes as well as inevitable failures that characterise the cyber leadership journey.

## Sustained by Our High Calling

Building and scaling a business is fraught with challenges – capital constraints, product-market fit and looming recession, to mention a few. Like most start-ups, we must manage these risks daily. But as Andy Groves, former CEO of Intel, famously said, 'Bad companies are destroyed by crises. Good companies survive them. Great companies are improved by them.'[9]

We keep pushing through obstacles. We are fuelled by the unshakable conviction that our mission is deeply connected to who we are. Our obligation to our members and the future generation has instilled a higher sense of purpose. We believe that without effective cyber leaders, digital resilience will remain a pipe dream. John Maxwell was right to say everything rises or falls on leadership.[10]

Building highly effective cyber leaders is our supreme calling, which we pursue with remarkable clarity. Our team is encouraged to share their ideas freely, maintain a dogged focus on the needs of our members and reject yes-man thinking. Only by embedding these virtues into CLI's DNA can we build the enduring enterprise we envisioned from the start.

## Like Sticks in a Bundle

But no matter how brilliant or determined our team and community can be, we cannot achieve this lofty goal in isolation. Over the years, we have developed partnerships with the Australian Information Security Association (AISA), Information Security Society Switzerland (ISSS), Australian Women in Security Network (AWSN), Info-Tech Research Group and many more. These strategic relationships continue to help us scale our impact and bridge diversity gaps. We are stronger together; as the African proverb goes, sticks in a bundle cannot be broken.

Our members have transformed CLI into the global brand it is today. They believed in our mission when we were relatively unknown. Even now when we boast more than 6,000 members across all geographies, we remain committed to understanding our members' individual needs because they are the ones to whom we owe our greatest obligation. But it would be impossible to make these achievements in such an unpredictable space without our extraordinary CLI team – who constantly punch beyond their weight to service our members.

## The Cyber Leadership Imperative

Recently, the World Economic Forum revealed that the CISO role represents one of the most dynamic careers today.[11] We share the same sentiment. We predict that over the next few years CISO salaries will continue to rise exponentially, more CISOs will gain unfettered access to their respective boards of directors, and report directly to CEOs, as well as have constant visibility with the media and investors. But these important changes only reinforce our strategic goal – to equip our members with actionable tools and skills to accelerate their organisations towards cyber resilience.

**We have written this end-to-end cyber leadership book with two interrelated aims, to provide:**

1. Actionable guidance to aspiring CISOs to break through the stubborn technical ceiling, land CISO roles and thrive in the C-suite – thus unlocking their full leadership potential, increasing their earning power and aligning their work with a bigger *why. As our mantra goes – 'Know You're Ready'.*

2. A detailed guide to experienced CISOs to further sharpen their cyber leadership skills, lead with courage during inevitable crises, build high-performing teams and impress key stakeholders with exceptional presentations.

role has been positioned to play a pivotal role in safeguarding the long-term survival of companies and the resilience of their internet infrastructure. Working towards a clear, higher goal is a rarity in corporate leadership – providing a powerful convergence between purpose and reward.

But despite the rising appetite, very little clear-cut guidance exists to help aspiring cyber leaders accelerate their paths to the top. Most cybersecurity professionals feel stuck in functional roles; their careers are rising at a slower pace than a snail trailing across wet cement.

When you search the phrase, 'How to become a CISO', Google will return more than 1.5 million results. Sifting through this content, most of which is substandard, is tedious and overwhelming. Granted, the domain of cyber leadership is vast and complex; there is no one path to the cyber leadership position. Therefore, this chapter provides practical insights for aspiring cyber leaders to accelerate their path into the C-suite and excel in those executive roles. If you are already a seasoned cyber leader, you can skip straight to Chapter 2.

## The Shift Towards the Business-Savvy CISO

About a decade ago, the cyber leader role was largely compliance-focused and widely regarded as a cost centre. IT security managers (most senior cyber leaders) deployed and maintained a portfolio of technical solutions, such as firewalls, internet proxies, intrusion detection systems, email security gateways and endpoint security. Some of these cyber leaders had remits that extended into IT infrastructure, systems development, and support. The role of the cyber executive certainly looks very different today. It has now expanded beyond a compliance focus into a strategic role that anchors licence to operate, business growth, customer trust and long-term brand success.

While the role of most cyber leaders has narrowed significantly to focus on business resilience, a significant proportion of cyber leaders now run large cybersecurity teams with complementary skill sets spread across geographic zones, supported by myriad highly specialised third-party vendors. Most of the skill sets that made cyber leaders excel in their roles ten years ago are now poor predictors of success. To build high-performing teams, manage multimillion-dollar budgets, leave lasting impressions with the board, drive organisational-wide cultural change, earn the respect of executive peers, lead through crises and face sceptical investors, cyber chiefs need to cultivate leadership, strategy execution, and influencing and negotiation skills. Unfortunately, very few of these leadership fundamentals are taught in technical certifications or academic degrees.

This certainly mirrors our experience training hundreds of cyber leaders from dozens of countries who go through our intensive **Cyber Leadership Program (CLP)**.[14] We have consistently observed that one's ability to formulate and execute high-impact cyber resilience strategies, win hearts and minds, lead through crises and cultivate a strong personal brand are better predictors of success than mere technical competencies. But before we delve into the how, let's unpack the cyber leadership role.

## What Exactly Do Cyber Leaders Do?

Before we dive deep into the nuances of cyber chief career paths, let's dissect the cyber leadership role. Based on our combined 70-plus years in the cybersecurity trenches, and training cyber leaders from more than 65 countries, there are six critical responsibilities that underpin a cyber leader's success:

1. **Leader:** The cyber transformation agenda must be anchored in a compelling mission and inspire everyone – from the board to frontline personnel – to go beyond the call of duty to protect the enterprise from the rising menace of cybercrime. Leading cyber leaders also implement highly adaptive learning

programs that align their team's work with their passions, accelerate individuals into leadership positions and actively promote diversity of thought. By building high-performing teams and empowering their direct reports with key decision-making powers, leading cyber chiefs free up time to focus on the big picture and nurture strategic relationships – building confident teams and avoiding burnout. The cyber leader, in short, is the army commander who builds a lean and lethal army during peacetime and leads with courage from the front lines during tumultuous times.

2. **Politician:** The ability to navigate entrenched political systems and turn potential detractors into supporters is crucial. Leading cyber executives are able to create a strong sense of purpose by wielding persuasion and influencing skills to enlist the support of the most critical decision makers, mostly the executive team and the board of directors. This helps build a strong tone at the top, sending an unequivocal message that cyber resilience is everyone's responsibility, from the board of directors to frontline staff.

3. **Trusted advisor:** To create a shared sense of purpose, the cyber leader must clearly translate deeply technical matters into the language of the business – helping executives and boards make confident, quality and risk-informed decisions. By rigorously tying cyber transformation initiatives to the broader mission, the cyber leader will radically transform the cybersecurity function from a traditional cost centre into a non-negotiable aspect of strategic decision-making whose effectiveness correlates both to the bottom line and the long-term survivability of the enterprise.

4. **Change agent:** The cyber leader must build a culture where cybersecurity is entrenched in all strategic and operational decision-making forums and inspire everyone. The cyber

leader must also proactively identify the 'pain points' new solutions will introduce, anticipate cultural resistance and implement a raft of measures to win hearts and minds – smoothing things over.

5. **Marketer:** Positioning cyber resilience as a powerful differentiator and business enabler involves evangelising critical capabilities to regulators, client prospects, insurers, investors, shareholders and business partners – helping to win new business, lower cost of capital and maintain license to operate. When hired to salvage their organisations from data breach messes, the cyber leader's role gets elevated into a critical part of management – one trusted with using lessons learnt from cyber incursions to fortify the organisation's digital defences and rebuild customer trust, attracting top talent, restoring share price and assuring business partners.

6. **Strategist:** Ruthlessly prioritising the protection of crown jewels – the most important digital assets that underpin their organisation's competitive advantage, intellectual property and most profitable business lines – and creating a business-centred strategy is essential to rapidly closing material risks and accelerating business growth. By focusing limited budgets on systems that matter the most, leading cyber leaders boost cyber resilience without burning the bank – thus cementing their reputation as a business-centred executive who possesses deep commercial acumen. Strategy execution is where the proverbial rubber hits the road for high-performing cyber leaders. They develop clear-cut road maps, persuade the board to fund the agenda and deliver beyond their promise.

A cyber leader's responsibilities are much broader, but these six essentials suggest that to succeed, it is vital for cyber chiefs to transform themselves from functional experts into well-rounded business leaders.

# Given the Significant Upsides, How Can Aspiring CISOs Accelerate into the C-suite?

So, you know you want to accelerate your career and land that top cyber leadership role, but how exactly do you get there? Here are five proven steps you can take to break the technical ceiling and accelerate into the executive space.

## 1. Make yourself the obvious choice

Traditionally, most cyber leaders rose through the ranks from technical roles: they were network managers, software development techs, security operation centre (SOC) managers, penetration testers or IT engineers. But as many cyber leaders can attest, today's cyber executives need much more than technical expertise to thrive. To stand out in a crowded marketplace, you need to position yourself as business cyber-savvy. This means a cyber leader with a holistic understanding of the business value chain; a deep insight into the business's major revenue lines; and a big picture perspective about cyber risk and its implications on business growth, mergers and acquisitions, regulatory compliance, and personal liability to corporate directors.

Equally important is the cyber leader's proven record of embedding cyber resilience into digital transformation – reducing cyber risk while helping the business tap into innovation's benefits.

## CASE STUDY: PHIL

Phil Zongo, one of the co-authors of this book, deployed this differentiating strategy with great success. He refused to play it safe when his organisation embarked on a complex, multi-vendor cloud transformation program years ago. The aspiring CISO put his hand up to lead the cyber risk stream of this high-visibility program. This move was a significant bet on his career. By that time, cloud security best practices were emerging; there wasn't much precedence for large enterprises migrating their mission-critical systems into the public cloud. Cloud-related regulations were non-existent to fuzzy at best.

Phil felt like he was paving his way through the woods. Through this high-risk move, he had unconstrained access to senior executive and global IT vendor expertise, as well as to the Australian Prudential Regulation Authority (the regulator of the Australian financial services industry). By stepping up and taking on a complex role most colleagues feared, Phil landed his first-ever head of cybersecurity role at a prominent company only two years later, much sooner than he ever anticipated. No doubt this was a challenging step, but pressure builds resilience and growth, both bedrocks of a successful cyber leadership career.

You must create, not wait, for opportunities to show up. If asked to sit on key cross-business risk committees or mission-critical projects, do not hesitate to roll up your sleeves. Volunteer yourself in difficult situations. Never assume that a change of title will automatically anoint you to lead. In our experience training hundreds of new cyber leaders via our flagship Cyber Leadership Program, cyber leaders who beat the competition during interviews proactively equip themselves in leadership, negotiation, stakeholder management and board communication skills. An army that engages in endless drills, simulating real-life battles, building their physical and mental resilience through tough situations, is likely to succeed in a conflict when compared to reservists who are called on unexpectedly to face a skilled adversary.

They easily stand out from the competition when opportunities inevitably arise – by stepping out of their comfort zones to manage profit and loss accounts, assuming deputy-CISO roles, leading complex transformations and intensely pursuing differentiating skill sets, for example.

## 2. Get your hands dirty

A growing number of cyber leaders are hired to salvage serious problems such as clean up a mess following a damaging data breach, restore dented customer trust, respond to pressure from major shareholders or the board to ramp up cyber resilience capabilities, replace a fired CISO or address serious regulatory undertakings.

Cyber leaders with practical experience containing and cleaning up complex cyber intrusions, responding to crises calmly and demonstrating personal resilience are highly sought after. As the adage goes, 'Always sail with mariners who have been shipwrecked, for they know where the reefs are'.

To differentiate yourself, you need to muster the guts to lead cyber crisis response exercises, facilitate tabletop exercises with difficult stakeholders and build robust assurance practices, such as red teaming and threat hunting. When the right opportunity shows up, you will be ready.

## 3. Be highly intentional about personal branding

One of the biggest mistakes many professionals make during the early phases of a career is to resist the idea of personal branding. But personal branding isn't just for self-anointed influencers (who may lack real depth). It's about developing a strong thought leadership record – publishing compelling opinions in peer-reviewed magazines, speaking at conferences and being featured on popular webcasts. A strong and consistent personal brand is the most definitive weapon to ward off the competition.

Authority matters in most life domains, and cyber leadership is no exception. Recruiters, employers and clients now place a huge premium on strong thought leadership records. The years of landing an executive cyber role based solely on years of experience and a chronological description of your employment history have passed. Personal branding requires that you show up consistently. Strong and persuasive writing takes time, but with deliberate action, persistence and patience, it's certainly achievable. The idea is to focus on skills that set you apart from the crowd. Identify a niche – specific skill sets that are extremely valuable to businesses in the long term – then align it with your passion and relentlessly sharpen those skill sets.

If you turn up for an interview with several pieces from high-quality publications, a newspaper article that quoted you, or even better, a cybersecurity book, you are likely to blow competitors out of the water. Additionally, a strong track record of thought leadership will boost your confidence during the interview and demonstrate an in-depth understanding of specific domains.

According to Stephanie Balaouras, research conducted on Fortune 500 companies revealed that first-time CISOs promoted from within are rare.[15] Organisations often reach out externally to fill this senior role. Some of these roles are not even publicly advertised. An effective thought leadership record will boost your visibility outside your corporate circles. Great candidates are often overlooked because they light their lamps only to leave them under a bushel.

## 4. Make your résumé stand out

**Michael Porter** once said, 'Competitive strategy is about being different. It means deliberately choosing a different set of activities to deliver a unique mix of value.'[16] In line with Porter's enduring wisdom, your résumé must stand out among hundreds of competitors and be convincing enough to land you the first interview. Your résumé is your potential hirer's first impression of you. Here are our top five tips for creating a killer résumé:

- Ditch the one-size-fits-all chronological résumé that tediously narrates your journey from high school to the present. It's all about context. Carefully study the job specification and problems the company is facing, then craft a résumé highlighting your specific strengths that align with their needs. For example, if the cyber leadership role results from a regulatory undertaking, highlight your experience in tightening governance processes. If the company frequently engages in mergers and acquisitions, talk about your expertise in simplifying redundant and complex security architectures, as well as combining disparate cultures.

- De-emphasise technical skills because, in most cases, they are a given. Instead, highlight your experience building high-performing teams, influencing decision makers, communicating with clarity and impact, delivering complex change, and leading through crises. Strong strategy, leadership and influencing skills are the hallmarks of the leading cyber executives.

- Scrap the traditional objective/personal goals statement and write a gripping summary of your career achievements. Clarify straightaway why you are the best candidate for the job. Remember, the most comfortable thing for someone reviewing your résumé is to stop reading and trash it. Hook the potential employer in from the first sentence and leave them craving to know more about you.

Remember, less is more. Prune each sentence and paragraph to its cleanest form. Even more importantly, back your résumé with a short and concise cover letter. As Mary Elizabeth Bradford wrote for **Forbes**, 'Be sure to get right to the point (with the cover letter). Share your focus of direction, respectfully call out a few examples of success, then invite them to learn more by looking at your resume.'[17]

- The truth is, when employers hear of a prospective candidate's name, they will likely jump on to your LinkedIn profile. Your LinkedIn profile represents your professional brand, so make it stand out. First, write an eye-catching headline, the proverbial elevator pitch. Second, invest in a professional, high-resolution portrait; simply cropping your wedding photo comes across as unprofessional and lazy. Third, stick to facts and make sure your LinkedIn and résumé align. We have seen exaggerated achievements come back to bite their creators at incredible speeds. Finally, and maybe most importantly, don't get entrapped by the habit of spewing negativity on LinkedIn. A victim mindset and leadership are mutually exclusive traits.

## 5. Once you land a cyber leadership interview, please don't mess up!

Always remember that you will be going head-to-head with dozens of other highly decorated and experienced professionals. If you show up unprepared, your chances are very slim. As Louis Pasteur said, 'Chance only favours the mind which is prepared.'[18] Before the interview, thoroughly research the company – understand its core products, value chain, stock performance, corporate values, strategic priorities, key executive players and the broader market issues the company is facing. An in-depth understanding of the company and its key executives demonstrates that you are taking the opportunity seriously.

The next step is to arm yourself with a well-thought-out 100-day plan. This proven concept can be traced back to Napoleon Bonaparte because that's how long it took him to return from exile, reinstate himself as ruler of France, and wage war against the English and Prussian armies before his final defeat at the Battle of Waterloo. So much can be achieved within 100 days, but it requires careful planning from the start.

This 100-day period represents an essential window for new cyber leaders to cement their credibility with the C-suite and enlist support during this formative stage. Readers can download a free comprehensive **CISO First 100 Days Playbook** from the **Cyber**

**Leadership Hub.**[19] The 100-day plan will markedly differentiate you from competitors because most candidates will show up to answer questions. **George Bradt** agrees: 'Shame on you if you walk into a late-round interview without a plan for what you are going to do leading up to and through your first 100 days. And shame on you if your plan is all about you.'[20]

## CASE STUDY: SAIRA HASSAN

Saira Hassan, a Cyber Leadership Program (CLP) graduate, successfully utilised the 100-day plan to land the top position. Saira always wanted to become a CISO. But when opportunities came knocking, she found herself struggling to close competitive CISO interviews. 'One of my key challenges was articulating how to design a robust cyber strategy that enabled the organisation to operate within its risk appetite in a compelling way,' **Saira recalls.**[21]

When Saira read a CLP post a friend shared on LinkedIn, she researched the program and joined the next cohort. She quickly immersed herself in the advanced program and executive toolkits. This was a turning point. The CLP sharpened Saira's strategy design and executive communication skills. With boosted confidence and a compelling 100-day plan, Saira nailed the next interview and landed her first CISO role at Zodia Markets. We congratulate Saira on her success.

### Five Additional Recommendations to Leave a Lasting Interview Impression

1.  If asked about your professional background, pick one or two career highlights that tie back to the role you are interviewing for. Avoid the common trap of trying to squeeze in every piece of your decades-long career.

2.  Leverage the STAR method (situation, task, action and result) to provide thought-through and compelling interview

responses. What was the situation or pain point? How did you turn the situation around? What specific actions did you take? How did that action benefit your organisation in tangible ways? Ensure you have at least two concrete case studies demonstrating your problem-solving skills.

3. Learn from previous interviews and close the loopholes beforehand. Be honest with the feedback you received during previous interviews, negative as it may sound. For example, if you were called out for being verbose, then script your introduction and case studies before committing key points to memory. Brushing negative feedback under the carpet only delays your ascension into the cyber leadership space.

4. The interviewer will certainly ask you if you have any questions towards the end of the interview. Identify three strategic questions and express them with clarity and brevity. Examples include measures of success, reporting structures, governance and executive participation in cyber risk governance, digital transformation agenda, cultural aspects and broader business goals. Stay away from operational questions or any expressions that convey a victim mindset, such as budget constraints or endless questions about why the predecessor left.

5. Anticipate any concerns the interviewer might raise and find convincing ways to close that gap. For example, when one hiring manager looked concerned about the candidate's young age, the aspiring cyber leader respectfully countered by sharing a recent case study in which she had successfully delivered a complex cybersecurity modernisation project, overseeing millions in capital spend, managing a wide range of senior stakeholders and functional experts, as well as negotiating multi-year vendor contracts. The age concerns were quickly allayed.

## Hit the Ground Running with CLI's First 100 Days Framework

Once they land the coveted role, new cyber leaders must hit the ground running and fast. They must deliver critical capabilities and secure the trust of critical stakeholders. To do so, the cyber leader must develop a strong grasp of the enterprise's critical risks and other hurdles that may delay or impede change. In our experience, cyber leaders lose credibility or, worse yet, get fired for making terrible purchasing decisions, failing to spot critical blind spots, souring relationships with influential executives or falling victim to an avoidable data breach. That's why we have developed a detailed Cyber Leadership Institute framework outlining how to best utilise your first 100 days as a new cyber leader while identifying and overcoming issues.[22] This framework has been deployed to wide success by hundreds of our members.

### Be SUPER

The SUPER acronym provides a framework for each phase in the first 100 days of a cyber leader.

### PHASE 1: S – START-UP  Days 0–15

Before starting the role, prepare thoroughly by conducting company research, reading annual reports, investigating whether there are headline breaches related to the company and exploring the executive team's critical members. The only way to develop a brand as a business-savvy cyber executive is by understanding how the business makes money, its mission and the topmost concerns for senior executives and the board.

### PHASE 2: U – UNDERSTAND Days 0–45

Meet with high-influence/high-interest stakeholders to learn about the business, its issues and opportunities for improvement.

Examine board reports, assessments, audit findings, existing strategy documents, policies and metrics to understand critical risks and issues. These vital interactions will give you valuable insight into cultural hurdles, potential detractors, technological constraints, digital transformation road maps and business priorities – all prerequisites for success.

## PHASE 3: P – PRIORITISE Days 15–60

Identify the quick wins and complex capabilities that take time to roll out. That way, you can rapidly secure credibility with key stakeholders while giving yourself enough time to plan more complex initiatives. **Tom Scholtz**, research vice president of Gartner, suggests identifying two projects that you can complete or show meaningful progress on in the first three months.[23] Once you identify the low-hanging fruit, develop a plan and enlist the buy-in of your manager, team and key stakeholders. Remain open to feedback and constantly refine the plan as new information emerges.

Consider this case: Upon starting a new role, a CISO determined that the approach by the predecessor to build an internal SOC was wrong. The new CISO decided to outsource this stalled project to a global threat prevention, detection and response firm. Within two months, by steering in the opposite direction, the organisation onboarded all its high-value digital assets on to the same SOC platform that several Fortune 500 companies used. This boosted detection and response capabilities without hiring expensive external staff.

The cybersecurity team eliminated billions of false positives and sharpened the focus on real threats by leveraging a global SOC's industrial-scale computing power, massive data sets and advanced machine learning algorithms. The decision to outsource freed money and time for the cybersecurity team to drive cyber transformation.

## PHASE 4: E – EXECUTE Days 30–80

While careful planning is the bedrock of leadership, resist the temptation of being drawn into endless risk assessments, a concept widely referred to as 'paralysis by analysis'. Execute your promise and deliver the quick wins you have identified. Put in place agreed plans to address some of the longer-term issues. Organise your team by creating security team roles and responsibilities, setting up your management system and ensuring governance effectiveness. Leverage the consulting budget to bring in external experts on a short-term basis, which helps improve cyber resilience posture while building your internal team.

## PHASE 5: R – RESULTS Days 45–100

Don't be shy to celebrate your team's successes. Leverage our **cyber risk reporting framework** to demonstrate back to your stakeholders the progress made and critical risks mitigated, as well as remind them of the key next steps.[24] Stay open to feedback, especially during the early days, as this helps you reaffirm business priorities and position your strategy as one whose success depends on the active participation of all stakeholders (technical or otherwise). Present a revised cyber risk profile demonstrating how your quick wins improved the resilience posture. We have developed the **CISO Playbook: First 100 Days, Setting the CISO up for Success** that further details our phases, including a daily guide to follow to ensure success in your first 100 days. This practical Action Plan can be found in **Appendix A**.

### Before 'Day Zero' – Prepare Thoroughly

Before a new leader embarks on a role as a cyber executive there are some essential skills and knowledge to acquire. It's no good having a great 100-day plan if you can't communicate it effectively. Nowadays cyber leaders need to demonstrate necessary soft skills as well as sound technical knowledge, skills such as establishing and maintaining effective lines of communication with a myriad of stakeholders and departments. According to **Deloitte**, '[the majority of CISOs] have to invest a lot of time to get buy-in and support for security initiatives'.[25] In other words, communication and credibility are now must-haves. The more effective a CISO's communication skills, the easier it is to secure the top job and, once in the role, gain executive support. To be blunt, if you can't communicate with clarity, confidence and persuasion, you will be unlikely to earn the respect of your executive peers.

## TOP TIP – FOCUS ON WHAT YOU DON'T KNOW

The road to the cyber chief role is not always linear. While many have risen the ranks through the broad range of information security disciplines, with many coming from engineering and network security backgrounds, some enter the profession via alternative routes, such as technology risk, legal, IT or program management. Wherever they come from, it's rare to reach the role of a cyber leader without some preconceptions built up during the course of a career.

People are most comfortable with what they know. However, we recommend that you develop deep self-awareness, step out of your comfort zone and focus on your weak spots. A good starting point is to drill down into your weakest areas and make the necessary improvements before applying the same process to your team. Understanding your blind spots will help you craft an effective career development plan and know which skill sets you need to prioritise for hiring.

A new cyber leader finding their feet should take their time to understand the cyber risks and issues, but just as importantly, to learn about the business: Who are its customers, how does it make money, and what are the organisational cultural dynamics? Having a clear understanding of what matters most to your organisation will also inform the highest priority in the confidentiality, integrity and availability (CIA) triad, ensuring that limited resources are directed towards the most important business goals.

## Combine Soft Skills with Technical Skills

To thrive in their roles, cyber leaders today must combine robust soft skills with a solid understanding of the technical environment and digital transformation road map. Learning about the company, both during the interview stage and once in the role, is essential to success. Here are three tips to accelerate your learning of the organisation's core values and goals:

1. Begin with the organisational mission statement (its core reason for existence). Understand what inspired the vision and mission, and the symbols management have implemented to bring the values to life.

2. Learn about organisational core activities, products, services, research and development, intellectual property, and mergers and acquisitions plans.

3. Research publicly available information such as the company's annual report, financial statements, press releases, news, audit statements, data breaches, patents, executive leadership team and board of directors.

This vital information will assist you in developing a high-impact, cost-effective and most importantly, business-centred cyber transformation strategy.

## Shape Cybersecurity as an Investment in the Brand

The cyber leader should develop a general narrative that clearly communicates that cybersecurity is no longer just a cost of doing business: it's a long-term investment in the brand – a strategic asset that contributes to the company's bottom line. Cyber leaders must develop a cyber resilience strategy focused on doing the right thing, not necessarily what's easy, to quickly position themselves as business-centred executives. That means carefully working with new product development teams, key customer segments and balancing consumer privacy and digital experience. The cyber leader must shape and push the narrative that cybersecurity is not merely a compliance matter but a critical business enabler that underpins long-term brand value, stock performance and profitability.

## Lead with Impact

Leadership is essential for the success of any organisation and without it, companies would not meet their objectives or deliver products and services to their customers. In 1946, **General Montgomery** defined leadership as the capacity and the will to rally together to a common purpose and the character which inspires confidence.[26] Similarly, a cyber leader must develop and nurture the skills to motivate large teams to get behind clear goals and go beyond the call of duty to contribute towards the organisation's cyber resilience. This requires individuals to think beyond their own key performance indicators and work as a cohesive unit. To achieve this, the cyber leader must develop compelling narratives that tie key cyber initiatives to the long-term mission and inspire their team towards a shared common vision.

## Foster a Positive Culture

Culture is about creating positive behaviours and buttressing them deep into operational routine, ensuring that everyone considers cyber risk implications in everything they do and proactively protects key digital assets from harm. Culture sticks when driven from the top down. Developing a people strategy will motivate and inspire the team by setting the agenda, articulating roles and responsibilities and prioritising goals aligned with the function's strategic capabilities and broader business mission. It is also important to establish an internal function culture, which includes leadership open door policy, psychological safety, growth opportunities, well-being, rewards and success.

## Meet the Team

It is essential to meet with all of the team in the very early days of a cyber leadership role. Ideally, these meetings should be one-to-one and face to face, followed by a team meeting. Start by meeting direct reports. These meetings will inform you of what is going on and help ease some of the anxieties that often characterise leadership changes by sending an unequivocal message that the views of your direct reports matter deeply.

The cyber leader must take time to carefully understand the key strengths of their team members, as well as skills gaps. This often calls for the cyber chief to shake things up, but always take a measured approach. Hasty action compromises trust and credibility, which may lead to inadvertently losing valuable team members. The following checklist of prompt questions will help structure your decision-making:

- **Competence** – Does this person have the technical skills and experience to execute?

- **Judgement** – Does this person exercise sound judgement under pressure?

- **Energy** – Does this team member bring the right kind of energy to the job? Or are they disengaged, burnt out or unfulfilled? Are they still motivated by their current role, or have they long outgrown their space? Do they inspire others to become their best or suck energy from the team by blowing problems out of proportion and endless complaining?

- **Focus** – Does this person get along well with other team members and work towards bigger team objectives or are they a self-centred individual who depletes energy from the team?

- **Trust** – Is this person consistent and reliable? Do they have a track record of delivering key promises and working autonomously or are they all talk?

Establish a team management system that includes key meetings, key reports, and major project governance. Pull this together into a consolidated tracker, even if you're just using a spreadsheet. This system will serve as another decision-making tool, one that provides transparency into the current workload and the heartbeat of the team.

## Stakeholder Management

Once appointed as cyber leader, take time to get to know everyone in the team. Understanding their personalities, quirks, concerns and goals will help the new cyber leader understand how they work together. This includes fostering good relationships with everyone with whom the cyber leader has regular contact. Understanding how each one contributes to company goals will help prioritise high-influence and high-interest stakeholders. We discuss stakeholder management in Chapter 2 in more detail.

The most crucial step is to gain top-down support. Cyber leaders are a strategic and integral part of the business management team and need to make sure there is buy-in from the board of directors. By establishing strong working relationships with key executives and the board, the cyber leader will accelerate budget approvals and ensure their critical initiatives are prioritised among competing business goals.

## Assessing Risk, Knowing the Issues and Measuring Capabilities

You don't have enough time to conduct a full-blown cyber risk assessment during your first 100 days. You should instead focus on performing a high-level maturity assessment and define the most critical risks the organisation faces. This initial executive report will also demonstrate the need for a more thorough independent third-party assessment to benchmark against industry standards.

Your report at the end of your first 100 days should provide answers to the following questions:

- How well protected is the organisation? What is our capability maturity?
- What are our most plausible threats/cyber risk scenarios?
- What risks could have the most significant negative impact on the organisation, should they materialise?
- What will it take to improve the organisation's security posture?
- How can the effectiveness of investments be measured?
- What is the anticipated return on investment (ROI) for security investments?
- What will the organisation risk if nothing changes?
- What executive and board support is required to accelerate change?
- What is being done well, and how can this be preserved during change?
- What are the critical blind spots? These are key areas whose risk profile is unknown, and that warrant greater assurance budgets.

## Be Ready to Respond to a Major Cyber Incident or Crisis

Cybercriminals work around the clock and don't care whether you are still bogged down in your first 100-day plan. There is a high likelihood that a significant breach could occur during the cyber leader's formative months. The executive team and board will look to the cyber leader for assurance from day one. In cyber leadership, there is no honeymoon period. Running cyber-simulation exercises will assess the team's incident management capabilities. The training will also provide an opportunity to increase awareness of the impact major security breaches can have on the business and reinforce the key message that business executives should fully fund the cyber transformation program. Equally important, the cyber leader must consider purchasing a cyber incident response retainer, providing assurance that the organisation will get prompt access to experienced cyber-threat responders while maturing its capabilities.

## Career Resilience for a CISO

The CISO role is a challenging one with constant pressure to demonstrate business value in the strategy. The first 100 days are perhaps the most challenging time. New cyber leaders must quickly decipher the key issues and risks facing the organisation and demonstrate their ability to address them. There may be no formal or public record of cyber leaders being given the boot, but it is clear that this happens often. Cyber leaders could depart from their organisation after suffering a damaging breach, failing to spot or report major vulnerabilities, poor purchasing decisions or because of unresolved conflicts with senior management. There are many things a CISO can do to reduce the risk of career failure and to protect themselves – but first, let's hear what some sacked CISOs had to say.

## CISOs Tell All

Several CISOs have described their experience of being fired and the lessons learnt. One who previously worked in the UK financial services sector said that his dismissal ultimately came down to 'a difference of opinion' between the CIO and him. 'The information security budget was part of the overall IT budget, and the CIO had to make cost reductions while information security still had to show savings in the budget; this increased risk in certain areas.'

He continued that, having explained the potential damages to senior management, the CIO took a nasty turn. 'The CIO did not like this, although agreed that the business should be responsible, which was a case of, do as I say, not as I do.' He felt he handled the departure well but believes he learned a lot from the experience. 'It is best not to report directly to technology and have your budget controlled by the CIO, who is under pressure to cut spend. The reality is that some business leaders don't want to face the truth or have transparent conversations, even if they publicly state that.'

Unfortunately, this tale is not unique. A head of InfoSec at a managed service provider also cites difficulties with the IT team, with this eventually paving the way for his own exit. 'The IT director constantly ignored the advice of information security, thought that he knew better, and while telling the board that we should improve, undermined my position by negatively influencing my peers, as he just did not like what I did.

'This resulted in a complaint to HR against my director for unbecoming conduct, and breach of our corporate ethics policy. Unfortunately, the HR team brushed this under the carpet. I was dismissed a month before my two-year employment period.'

Another CISO, working in the US pharmaceutical industry, explained why he resigned after blowing the whistle on insider fraud. 'There was a merger with a bigger US company with a global reach. As this was a publicly traded business, we had Sarbanes-Oxley and SEC compliance, which fell under my remit, as the parent organisation's information security function was less mature than ours.

'There were a number of financial irregularities throughout the year, and while carrying out some analysis on data loss prevention, [I] came across what looked like fraud and insider trading. One of these was a regional CFO, who I got on well with. The information was not conclusive, and after debating with myself for a week on what to do, I passed on the information in confidence to the new CEO in accordance with our own policies: ethics and whistleblowing. The CEO then forwarded my confidential email to the person I reported, asking what was going on, in [response to] which I straightaway received retaliatory action against me.'

He resigned the day after, but four months later, the company filed for bankruptcy. Later on, the CEO and CFO were investigated by the SEC.

However, not all CISO dismissals result from toxic cultures or political infighting. Some cyber leaders dig their own career graves. Consider one such CISO we collaborated with: soon after stepping into a new role, the CISO engaged a global consulting firm to draft a fresh road map based on 'industry best practice'. But a few months prior, the board had already approved a solid strategy developed by the previous CISO. When the CISO presented their rushed strategy, everyone was rattled, especially fellow executives who thought the new CISO should have known to consult widely before wasting time and resources. The new CISO's leadership team, most of whom had worked with the previous CISO, felt disrespected and ganged up to undermine the new strategy.

New cyber leaders often seek to make their mark through bold acts. But without a delicate balance, hasty changes can create fault lines that lead to mistrust, lost credibility and resentment.

## So, What Can a Cyber Leader Do to Prepare for the Role and Protect Themselves?

Here are six top tips:

1. It's essential to get off on the right foot. Develop a 100-day plan like the one outlined in **Appendix A**. It provides structure and an effective communication tool to all your key stakeholders. Working off a well-structured plan positions the cyber leader as a consummate professional and sets realistic yet ambitious expectations from the start.

2. Know your scope and your boundaries, where you can add value (and where you could break the business if not careful).

3. Take time to get to know key stakeholders and understand the business, how it makes money, its customers and its priorities.

4. Set clear-cut expectations by using benchmarks and maturity assessments to show how the company stacks up to competitors and best practices. What assets do they really care about (i.e. the crown jewels), who are the most likely threat actors, and what are the few critical projects to execute?

5. Develop your community of peer cyber leaders to share common toolkits, exchange ideas and encourage each other through the inevitable obstacles you will face in your role. Why spend days creating a playbook for running joint board and executive team tabletop exercises if you can leverage what your community has done without diminishing each other's competitive advantage?

6. And finally, consider undertaking leadership training, such as the **Cyber Leadership Program**, to gain valuable insights from mentors and gain free access to tools, templates and much more.

## Five Critical Mistakes New Cyber Chiefs Should Avoid

Now that we have mastered strategies to land a cyber leadership role and quickly build credibility, let's conclude this section by discussing five career-ending mistakes you should avoid as a new cyber leader. Through our work training hundreds of cyber leaders, we have found that a significant proportion of new CISOs fail to make an immediate impact, while some fail completely. Five key mistakes stand out.

### 1.  Overreliance on Technical Skills

Predictably, most cyber leaders hail from technical backgrounds. But as new cyber leaders quickly discover, technical skills are a small part of the job. The technical competencies that earned them praise in functional roles are ill-suited to commanding respect from executive peers and leading complex change. If they fail to detach from operational tasks, 'techie' cyber leaders abdicate their leadership and strategy execution responsibilities. Without the C-suite and board on their side, their cyber transformation programs are quickly thrust into rough waters.

We once heard of a CISO who spent weekends bunkered in a data centre configuring internet proxies and security alerting tools. The result was predictable: the CISO wasn't visible to executive committees, burned out, and the team felt disempowered.

As the **ISACA's 2022 State of Cybersecurity Survey** brings to light, there is a rising demand for innovative CISOs with proven leadership skills, strategic thinking and the ability to take smart risks.[27] This reality may be uncomfortable, but it must be faced. To boost their chances of success, new cyber leaders must proactively nurture deep relationships with decision makers and translate complex technical matters into business language while empowering their direct reports to make key technical and operational decisions.

## 2. Changing What Already Works

Overtaken by excitement, some new cyber leaders make the strategic mistake of attempting big changes too quickly. This is more likely if the CISO is an external hire with little visibility into the existing political dynamics or technical constraints of the business.

Consider the earlier case: the new CISO who engaged a global consulting firm to draft a fresh road map based on 'industry best practice' when the board had already approved a solid strategy just months prior.

Slow down and incorporate key stakeholders' perspectives into cybersecurity strategies. With a strong and shared sense of purpose, stakeholders are more likely to support cyber transformation programs.

## 3. Feeding Their Insecurities

The fear of failure drives some new cyber leaders towards irrational behaviour. They fall into the perilous trap of hiring direct reports who pose no threat to their positions, reports who conform and do as they are told. This irrational behaviour is fertile ground for inefficiencies, backbiting, project delays and costly mistakes – by leaving critical strategy execution, leadership or board communications exposed.

Winning CISOs develop self-awareness and use proven competencies as a yardstick for building high-performing teams. They unlock the power of diversity by hiring individuals who compensate for their weak spots and amplify their strengths; they fearlessly challenge assumptions and openly embrace opposing perspectives. Getting this right requires not only self-awareness but courage and humility.

## 4. Neglecting Hearts and Minds

When drafting strategies, some new cyber leaders are enticed to focus on flashy concepts – zero-trust tools, defence against zero-day threats, machine learning algorithms and so on. But, by placing exaggerated faith in technical solutions, they overlook the people and change management aspects of transformation. Most cybersecurity projects – such as data loss prevention, mobile device management, and multi-factor authentication (MFA) – require staff to fundamentally alter their entrenched habits and ways of thinking. Forcing users outside of their comfort zones without careful planning turbocharges resentment, undermining the potential of security investments.

Leading cyber leaders put people's hearts and minds, not technology, at the centre of their strategies. They hire experienced change managers to work closely with the technical teams to identify the pain points new solutions will introduce, anticipate cultural resistance challenges and implement a raft of measures to smooth things over. By empowering the program manager with key decision points, they free up time to manage key stakeholders, mentor direct reports and engage deeply with the board.

## 5. Positioning Cybersecurity as a Necessary Evil

The primary role of most cyber leaders is to mitigate risks. But solely focusing on risk mitigation positions cybersecurity as a traditional cost centre with a weak link to broader business goals. New cyber leaders without a compelling mission often struggle to enlist the support of the board and executives – a prerequisite for success. Consequently, the cyber leader's views are quickly shot down, and their budget requests hit brick walls, making them feel like glorified systems administrators.

To succeed, new cyber leaders must ruthlessly tie cybersecurity budget requests to business goals. For example, take SOC 2 Type II reports: globally accepted, independent reports on the effectiveness of an organisation's controls relating to data security/availability, processing integrity, confidentiality and privacy. A proposal to move the organisation towards SOC 2 certification that highlights the goal of accelerating reviews by prospective clients is more likely to obtain funding than a proposal that simply asks to improve compliance.

## Appendix A – First 100 day plan for a new CISO

### PHASE 1: S – START-UP

Before starting the role, conduct thorough research into the company, read the most recent company annual report, what headline breaches the company has had, who's who in the executive team and so on. Engage with your EA/PA (if you have one), start setting up meetings. Refine your plan and begin.

| TIMING | KEY ACTIVITIES |
|---|---|
| Before day 1 | Reinforce new connections with people already talked to in the company during the interview process. |
| Before day 1 | Gather and consolidate external industry analyst research reports, identify key industry security conferences, memberships/associations (such as the cyber leadership hub) – document and pull together costs. Prioritise subscriptions that will add tangible value, boost your team's performance and create valuable executive networks. |
| Before day 1 | Set logistics with the manager, HR, EA, etc. Achieve readiness for day one (who will meet you, technology set up, access, badges, company induction, etc.) |

| TIMING | KEY ACTIVITIES |
| --- | --- |
| Before day 1 | Identify key templates for documentation, frameworks, presentations, reporting, etc. and align with each row in the reference section of the 100-day plan. |
| Before day 1 | Begin discovery conversations with external security consultants for the independent maturity assessment – references, pricing, availability, etc. |
| Before day 1 | Ideally, using admin support, gather a list of key stakeholders and agree with the manager who should be the priority to meet in the first two weeks. Admin support should schedule these before arrival. |
| Before day 1 | Prepare introductory communication about yourself, including thoughts on joining the company and key priorities in life/work. |
| Before day 1 | Prepare stakeholder and staff discussion guides that can be used in one-to-ones and meetings (questions should be open and specific). |
| On day 1 | Communications – meet/call with your manager, send introductory emails to key stakeholders and to the wider organisation, e.g. company intranet posting. |
| On day 1 | Regroup with your manager. From your manager's perspective, understand the key challenges/opportunities/known issues. Schedule a regular communications schedule between you and your manager. |

| TIMING | KEY ACTIVITIES |
|--------|----------------|
| On day 1 | Regroup with the manager. Discuss the introductory vision for information security in the company and document the key asks/requests to support the new role. |
| Week 1 | Set up calendar invites for one-to-one meetings with key stakeholders and teams responsible for delivering information security. Request invites to current recurring calls/meetings required for the role, including company communications. |
| Week 1 | Request organisation structure, reporting lines and in particular those in legal, security, risk and compliance. Meet regularly with your manger to confirm security teams. |
| Week 2 | Establish name/links with third-party information sharing forums specific to the industry, including national law enforcement and government agencies. |
| Week 2 | Request access to security and risk-related data such as current security strategy/program, pen test, vulnerability assessments, policies/standards, audit findings, and risk management tools. |
| Week 2 | Confirm with manager key memberships/associations and provide business case and costs. |
| Week 2 | Understand pricing and scope for independent security assessment activity and external benchmarking. |
| Week 2 | Establish personal management systems and communications |

## PHASE 2: U – UNDERSTAND

Meet the important stakeholders first, rank them, and learn about the business. What are the issues and opportunities to improve the situation? Gather reports, assessments, audit findings, existing strategy documents, policies, metrics, board reports and so on.

| TIMING | ACTIVITIES |
| --- | --- |
| Week 1/2/3 | Gain business insight. Meet with key stakeholders who were prioritised by your manager, business leaders and operational teams (security, risk, compliance, etc.) Establish opinions on current security program and what key stakeholders believe are the priorities. Capture output in a report. |
| Week 2 | Assess how many resources are in place globally to manage the security organisation, including financial parameters and operational security budgets. |
| Week 2/3 | Review existing security governance, strategy, policy, standards, and overall framework architecture, and where this is stored – central or distributed. Look for good practice and document findings. |
| Week 4 | Review recent high-level executive summaries of audit findings, vulnerability assessments, penetration test reports and recent security incidents. |
| Week 4 | Seek at least one executive mentor internally, one externally, and formally join the priority industry information sharing forum. |
| Week 5 | Review cross-business projects and initiatives. What is currently underway across the business, what is security's involvement, e.g. M&A activity? |

| TIMING | ACTIVITIES |
|--------|-----------|
| Week 5 | Assess scope of the CISO role and overall remit following previous meetings and company discovery (information security, IT, risk, compliance, privacy, fraud, physical, business continuity, etc.) |
| Week 6 | Review security- and compliance-specific projects and initiatives. Which projects currently underway are seen by the business as being a priority, what is security's involvement? |
| Week 6 | Understand at the macro level what is functioning well and what requires improvement. |

## PHASE 3: P – PRIORITISE

Know the quick wins, understand which issues will take longer to resolve, what current processes are working well and should continue to be executed on. Develop vision and share it with your manager, your team and your key stakeholders. Get feedback and refine.

| TIMING | ACTIVITIES |
|--------|-----------|
| Week 3 | Build requirements for security education packages and identify external specialist security companies. |
| Week 3 | Identify an appropriate tool for measuring ongoing information security, risk and compliance globally for the company. |
| Week 3 | Tightly scope an information security assessment to measure general maturity and provide a benchmark score. |
| Week 4 | Plan global site visits, arrange to meet security, risk, compliance personnel and any key stakeholders face to face. |

| TIMING | ACTIVITIES |
|---|---|
| Week 5 | Design a draft of the information security assessment that could operate within the company. Consider both IT and business security roles and identify headcount for security role gaps. Align to budgets (OPEX and CAPEX). |
| Week 5 | Plan an operational security budget for the next three months. Work with assigned financial analyst and consider ROI metrics and specific headcount shifts/new hires. |
| Week 5 | Schedule monthly calls with current identified security-related personnel. Amend as required as the team shapes up during the next six months. Share executive communications, review individual activities, allocate actions and track. |
| Week 6 | Review the existing (or prepare a new) information security charter and prepare materials for information security steering committee. |
| Week 7 | From the assessment of major issues, prioritise two or three key issues to focus on over the next two months. |
| Week 8 | Draft and socialise an interim information security strategy and vision – where we want to be, where we currently are. Show current/proposed projects to close the gap (two or three focus areas). |

## PHASE 4: E – EXECUTE

Deliver on some of the quick wins and put agreed plans in place to address some of the longer-term issues. Organise your team, set up your management system, and ensure governance effectiveness.

| TIMING | ACTIVITIES |
|--------|-----------|
| Week 5 | Refine new global information security organisation, operating model, and request additional headcount. Create cybersecurity team roles and responsibilities (leaders, analysts, engineers, PMs, etc.). |
| Week 5 | Visit key global sites, and meet security, risk, compliance personnel and any key stakeholders face to face. Review high-level physical security of data centres/server rooms. |
| Week 6 | Begin a tightly scoped information security assessment to measure general maturity and provide a benchmark measurement. |
| Week 7 | Appoint security champions globally, clarify roles and responsibilities, arrange a kick-off call and publish a summary internally. |
| Week 7 | Get directly involved in projects and, where appropriate, challenge their relevance. Ensure the teams are focused on the business value, executing in line with agreed milestones and project risk assumptions issues dependencies (RAID) are clearly documented/maintained. |
| Week 8 | For new projects, validate and identify security leaders assigned, and ensure the status is reported back to the cybersecurity program office. |
| Week 8 | Draft and socialise an information security charter with the executive leadership team. Obtain approval from key stakeholders. |

| TIMING | ACTIVITIES |
|---|---|
| Week 9 | Establish (or re-establish) the information security governance process and forums based on previous maturity assessments (instituting effective decision-making linked to accountability, responsibility, and authority, as well as budgeting and reporting). |
| Week 9 | Facilitate executive cyber education workshop and develop a quarterly schedule with a repeatable format. |
| Week 9 | Deliver basic security awareness/education in priority areas of the business. |
| Week 10 | Engage in planning activities for the next six to twelve months and assign resources/funding. |

## PHASE 5: R – RESULTS

Re-engage with all your key stakeholders, reconfirm the key actions and progress made, as well as where you might need their help and feedback on your first 100 days. Form an executive assessment report of key risks and issues.

| TIMING | ACTIVITIES |
|---|---|
| Week 7 onwards | Monitor status and measure the success of existing security-related programs and build into regular reporting. Include planned projects as initiated. |
| Week 10 | Deliver an effective, executive monthly information security scorecard/dashboard. It is important to gain feedback and amend as required. |

| TIMING | ACTIVITIES |
|---|---|
| Week 11 | Measure the performance of current security personnel, using a 360-degree feedback process. Ensure low performers have a plan to improve and high performers are recognised for their contribution (objectives set). |
| Week 13 | Highlight any early wins, successes and challenges, and schedule a meeting with your manager, team leaders and key stakeholders. Refine reporting based on feedback. |
| Week 13 | Complete an executive report that includes a maturity assessment, SWOT analysis, critical controls deployment rate, etc. |
| Week 14 | Conduct a status meeting for senior executive management that includes early wins and plans for the next six to twelve months. Use presentation format from earlier meetings and develop a quarterly schedule with a repeatable format. |

# Chapter 2

# STRIKE Framework - Six Pillars of Cyber Leadership Performance

### EQ a Better Predictor of Success Than IQ in Cyber Leadership

In his bestselling book *Emotional Intelligence*, Daniel Goleman argues that emotional intelligence (EQ) can be as important as, or even more important than, one's intelligence quotient (IQ) for determining success in life.[28] Emotional intelligence is the ability to effectively understand and manage one's own emotions and influence the emotions of others. According to Goleman, emotional intelligence contributes to much better personal relationships and higher professional performance, as well as greater mental health.[29]

Ever since Daniel Goleman published his first book in 1995, EQ has become one of the hottest topics in corporate circles. In 1998, Goleman wrote an article for *Harvard Business Review (HBR)* titled 'What Makes a Leader?'[30] It attracted a higher percentage of readers than any other article published in that periodical in the last 40 years. It is said that the CEO of Johnson & Johnson was so impressed by the article that he sent out copies to the 400 top executives in the company worldwide.[31]

The significance of EQ to the cyber leadership domain is hard to overstate. The cyber chief role has quickly morphed from an IT-centred executive whose mandate was limited to defending networks against cyber threats to an integral member of the

C-suite responsible for building inspired teams, maintaining business resilience, lowering the cost of capital, educating the board and directly contributing to the bottom line.

But a major challenge exists. Traditional academic degrees and technical certifications have failed to keep up with these increasing demands and build business-centred cybersecurity executives. No doubt, technical depth plays a significant role in building well-rounded cyber leaders, but the future of cybersecurity leadership demands more – it calls for a harmonious blend of technical depth, commercial acumen and decisive leadership.

Technical certifications have historically succeeded in building functional leaders. Yet, a significant gap exists at the top – most cybersecurity professionals haven't yet mastered the commercial acumen, emotional intelligence, leadership and other soft skills required to command respect in executive circles and execute complex transformational programs.

One highlighted concern is the industry's overemphasis on technical knowledge and certifications, often sidelining essential soft skills, business acumen and business collaborations – all must-haves to survive the demands of executive roles. But as mentioned earlier, with obstacles come opportunities. At the Cyber Leadership Institute, we have built a range of complementary programs to radically transform functional leaders and technical professionals into well-rounded cyber leaders who can confidently lead their organisations towards cyber resilience.

Now that we have laid the foundations on how to land an executive cyber role and how to secure early credibility with executives and the board, let's dive into the Six Essential Pillars of Cyber Leadership – a CLI proprietary framework (The STRIKE Framework).

At its core, the STRIKE framework provides a comprehensive and objective approach for cyber leaders to assess their key competencies, uncover critical blind spots and formulate a strategy to position themselves as business-centred and high-performing cybersecurity leaders.

Central to this journey is the STRIKE Six Pillars of Cyber Leadership Performance Framework, our innovative framework that holistically addresses the multifaceted challenges businesses encounter today in cybersecurity, providing professionals with a comprehensive tool to effectively navigate their career trajectories.

## Top Ten Recommendations

1. **Prioritise Holistic Cybersecurity Training**: Cybersecurity leaders need to focus on a blend of technical, leadership and business insights, going beyond traditional training paradigms.

2. **Move Beyond Certification**: Cybersecurity certifications have their place, they impart invaluable technical knowledge, but as cybersecurity professionals move up the ladder, they must recognise that certs have their limits. They must work on new skill sets to demonstrate strong mastery of strategy execution, team leadership, crisis management and other essential leadership disciplines. Only that way can they break the technical ceiling and reach their leadership potential.

3. **Embrace Soft Skills**: Soft skills such as communication, conflict resolution, negotiation, commercial acumen and team leadership are no longer nice-to-haves for cyber leaders but essential pillars to accelerate into the C-suite and earn the respect of the board and fellow executives. The CISO is, first and foremost, a politician, carefully navigating complex organisational dynamics to get key decision makers on their side, access critical resources and ensure cross-organisational buy-in. This can only be achieved through soft power, not technical brilliance.

4. **Strengthen Business Acumen**: Cybersecurity professionals must develop an in-depth understanding of the business value chain, its competitive advantage, the most profitable business lines and how mission-critical decisions are made. This requires spending a great deal of time interacting with the product teams and key decision makers. Doing this enables the cyber leader to act with extreme frugality, creating a differentiated strategy that prioritises the protection of digital assets that underpin the organisation's competitive advantage (trade secrets, intellectual property, etc.) and supports products that bring the most revenue to the business.

5. **Promote Collaborative Learning**: Leadership is too deep and broad a discipline to be mastered in isolation. The days of the lone wolf are gone. To move up and stay relevant to dynamic business needs, cyber leaders must shift from isolated training methods to collaborative, community-driven learning experiences, underlining the importance of peer support and mentorship. As the adage goes, iron sharpens iron. Active cross-industry collaborations facilitate the cross-pollination of ideas, helping cyber leaders to bring the outside in to challenge invalid assumptions and tired ideas. By joining a global community of peer leaders, you gain access to the collective insights from leaders who understand the stresses and expectations of executive leadership.

6. **Implement the STRIKE Six Pillars of Cyber Leadership Performance Framework**: The STRIKE framework provides a comprehensive and objective approach for cyber leaders to assess their key competencies, uncover critical blind spots and formulate a strategy to position themselves as business-centred and high-performing cybersecurity leaders. In our experience mentoring dozens of aspiring cyber leaders through interview processes, we have noted that it's often the ignored weaknesses that impede cybersecurity professionals from breaking into executive roles. By taking a holistic approach, STRIKE will help you amplify core competencies while closing career-derailing gaps.

7. **Commit to Continuous Self-Assessment**: Leadership is a journey with no finish line. To remain relevant in the face of rapid business change, tightening external stakeholder expectations and an intergenerational workforce, forward-leaning cyber leaders must regularly self-evaluate against industry-leading frameworks. Only that way can they drive continuous improvement, adapt their own teams and continue to exceed expectations.

8. **Nurture Leadership at All Levels**: Foster leadership qualities across all tiers of the organisation to ensure constant movement towards cybersecurity goals. Why? Because cyber leadership is a team sport whose success is only guaranteed when the cyber leader creates a shared sense of purpose and drives risk ownership where it belongs – within the business front lines.

9. **Prioritise Mentoring and Coaching**: Invest in structured mentoring and coaching programs, pairing less experienced professionals with seasoned leaders. This bridges knowledge gaps, aids in the faster adoption of best practices and builds a culture of continuous learning and leadership development within the organisation. Creating a fluid pipeline of cyber leadership frees up time for the cyber leader to manage upwards and outwards – cementing their credibility and evading the burnout that comes with being drawn into technical and operational weeds.

10. **Engage with the Community**: Actively engage with the broader cybersecurity community to remain up to date with the latest threats, risks and trends, and to scale your leadership impact beyond your organisation.

Incorporating these recommendations will help organisations create a highly capable and adaptive workforce, one with a good blend of technical prowess and business acumen that can quickly build and maintain cyber resilience in today's dynamic environment.

## MAJOR BUSINESS PAIN POINTS

As cyber threats have grown in complexity, the demand for skilled cybersecurity professionals has surged. However, traditional cybersecurity training programs have often been too narrowly focused, emphasising technical skills at the expense of broader leadership and business acumen. This oversight has resulted in a gap in the skills required to transition from mid-tier roles to senior cyber executive positions. Let's delve deeper into how traditional training has missed the mark.

**Overemphasis on Technical Knowledge**: Most foundational cybersecurity training programs prioritise mastering technical tools, protocols and methodologies. While these skills are undeniably crucial, a senior cyber executive also needs to possess a wider view of the organisation and its business needs. Most technical courses completely neglect this broader perspective, limiting participants to functional roles. In fact, as one rises through the ranks, soft skills become better predictors of success.

**Certification Obsession**: The industry has seen an explosion in the number of cybersecurity certifications. While these certifications help demonstrate proficiency in specific areas, they rarely touch on leadership, strategy or business alignment – all essential for higher managerial and executive roles.

**Lack of Soft Skills Training**: Soft skills such as communication, team leadership and conflict resolution are leadership essentials. Traditional cybersecurity courses, however, seldom cover these topics, leaving professionals ill-prepared for the interpersonal challenges and complex corporate dynamics they will inevitably have to deal with to get things done in senior roles. As soon as they step into leadership positions, these glaring skills gaps are severely exposed.

**Neglecting Business Acumen**: Cybersecurity isn't just an II concern; it's a business concern. Understanding risk management, organisational strategy and the financial implications of cybersecurity decisions is vital for a senior executive. Yet, many traditional courses gloss over or entirely omit this crucial area of knowledge. The modern cyber leader is as much a transformational leader as a voice of financial prudence.

**Isolated Learning Environments**: Traditional training often happens in silos, whether in isolated online courses or classroom settings. These environments lack the collaborative and community-driven learning experiences that can foster peer support, mentorship and the sharing of diverse perspectives – all invaluable for holistic professional development. Most cyber leaders fail to make an impact because their ideas are never challenged, they shelter themselves from opposing ideals and waste precious time reinventing the wheel. As Hal Gregersen wrote, 'This dangerous 'white space' where leaders don't know what they don't know is a critical one. But often, leaders – especially senior ones – fail to seek information that makes them uncomfortable or fail to engage with individuals who challenge them. As a result, they miss the opportunity to transform insights at the edge of a company into valuable actions at the core.'[32]

**Navigating Setbacks and Growth Opportunities**: Many aspiring cyber leaders are crushed by obstacles. But setbacks are golden opportunities to stand apart, shine and develop personal resilience – must-haves to survive the pressures of the C-suite. This fundamental aspect of leadership is hardly touched on in technical certifications and academic qualifications. By the time aspiring cyber leaders interview for executive roles, unfortunately, most find themselves poorly prepared.

**Overlooking Peer Influence and Mentorship**: Without an effective mentor to provide strategic direction, one risks repeating avoidable mistakes and reinventing the wheel, thus derailing their career by many years. Having access to experienced coaches and complementary self-assessment tools facilitates candid conversations, and helps cyber leaders gain a deeper understanding of their strengths, weaknesses and leadership styles.

Cybersecurity technical training still holds an important role in securing the digital ecosystem. But given the enormity of the challenges we face, a radical shift in cybersecurity capability development is required that focuses on deeper self-awareness, executive communication, strategic communication, business savviness, conflict resolution, negotiation and stress management.

## Traditional Training vs Extended Career Paths Through Cyber Leadership Institute Programs

Traditional cybersecurity training has undoubtedly laid a robust foundation for many in the industry. These programs, with their emphasis on deep technical knowledge and certification-focused curricula, can offer a clear pathway to intermediate roles, allowing professionals to excel in functional roles. Yet, what distinguishes a technical expert from an influential cyber leader? The nuanced capability to communicate complex technical challenges and opportunities in a language that stakeholders at all levels can understand is the answer.

*Figure 1.1*

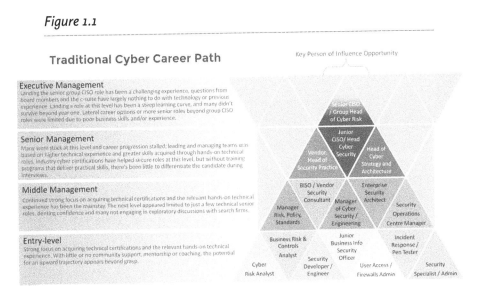

Programs that emphasise not just technical acumen but also hone executive leadership capabilities open career doors to a broader array of senior leadership roles.

Courses at the Cyber Leadership Institute go beyond the technical – they nurture these crucial bridging skills. These programs don't just prepare professionals for the next role on their career ladder – training individuals to communicate effectively, lead with vision, make bold decisions with conviction and align cybersecurity strategies with broader business objectives. These programs catapult them into boardrooms and on to decision-making tables where their expertise can have a far-reaching impact. CLI programs have positioned alumni as voices in demand across the industry, amplifying their brands, earning power and influence.

*Figure 1.2*

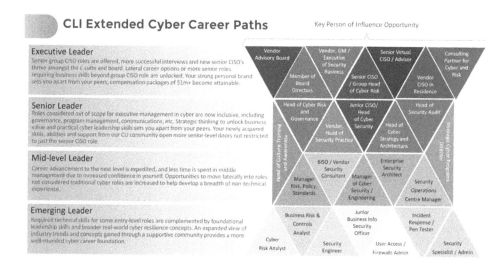

While traditional cybersecurity training offers a stepping stone for career advancement, programs like those at the Cyber Leadership Institute provide a launchpad for those aspiring to shape and lead the future of cybersecurity at a senior organisational level, even on a global scale. The more we have collaborated with experienced cybersecurity professionals over the years, the more we have recognised that there is a substantial number of professionals who aspire for cyber leadership roles beyond the traditional CISO roles. Through careful career planning and guidance, some of our alumni have landed roles in vendor advisory boards, second line of assurance (e.g. heads of cyber risk), Big Four consulting partnerships, virtual CISOs or as board members for reputable firms.

## Introducing the STRIKE Six Pillars of Cyber Leadership Performance Framework, Developed by the Cyber Leadership Institute

In the rapidly evolving landscape of cybersecurity, leaders are often inundated with a plethora of frameworks, each promising a comprehensive approach to mastering the respective domain. While these broader frameworks provide valuable insights, the true essence of effective leadership can often be distilled into a more concentrated set of principles. This is where the STRIKE framework shines.

Harnessing the wisdom of the 80:20 rule, STRIKE encapsulates the idea that 20% of focused effort can lead to 80% of the desired results. Instead of navigating the overwhelming expanse of information, STRIKE offers leaders a streamlined path to success, emphasising the core elements that truly matter.

The benefits of adopting the STRIKE framework are manifold. It provides a tailored approach to introspection, allowing leaders to reflect deeply on their strengths and areas for improvement. Great leaders are self-aware. By focusing on these pivotal elements, cyber leaders can achieve tangible outcomes, driving real change and progress in their organisations. Our extensive research in the field has consistently shown that those who embrace the key attributes of STRIKE methodology not only understand the intricacies of cybersecurity but also amplify their leadership prowess.

While the allure of broader frameworks can be tempting, it's essential for leaders to recognise the power of focused learning and growth. Effectiveness requires extreme focus. The STRIKE framework offers just that – a laser-focused approach to the most effective leadership attributes while closing blind spots that, if left unchecked, could significantly hamper career progress.

STRIKE is an essential tool for any cyber leader keen to rise above the competition and reach their leadership potential.

*Figure 1.3*

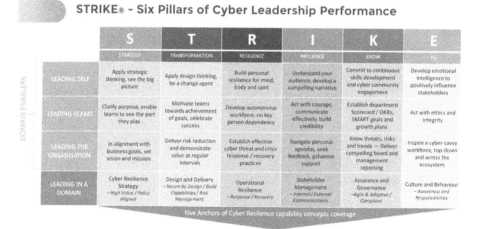

STRIKE® - Six Pillars of Cyber Leadership Performance

| | S STRATEGY | T TRANSFORMATION | R RESILIENCE | I INFLUENCE | K KNOW | E EQ |
|---|---|---|---|---|---|---|
| LEADING SELF | Apply strategic thinking, see the big picture | Apply design thinking, be a change agent | Build personal resilience for mind, body and spirit | Understand your audience, develop a compelling narrative | Commit to continuous skills development and cyber community engagement | Develop emotional intelligence to positively influence stakeholders |
| LEADING TEAMS | Clarify purpose, enable teams to see the part they play | Motivate teams towards achievement of goals, celebrate success | Develop autonomous workforce, no key person dependency | Act with courage, communicate effectively, build credibility | Establish department Scorecard / OKRs, SMART goals and growth plans | Act with ethics and integrity |
| LEADING THE ORGANISATION | In alignment with business goals, set vision and mission | Deliver risk reduction and demonstrate value at regular intervals | Establish effective cyber threat and crisis response / recovery practices | Navigate personal agendas, seek feedback, galvanise support | Know threats, risks and trends — Deliver compelling board and management reporting | Inspire a cyber-savvy workforce, top-down and across the ecosystem |
| LEADING IN A DOMAIN | Cyber Resilience Strategy – High Value / Policy Aligned | Design and Delivery – Secure by Design / Build Capabilities / Risk Management | Operational Resilience – Response / Recovery | Stakeholder Management – Internal / External Communications | Assurance and Governance – Agile & Adaptive / Compliant | Culture and Behaviour – Awareness and Responsibilities |

Five Anchors of Cyber Resilience capability concepts coverage

STRIKE®: Reference Architecture Model for 'Leading in a Domain' skills. Aligned to *The Five Anchors of Cyber Resilience* capability concepts.

## STRIKE®: Six Pillars of Cyber Leadership Performance

*Figure 1.4*

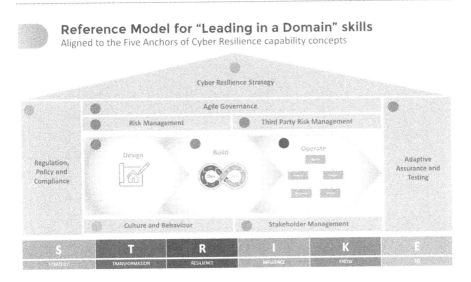

### Reference Model for "Leading in a Domain" skills
Aligned to the Five Anchors of Cyber Resilience capability concepts

## Empowering Self-Assessment with the STRIKE Framework

The STRIKE framework is a comprehensive tool that encapsulates the vital dimensions of cyber leadership. The true value of STRIKE lies not just in understanding the framework but in applying it as a mirror to reflect on one's own capabilities. To embark on this self-reflective journey:

**Begin with Our Digital Assessment**: To make this process streamlined and insightful, we have curated an online assessment. By visiting www.cyberleadershipinstitute/STRIKE, you can get a comprehensive evaluation mapped against the STRIKE parameters.

**Answer Our Series of 'the Right' Questions**: As you navigate through the assessment, you will encounter a series of probing questions tailored to gauge your proficiency in each pillar of the

STRIKE framework. These aren't just queries, but rather thought-provoking prompts encouraging deep self-examination.

Each question serves as a touchpoint, urging you to reflect on your strengths, identify gaps and ultimately understand where you stand amid the vast expanse of cyber leadership competencies. Have a look at some of our example questions below before taking the full online digital assessment. How many of these can you say 'yes' to?

## STRATEGY

Do you have a clear vision and mission for cybersecurity initiatives aligned with overall business goals?

Are you able to develop a cyber resilience strategy that delivers regular risk reduction, demonstrates the value of cybersecurity investments and supports the achievement of longer-term policy compliance?

## TRANSFORMATION

Do you embrace design thinking principles and actively drive change within your organisation?

Are you agile, adaptive and compliant in transforming the organisation's cybersecurity posture?

## RESILIENCE

Have you built personal resilience to handle the challenges and pressures of cybersecurity leadership?

Have you established effective cyber threat and crisis response practices to minimise the impact of incidents?

## INFLUENCE

Are you able to positively influence stakeholders through effective communication and compelling narratives?

Do you understand your audience and tailor your message to resonate with them?

## KNOW

Do you commit to continuous skills development and engage with the cyber community to stay updated with the latest threats, risks and trends?

Can you deliver compelling board and management reporting to keep key decision makers well informed?

## EQ (EMOTIONAL INTELLIGENCE)

Have you developed emotional intelligence to enhance interpersonal skills and navigate complex relationships?

Are you able to understand and manage your own emotions while empathising with the emotions of others?

### STRIKE SELF-ASSESSMENT

**LEADING SELF** – Assess your personal leadership qualities and skills needed to excel in the cybersecurity domain by reflecting on the following points:

- Are you applying strategic and design thinking to drive change?

- Have you built personal resilience to withstand the challenges of cybersecurity leadership?

- Can you develop a compelling narrative to influence stakeholders effectively?

- Do you commit to continuous skills development and engage with the cybersecurity community?

- Have you developed emotional intelligence to positively influence and connect with stakeholders?

**LEADING TEAMS** – Evaluate your ability to lead teams effectively by considering the following:

- Do you clarify the purpose of the team and help individuals see their role in achieving organisational goals?

- Are you fostering a high-performing team culture through motivation and celebration of success?

- Can you develop an autonomous workforce, reducing dependency on key individuals?

- Are you communicating effectively, acting with courage and building credibility?

- Have you established department scorecards, OKRs and growth plans?

- Do you operate with ethics and integrity in all aspects of leadership?

**LEADING THE ORGANISATION** – Assess your strategic approach to leading the organisation in the cybersecurity domain:

- Have you set a vision and mission aligned with business goals?

- Are you delivering risk reduction and demonstrating the value of cybersecurity at regular intervals?

- Have you established effective cyber threat and crisis response and recovery practices?

- Can you navigate personal agendas, seek feedback and galvanise support from stakeholders?

- Do you have a deep understanding of threats, risks and trends, and can you deliver compelling board and management reporting?

- Are you inspiring and promoting a cyber-savvy workforce throughout the organisation and across the ecosystem?

**LEADING IN A DOMAIN** – Evaluate your leadership and management skills within specific areas of the cybersecurity domain.

## Cyber Resilience Strategy:

- Are you developing a high-value and policy-aligned cyber resilience strategy?

- Have you incorporated secure-by-design principles and built necessary capabilities?

- Are you effectively managing risks through robust risk management practices?

## Design and Delivery:

- Do you ensure that cybersecurity initiatives are secure by design?

- Have you built the necessary capabilities to implement and deliver cybersecurity solutions?

- Do you focus on risk management throughout the design and delivery process?

## Operational Resilience:

- Have you established effective response and recovery practices to maintain operational resilience?

- Do you have strategies in place to mitigate the impact of cyber incidents and recover swiftly?

## Stakeholder Management:

- Are you maintaining strong internal and external communications to manage stakeholders?

- Can you develop compelling narratives to engage and influence stakeholders effectively?

### Assurance and Governance:

- Are you adopting an agile and adaptive approach to cybersecurity assurance and governance?

- Do you ensure compliance with relevant regulations and standards?

### Culture and Behaviour:

- Are you promoting cybersecurity awareness and responsibilities top down, and rolling out sustainable culture change programs?

- Are you fostering a risk-aware culture by encouraging proactive behaviours throughout the organisation?

## Self-Introspection, a Never-Ending Journey

This process of introspection is crucial for identifying aspects that demand your full attention, acknowledging that leadership development is an ongoing journey. It's essential to routinely engage with these questions, evaluate your progress and adjust your course as needed. This approach not only enhances self-awareness but also guides you towards leadership excellence over time.

The dynamic nature of cybersecurity requires a commitment to continuous learning. By aligning our educational pathways with the STRIKE framework, we offer a structured approach to achieving your career objectives. The insights gained from your assessment will direct you towards courses that best match your career ambitions and areas for improvement. Moreover, applying what you've learned is akin to exercising muscles – the more you practice leadership skills, the stronger and more effective they become. This cycle of action, coupled with accountability and tangible results, propels you forward, fuelling your motivation to persist in your development journey.

Additionally, success in cybersecurity is not solely a result of individual effort – it thrives on the collective wisdom of the community. Identifying and leveraging your strengths while tapping into the expertise of a network of seasoned professionals can significantly enhance your growth. Engaging in collaboration and co-creation with others, especially as you progress to more senior roles, fosters a culture of continuous learning and improvement, reinforced by the accountability and support a professional community offers.

Career success has broadly three elements, split roughly 40:20:40.

**Skills Development and Strategic Choices (40%):** This encompasses the deliberate decisions we make, beyond inherent talents and the synthesis of developed skills and ideas – from the leadership we choose to align with, to our knack for strategic planning, to the experience we gain from working alongside exemplary colleagues, volunteering on strategic projects and engaging with a supportive community.

**Good Fortune (20%):** This is the uncontrollable serendipity of success – the instances of being in the right place at the right moment. While some believe we curate our luck, this element acknowledges the unpredictable – you get a great new boss or a new regulation is introduced, and your department is given the opportunity to deliver on it. The idea, however, is to proactively sharpen your leadership skills so that when the opportunity comes knocking, you know you're ready.

**Hard Work and Dedication (40%):** The 'hard yards' matter as we have learnt from our own journeys. Success requires a great deal of personal sacrifice. It requires special attention to cyber leadership roles that often stretch beyond the norm. It's about recognising which additional projects or professional gatherings to partake in, approaching each with a 'soft yes and fast quit' mentality. Sometimes, the passions we pursue lead to unforeseen career gains. But as we have witnessed during our combined five decades on the front lines of cyber leadership, not all sweat is sweet – toil by itself is not enough. In today's fast-moving world, cyber leaders need to work both harder and smarter. This means disproportionately focusing your limited time and resources on skill sets that multiply your leadership effectiveness, closing career-derailing skills gaps, and setting out on a continuous learning curve, one enriched with the perspectives of seasoned mentors to further clarify your vision.

That's exactly why we established the STRIKE framework – to catapult your cyber leadership journey.

However, the essence of career advancement isn't rooted solely in individual achievement. True success blossoms when varied expertise and visions interlace. In our hyper-connected era, no achievement stands isolated. Every accomplishment sings the praises of teamwork, mentorship and a collective dream. The Cyber Leadership Institute stands ready to guide your journey, reminding all that while the might of a team lies in each member, each member's true power is amplified by the team.

# Chapter 3

# Driving Change Through Persuasion and Influence

## Effective Stakeholder Management the Bedrock of Cyber Leadership

Cyber risk has zoomed to the top of many boards' agendas. Corporate directors clearly understand that if they do not take decisive steps then their respective organisation could be the next victim of a debilitating cyberattack, wiping shareholder value, leaving a lasting dent in their professional legacy.

Consequently, the past decade has seen drastic changes in cyber leadership. Once a peripheral technology role, an increasing number of cyber leaders are getting elevated into the C-suite, interacting with board members and presenting to investors and journalists. This trend is not surprising.

Cyber resilience has become an essential aspect of doing business, materially impacting regulatory compliance, business growth ambitions, success in mergers and acquisitions, brand perception, cost of capital and every critical aspect of the business value chain. As one expert wrote, 'The old tale of CISOs as mere digital gatekeepers is getting a rewrite. They are now key players in big boardroom chats, breaking down geeky cybersecurity jargon into business talk and having a say in the big decisions.'[33]

But as these changes unfold, most cyber leaders are finding themselves woefully unprepared. Cyber leaders who rise through the ranks from technical engineering and operational roles often have their roots in technology. Their deep technical expertise and range of cybersecurity certifications equip them to excel in middle managerial roles, not leadership.

An enduring lesson has emerged from our experience on the cyber leadership front line and our collaboration with cyber leaders from dozens of countries who have gone through our intensive Cyber Leadership Program (CLP). Success in cyber leadership is less about technical prowess and more about the ability to deftly navigate entrenched political systems and enlist the buy-in of highly influential individuals, some of whom may not like the cyber leader.

For many cyber leaders, their appointment to the executive role represents a moment of great delight. But as soon as they step into this high-pressure role, they discover that the situation is much more complicated than they perceived. Although they may sit at the top of the cyber hierarchy, their success in rolling out important transformation programs depends on their ability to persuade key executives and the board. Their mission crashes during take-off in the absence of these must-have soft skills. Effective stakeholder management is the cornerstone of cyber leadership.

## Cultural Obstacles

Through our work at the Cyber Leadership Institute, we have identified several major cultural obstacles that severely threaten most cyber leaders' missions.

Predictably, the majority of cyber leaders hail from technical backgrounds. The technical competencies that earned them constant praise in functional roles give them distorted self-images. Without self-awareness, unfortunately some of these new cyber leaders stubbornly stick their heads in the sand like ostriches – and they pay dearly. They struggle to detach themselves from technical and operational decisions, and in the process abdicate their stakeholder management responsibilities. Thrust in front of boards and regulators and investors, their leadership gaps loom large. Consequently, without key decision makers on their side, their cyber transformation programs are quickly thrown into rough waters.

Some cyber leaders are hired to salvage their companies from serious data breaches. A cyber crisis certainly offers justification for dramatic action. Without much intuition, these cyber leaders rush to allocate resources to independent reviews and remediation efforts, overlooking some foundational measures required to sustain cyber resilience in the long term. In their haste, these cyber leaders resemble doctors who administer strong medication without conducting a proper diagnosis. They overlook major cultural obstacles that come back to bite them at stunning speed.

Other cyber leaders are simply hired to fulfil some external mandate. The board is pressured by investors, clients or peers to fill this important role. Sometimes, the board is forced into panic mode by a looming regulation. The hiring represents only form and has zero substance. These cyber leaders step into ceremonial positions and struggle to overcome the inertia exerted by toxic cybersecurity cultures.

In such an environment, the cyber leader's views are quickly shot down, and their budget requests hit a brick wall. This makes them feel like glorified systems administrators. The cyber leader lacks organisational stature, they have no access to the board, their budgets are underfunded, they have disproportionately small teams who are under constant pressure, and they fail to overcome entrenched business routines that deprioritise security.

When the cyber leader makes a recommendation and nothing happens – but on the other hand, when an external consultant or advisor conveys the same recommendation and the business acts – this indicates a problem with the messenger, not the message itself.

In short, the leader severely lacks visibility and presence. Executives default to risk acceptance, including obviously fixable high-risk control gaps. Senior business leaders barely show up at cyber governance committees. At best, they delegate cyber risk governance meetings to middle and junior managers.

One cyber leader vented their frustrations to us as the chief financial officer kept sending their finance manager, with zero organisational clout, to attend monthly cyber risk governance meetings. As the saying goes, 'Culture eats strategy for breakfast'.

The new cyber leader positions themself as a highly technical cybersecurity virtuoso who can communicate flawlessly, build a world-class cybersecurity team and solve all the problems that have haunted the organisation for decades. The new cyber leader talks a big game during the interview and delivers glossy slides, but they soon discover that talk is easy and cheap; cyber resilience transformation is a detailed exercise fraught with risk. When the new leader pivots away from the promised utopia and delivers a severely watered-down strategy, their credibility is irrevocably shattered.

The cyber leader does not have cordial working relationships with critical business functions. Project development teams try to bypass the security function because the cybersecurity function has a reputation for summarily shooting down business proposals without offering viable options. The CIO's relationship with the cyber leader is tense because the cyber chief maintains a hard-line stance on security and doesn't compromise their position.

These cultural obstacles frustrate cyber leaders, some of whom respond by leaning back, just hoping that these entrenched issues will magically vanish, or by resigning. Some bottle their frustrations, leading to serious mental health issues. Whereas we – based on our experience 'deep in the trenches' and our training of fellow cyber leaders – have discovered proven strategies to overcome inertia and persuade senior business leaders to throw their full weight behind the cyber transformation plan.

## 1. Conduct a Thorough Stakeholder Assessment

Leading cyber leaders know how to prioritise what matters. Not all stakeholders are created equal. With limited time at your disposal, you must be deliberate about your networking plan. Stakeholder mapping is a simple but effective stakeholder analysis technique, which plots stakeholder significance as a function of two factors: first, the degree to which the stakeholder can derail the program, and second, how much they care about the program's success. The result of this analysis is a four-quadrant map, as shown in Figure 2.1.

*Figure 2.1*

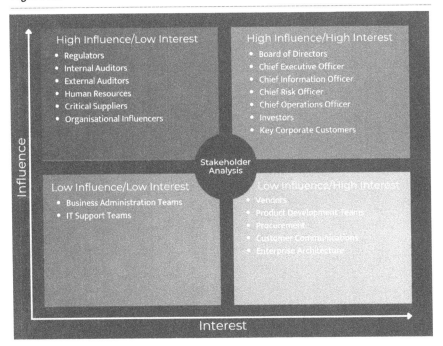

### High-Influence, High-Interest Stakeholders

This group has significant clout – they can squash or sustain your transformation program. They are widely respected across the organisation and no major decision is made without their consent. They also have a high interest in the success of your cyber transformation program – the proverbial skin in the game. While most of your C-suite members sit in this space, you should never confuse rank with influence. A good example is that enterprise architect whose perspective the CIO always seeks before making any strategic decisions. You should also pay closer attention to those external stakeholders who may hold significant organisational clout, for example:

An external cybersecurity strategic advisor (likely a partner at a large consulting firm, a veteran CISO or an ex-intelligence officer) who is retained to 'bring the outside in'. Given their industry authority and long-term personal relationships with some board members, you must proactively develop positive relationships with these stakeholders because the misalignment of your views with theirs will sink your mission.

External audit partners with unfettered access to the audit, risk and compliance committees. While external audits traditionally focused on IT general controls, intensified focus on the effectiveness of cybersecurity controls as a prerequisite for signing financial statements demands closer collaboration with this group.

Cyber leaders must follow a disciplined approach to understand these critical stakeholders' perspectives early and keep them highly engaged throughout their tenures. According to McKinsey, getting influential stakeholders on your side multiplies the odds of success by four times.[34] You must, therefore, actively manage these stakeholders. Develop deep and personal relationships with them, infuse their perspectives into your cybersecurity strategy, as well as seek their buy-in before key meetings. Make every effort to meet with these stakeholders at least monthly, ideally face to face, because, as the saying goes, 'out of sight, out of mind'.

As a cyber leader, you must actively manage these stakeholders through one-on-one meetings, email updates on cyber transformation progress, social events and debriefing on key papers before presenting them to committees. Finding some mutual personal interests – such as sports, books or personal stories – can also help deepen your connection with stakeholders. In short, do your best to keep this group satisfied.

Online collaboration tools have revolutionised how we remotely interact but none of these beat the power of old-school, face-to-face human interactions. They provide a deep sense of comradeship, connection and empathy that is almost impossible to replicate online. Cyber leaders can also leverage the proven power of reciprocity to influence their key stakeholders. They can create a deep sense of obligation to their stakeholders by actively participating in their activities, supporting their initiatives in governance forums or volunteering their direct reports to assist with critical deadlines. Human beings are hardwired to return favours.

Reciprocity is so powerful in influencing and persuasion that Dr Robert Cialdini, a leading social scientist in the field of influence, asserts in his book *Influence: The Psychology of Persuasion,* 'People we might ordinarily dislike – unsavoury or unwelcome sales operators, disagreeable acquaintances, representatives of strange and unpopular organisations – can greatly increase the chance that we do what they wish by merely providing us a small favour before their requests.'[35]

Done right, the principle of reciprocity has the profound power to get your critical initiatives swiftly through cyber risk governance committees and your unplanned discretionary expenditures approved. Putting your hand up to help fellow executives is doubly beneficial – it evokes a deep sense of social obligation and positions you as a valuable helper.

But remember – and we cannot emphasise this enough – the most important stakeholder is your boss. This is the relationship you must manage carefully, especially if you report to a non-technical business executive. As Robert Greene writes in his bestselling book *48 Laws of Power,* 'Never outshine the master. Always make those above you feel comfortably superior.'[36] You must, therefore, meet them regularly and ensure that they have a clear understanding of the issues you face and that your strategy is adapted in line with your manager's changing expectations.

## High-Influence, Low-Interest Stakeholders

This group is often not actively engaged in the cyber transformation program's nuances but wields enormous influence on the cyber leader's success. A good example is the internal audit team, whose views about your cyber resilience posture have the attention of the board audit committee.

As you engage with this group, you might discover potential candidates to shift to the top right quadrant. For instance, if you operate in an industry where the license to operate is underpinned by compliance with strict data protection laws, then it might be worthwhile to engage with your regulators or auditors proactively. You might discover that some stakeholders initially plotted in the top right quadrant are not that interested in the program in the same vein. So, you push them left and focus on nurturing a small set of strategic decision makers.

## Low-Influence, High-Interest Stakeholders

A good example of those in this quadrant is the enterprise architecture team whose work is significantly impacted by security decisions but who may not possess the same influence as the CIO. It is essential to keep this group informed and align your strategy with their views.

## Low-Influence, Low-Interest Stakeholders

IT support and administration teams are in this quadrant. You can keep these groups informed and engage with them at a deeper level when the need arises.

## 2. Struggling to Be Heard? Here's How to Fix It

While the board may on the surface understand the importance of cybersecurity, entrenched, toxic, cyber-resistant cultures can be hard to fix. Frustrating as these issues may be to a cyber leader, they will not magically vanish on their own.

### Actively Engage and Listen

Spend time in the formative stages of your executive role developing a strong rapport with your most critical stakeholders, such as the chief executive officer (CEO), chief operations officer (COO), product development executive, chief information officer (CIO), chief customer officer and the chief risk officer (CRO).

Understand their key concerns and expectations and embed their perspectives into your cyber resilience strategy. People want to feel heard and respected. This is even more important when you are dealing with big egos that occupy the C-suite. Top leaders want to feel on top. Active listening is the cyber leader's most powerful weapon to deliver transformation. The most important insights don't lie within cybersecurity frameworks but within key stakeholders' heads. That's OK – give them the illusion of control – it's their business that you are charged with protecting. Once you create a shared sense of purpose and build key stakeholders' perspectives into the cybersecurity strategy, they will throw their full weight behind its execution.

Always resist the urge to rush into execution mode. Develop a deep understanding of the lay of the land – painstakingly reviewing company prospectuses, board papers, financial statements and other pertinent reports – an in-depth understanding of the business value chain. Approach your key stakeholders with a blank piece of paper and an open mind. Ask your stakeholders: What would you prioritise if you were in my shoes? How does the business make money? What are your top business unit priorities and how can my team help you achieve those goals? Simply put, executives will do their best to support you if they know, trust and like you.

## Don't Play the Victim

Tell business leaders what you will do, do it, and then tell them what you have done. An effective way to do this is to use strong visuals, such as the Active Cyber Risk Profile, which we strongly advocate in the Cyber Leadership Program. Let us illustrate with a practical example. One cyber leader in the oil and gas sector was hired to salvage the business from a brand-damaging crisis. During the formative weeks, the cyber leader scoured through risk registers, board reports, strategy decks and audit reports. They identified six critical risks sitting outside of appetite and requested funding to bring each of these material risks within appetite, which the board approved.

Over the next 12 months, the cyber leader ruthlessly focused on initiatives that reduced the likelihood or impact of these material risks and successfully delivered on their promise. The next update to the board demonstrated how the approved funding shifted the Active Cyber Risk Profile from the red zone to the amber or green. This clear demonstration of the value delivered by the transformation program using a simple but proven methodology made it easier for the cyber leader to request more funding.

Avoid telling the executive team and board why specific initiatives are 'impossible'. Leadership is about taking challenges head-on, pushing through obstacles, and not playing the victim. Of course, in any cyber transformation, you will face challenging situations but always aim to provide alternate ways to solve the problem. A can-do attitude is essential to thriving in this high-pressure role.

While not always avoidable, limit the amount of negative language in your cybersecurity reports. Contrary to widespread beliefs in the cybersecurity industry, fearmongering projects a tone of weakness. Leave doomsday scenarios to news anchors and meteorologists; these only undermine your credibility in the long term. As Cialdini puts it, 'There is a natural human tendency to dislike a person who brings us unpleasant information, even when that person did not cause the bad news. The simple association with it is enough to stimulate our dislike.'[37]

## Contextualise Messages with Key Stakeholders

The cyber leader must be deliberate about internal networking by organising regular catch-ups with critical stakeholders. There is no one-size-fits-all in terms of relevant stakeholders, but here are four vital executives they will need on their side, as well as some exploratory questions:

**CEO** – As the linchpin of management, the CEO is one of the most important stakeholders for the cyber leader to win over. Once you have the CEO on your side, the probability of success materially improves. Use the initial meeting with the CEO to gain an in-depth understanding of the business strategy, organisational culture, immediate- and long-term priorities, planned expansions or acquisitions and the CEO's most significant concerns and expectations. If your role reports directly to the CEO, discuss the preferred engagement model and critical attributes for success.

**CIO** – Discuss the digital transformation strategy and how it supports corporate goals. Map out the technical landscape (such as public cloud), outsourced critical services, vendor governance models, project management methodology, IT governance models, technical debt and key influencers within the IT department. Understand how the engagement model with the previous cybersecurity head worked and what you can improve. Determine if there is any cybersecurity capability financed by the IT budget and plan to change it.

**CFO** – Understand the budgeting processes and schedules, out-of-cycle expenditures, delegations of authority, cyber insurance, provisions to absorb unforeseen cyber breaches and preferences over fixed or variable costs. Getting the CFO on your side early in the game softens the ground, making it quicker to get your budget approved.

**CRO** – Understand what keeps them awake at night, such as the critical cyber risks that sit outside of appetite. Discuss the risk management culture and potential roadblocks, the process of granting exceptions and the linkage to a board-approved cyber risk appetite statement. Understand existing key governance forums (their cadence, mandate and authority) and how you can leverage them to accelerate cyber governance. Understand how cyber risk is communicated to the board, by whom and how often. Determine crucial external obligations and the implementation of the three lines of defence.

Take time to listen to the fears and aspirations of key executives and connect with them at a deeper, personal level. Equally important, organise one-on-one catch-ups with key members of leadership committees before you pitch your strategy, risk paper or budget request. Most important decisions are made way before, not during, governance meetings.

Here are some additional questions you can ask during meetings with various stakeholders.

**About Them and Their Function:**

- What are the biggest challenges the business is facing (or will face) shortly, and why?

- What are the short-term priorities of your business or function? Are any of these at risk?

- What are the long-term strategic objectives for your business or function?

- What are the most promising but unexplored opportunities for growth? What is needed to exploit these?

- Do you have direct cybersecurity responsibilities in your function?

## About the CISO Function:

- How well has the function delivered value in the past three years? Where has it succeeded, and where has it struggled to provide value?

- How do you see the value-add of the CISO function in your business priorities?

- What are your suggested methods to collaborate more effectively with you and your team? One-on-one, briefings, working groups, team meetings, governance, etc.?

- Are there specific issues or needs in your business or function that require focus?

- What will success look like for our partnership in the first year? What about in the first three years?

- Which people outside your team are detractors, and which are supporters?

- If you were me, what would you focus on?

## 3. Identify and Manage Potential Detractors

Succeeding in this high-pressure, cyber leadership role is not merely about getting key decision makers or power brokers on your side – it is equally important to know who the potential detractors are and then to proactively manage them. Left unchecked, the pressure from powerful detractors may get so intense that it derails the cyber leader's mission. The first step in managing potential detractors is to identify and then closely watch them. Here are some illustrative examples:

- Entrenched insiders who are stuck in obsolete corporate routines, scared of what a sharp change in direction will do to their value or even jobs. This group will tell you, 'We have always done it this way; why change now?' Their unwillingness or inability to adapt to a new management style or accelerated change can exert untenable inertia on your plan.

- Direct reports or peers who were competing for the position you filled. If you were promoted internally, previous peers must now swallow their pride and report to you. If you were hired externally, these aspiring cyber leaders could connive to oppose you, derailing the transformation program's success.

- A senior executive who thinks the cybersecurity function must report to them. In situations where the cyber leader sits one or more layers under the CEO, the struggle to control the cybersecurity function is common.

- Product development managers who have long perceived the cybersecurity team as a 'blocker' that needlessly delays new product launch, compromises customer experience and raises the product development cost.

*Once you know who these potential distractors are, the next step is to use the scale (ranging from –2 to +2) shown in Figure 2.2. Stakeholders at the right end of the scale are your potential supporters with a sizeable stake in the game; they perceive your success as their own. At the left end of the scale are those opposed to your mission – or just keen to frustrate your mission for personal gain or ego. In the middle are the neutrals – they are indifferent about whether to throw their full weight behind you or just 'watch and wait'.*

*Figure 2.2 Sample Detractor Assessment Scale*

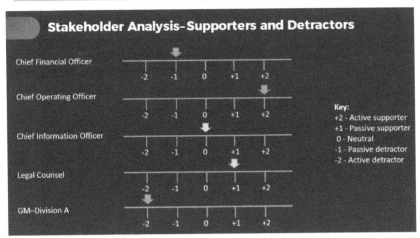

Managing difficult stakeholders is not for the impatient and short-tempered. It is important to remember that staying calm under pressure and actively listening to discern the root cause of frustrations are proven tools to disempower hostile stakeholders. Just by being friendly and patient, you can thaw most of your stakeholders who are hostile to your project.

The last step, and probably the most vital, is if you find someone incredibly challenging to deal with but notice that another stakeholder has a cordial relationship with them, then you can indirectly leverage that other relationship to get the problematic stakeholder on your side.

## 4. Acknowledge the Past but Focus on the Future

Some cyber leaders are hired to rescue their companies from highly damaging data breaches, regulatory undertakings and severely underperforming teams. Sometimes, the new position is created because of insistent lobbying by an influential investor, a business partner, or even the board telling the CEO that it is high time they fill this critical role. Naturally, the newly hired leader is inclined to delete the past and swiftly forge forward with the new plan. But this is a common and dangerous trap we see all the time.

85

Unless the new role is completely greenfield, you may not need to define an entirely new strategy. Imagine this scenario. The business fired CISO X after CISO X failed to execute the cyber resilience transformation strategy. It had taken CISO X six painstaking months working with various stakeholders – the CEO, CFO, general counsel, CIO, CRO, etc. – to identify critical blind spots and agree on priorities. The business had paid a reputable consultancy firm a substantial sum to bring external perspectives into the strategy. After several iterations the board had finally approved the comprehensive strategy. Unfortunately, CISO X was fired after failing to execute on a clear mandate, but the old strategy was robust and supported by business stakeholders. The replacement, CISO Y, was determined to reinvent the cyber resilience strategy quickly. CISO Y quickly started developing a new strategy, using their own 'proprietary methodology'. This needless and complete change of direction incensed several stakeholders, who had thrown themselves entirely behind the previous strategy.

To avoid this common mistake, you must acknowledge the work done by your predecessors, deliberately and carefully assess the lay of the land, and know what should be left unchanged. For instance, you can use the first slide of your strategy deck to portray critical initiatives already delivered and positive aspects of the organisational culture that will support rapid cyber resilience transformation. Let's illustrate with five examples where previous work has been overlooked:

1. Immaturely trying to transition cybersecurity services to your preferred supplier and replacing existing vendors who have developed long-term excellent working relationships with the CIO.

2. Haphazardly changing external assurance teams. If a specific organisation conducted independent red teaming exercise the previous year, and they did a decent job, retain them so they can validate the closure of issues previously reported to management, and leverage their internal knowledge to prevent friction with IT teams.

3. Killing projects whose proof of concepts has already been completed just because you prefer a tool that you are used to.

4. Establishing unnecessary working groups and governance committees when you can leverage existing forums.

5. Constantly undermining the work done by the previous team by labelling the function 'immature', 'below industry practice' or other demeaning terms.

Balancing past work with future needs requires cyber leaders to slow their pace down and rigorously engage with internal and external stakeholders. This way, they will also be able to accelerate their learning curve, know where their predecessors went wrong, and maximise their chances of success. There is no need to consciously ignore the excellent work done before you joined simply to serve your ego. Once you genuinely demonstrate that the organisation's cyber resilience matters more than your agenda, your chances to succeed materially rise.

## 5. Remember, Be Ambitious but Be Careful Not to Overpromise

To maximise your chances of success, you must take a disciplined, strategic approach to cyber resilience by working on a clearly articulated cyber transformation road map, one that is fully sponsored by the executive team and supported by the board. Here, it is essential to strike the right balance between ambition and caution. Your credibility is boosted if you deliver more than you promise.

Attempting to boil the ocean is a common blunder among cyber leadership teams. Predictably, these exaggerated promises always come back to bite at a breathtaking speed. Creating beautiful slides is the easy bit; delivering new capabilities is much more complicated than is often perceived. Here is an example to illustrate this common mistake:

- A CISO commits to encrypting large sets of databases within the next three months, only to discover after the strategy has been endorsed that the business is saddled by jumbles of complex, aged and proprietary applications referred to as 'legacy spaghetti'. Attempting to encrypt these legacy platforms will break their functionality. Such a swift and radical pivot from a control (encrypting data at rest) touted by the information security chief as 'non-negotiable' sowed doubt.

It is always dangerous to promise a Ferrari and then deliver a Toyota Corolla. Of course, no strategy is set in stone – but still, going back to the board with revised targets or apologising for 'miscommunication' will send your credibility flying out the window.

As Rory McDonald and Robert Bremner underscored in their article 'When It's Time to Pivot, What's Your Story?', 'Pivots can incur a penalty if they're not correctly managed. A reorientation is an implicit admission that the plan to which the founders were once deeply committed was flawed. This deviation can be jarring and can suggest a lack of consistency and competence.'[38] Although explicitly talking about entrepreneurs, the lessons are universal and apply to cyber transformation programs.

Take time to understand where the business is headed, its technical constraints and your team's capabilities. An essential part of strategic planning is understanding what can go wrong and making relevant provisions.

## 6. Share the Glory

No matter how brilliant you are, you will never be able to drive complex change by yourself. Successful cyber resilience results from a combined effort from many teams – program delivery, IT, legal, procurement and so on. However, because the cyber leader's role has become crucial to any organisation's ongoing concern and long-term success, you will continuously have access to the board and a range of organisation-wide events. If you are not careful, hubris will quickly kick in.

You must resist the temptation to be self-centred and remember to share the glory. This is even more important when you do not report to the CIO because successful cybersecurity solutions and integration with core systems hinge on strong IT involvement.

When you give credit where it's due, stakeholders feel obliged to support you. Conversely, stakeholders feel snubbed, overlooked, or worse, betrayed every time a cyber leader self-congratulates when the team ticks big-ticket items or when they cast blame on others when projects fail.

During your board and town hall debriefs, acknowledge the efforts of other leaders who have contributed to the cyber resilience strategy's success. Taking all the credit for the team's success and using the word 'I', not 'we', severely harms your ability to inspire action. No one wants to follow a selfish leader or, worse, a peer who continually seeks collaboration but never shares the glory.

It is even more critical that the cyber leader always acknowledge the contributions of their direct reports, including cascading messages of praise from the C-suite, the board, or risk management committees. An even more effective approach is asking the senior leaders to recognise your team members directly. Celebrating your team's success will also improve their confidence and motivate them to take intense pride in their work.

## 7. Deliberately Cultivate Your Credibility

The mention of personal branding turns many stomachs. It reminds people of the self-anointed influencers who make a lot of noise on social media but who do not have much to offer deep down. However, we are talking about something different: developing excellent and irrefutable skills in your domain that help you run away from the competition. Leading cyber leaders understand that personal branding, when done with the right intentions, is a potent tool that can accelerate their careers and enhance their standing within leadership teams.

To paraphrase Steven Martin, writing for *Harvard Business Review*, decision makers often place less faith in what is said and more in who is saying it; it's the messenger who carries the sway, not necessarily the message itself.[39]

Cyber leaders often complain that they have no access to the board or that their messages are ignored. But to thrive in any executive role, authority matters. Cyber leadership is no exception. Business leaders will believe your story if you have a strong standing in the industry and are respected by your peers.

Some of the strategies we have seen that consistently deliver tremendous results are rigorously pushing thought leadership articles, collaborating extensively with fellow cyber leaders and speaking at industry events. The credibility you build externally naturally trickles down to your professional role. Over time, your messages will become more believable. You start to project a more assertive or confident tone and get access to meetings you would otherwise not have been invited to. If the CEO respects you, then you will have access to the board; it is as simple as that.

Leveraging the power of existing internal forums and networks is another powerful strategy. For instance, once your strategy is approved, find ten-minute slots to share core, cyber resilience transformation program priorities via town hall sessions, risk governance forums, and newsletters.

Another strategy is to create an employee cyber ambassador program, where essential volunteers champion the cybersecurity message within their business units of their own volition.

One of the most effective ways to cultivate credibility and expand your influence is to work on your business communication skills.

Let's face it – cybersecurity is a highly technical and expansive subject. No wonder that most senior business leaders find it too ambiguous and frustrating. Cyber leaders who master the art of persuasive communication will easily stand out. The ability to communicate persuasively and with impact is necessary to thrive as a cyber leader. Because you are competing for the board's and C-suite's limited time, you must deliberately communicate cyber risk information in a way that is easy to understand.

Here are some effective strategies:

- Link cyber resilience to strategic matters executives and directors care about, such as business growth, customer retention, capital raising, and success in mergers and acquisitions. Avoid high-flying technical jargon that you think makes you sound important, as this only harms your credibility. Most senior business leaders are not interested in how much spam you stopped but care if a system that supports 40% of their revenue line is crippled by a ransomware attack with no offline backups.

- Tie the strategic cybersecurity initiatives to corporate values – something bigger than you, your team or other individuals. For example, a cyber leader successfully convinced product development teams to train developers in secure coding because shipping safe products to consumers aligned with the firm's value of 'always doing what is right, not what is easy'.

- Leverage your cyber assurance program to secure early wins and drive the critical message to senior business leaders and the board. Consider this scenario. A CISO faced significant hurdles trying to roll out multi-factor authentication, with the business saying this move would degrade user experience.

But when the cyber leader engaged an independent party to conduct Active Directory password testing that cracked 90% of all corporate network passwords using trivial tools within minutes, the message finally sank in. You can also engage third parties to conduct a digital footprinting exercise for targeted executives – scouring through the darknet to identify hacked, personally identifiable information for senior leaders, and presenting the findings via one-on-one meetings. That is a proven way to win hearts and transform minds.

- Meet with key board members and the C-suite before important meetings. Brief them on critical matters and solicit their support. It is undoubtedly impractical for a cyber head to meet with every executive before the meeting. So, it is essential to focus on critical executives impacted by your proposal, crucial swing voters, or power brokers. For instance, if you propose to drive significant cultural change, it is imperative to secure the head of human resources and the CEO before the meeting.

The cyber leader must pay special attention to external reports likely to be read by their boards or executives and pre-emptively contextualise key messages to their organisation. For example, your Big Four audit firm will likely email the results of its critical survey to the audit risk committee chair, or your CEO will read an industry cybersecurity benchmarking exercise.

## 8. Be a Courageous Leader

The CISO role is fraught with demanding situations, and your courage as a leader will inevitably be regularly tested. Here are a few situations:

- Excessive pressure from senior business officers to approve a supplier without proper due diligence because an audit will delay a project that's already in the red

- Inheriting some poor performers who have kept their roles by playing dirty corporate politics

- Feeling pressured to accept a risk you consider critical or revise the risk to low or moderate

Your role as a cyber leader is to empower business executives to make risk-informed decisions – you are not hired to accept risk. Cyber leaders often run into situations where they feel pressured to downgrade a risk because the business is unwilling to act. It is essential to be courageous, be realistic about risk scenarios and resist the pressure to sugar-coat situations. This is called 'Please now, suffer later' because if you downgrade a material risk to please stakeholders and then the inevitable happens, your credibility will tank.

An essential trait of effective leadership is mustering the guts to make decisions, even when you don't have enough information. Unfortunately, in our experience engaging with cyber leaders from dozens of countries, this is much easier said than done. Many cyber leaders are hesitant to cut through the fog and pass strong opinions on to business leaders. They waste time drafting lengthy risk papers.

To reinforce your trust with leadership teams, you must clearly state where you stand. If you think going live with an application with unmitigated critical vulnerabilities will expose the business to excessive risks, then be assertive with your recommendation. Tentative responses harm your credibility.

## Conclusion

John Baldoni summed up this subject beautifully when he said:

> Credibility is a leader's coin of the realm. With it, she can lead people to the Promised Land; without it, she wanders in the desert of lost expectations. Once lost, it may be impossible to

regain, and so the lesson to any manager who has any aspiration of achieving anything is to guard your credibility and take care you never lose it.[40]

Remember that job titles don't necessarily equate to influence. Spend time with your boss and understand who the critical power brokers are: the individuals able to persuade essential executives or the board. Your success as a cyber leader certainly depends on many factors, but your ability to persuade and influence key stakeholders is the most important.

# Chapter 4

# Embedding a Cyber Resilience Culture Deep into the DNA of the Enterprise

This chapter was a collaboration between the Cyber Leadership Institute and Jasmin Krapf, a senior cyber awareness expert and thought leader. She is reachable via LinkedIn - https://www.linkedin.com/in/jasmin-krapf-seo/

## Cyber Security and the Human Factor

Back in 2015, James A. (Sandy) Winnefeld Jr., Christopher Kirchhoff and David M. Upton published a compelling article in *Harvard Business Review* titled 'Cybersecurity's Human Factor: Lessons from the Pentagon' in which they extrapolated lessons from the military to provide a framework through which organisations can foster cyber resilience by placing disproportionate weighting on human elements of cybersecurity, not technology. 'One key lesson of the military's experience is that while technical upgrades are important, minimizing human error is even more crucial. Mistakes by network administrators and users – failures to patch vulnerabilities in legacy systems, misconfigured settings, violations of standard procedures – open the door to the overwhelming majority of successful attacks,' the authors argued.[41]

Almost a decade later, these enduring principles remain as relevant as ever. Studies show that over 65% of all breaches start with someone clicking on a seemingly safe link, which explains why phishing is used by adversaries to begin 80% to 95% of all attacks.[42] Just think about this: the 2016 hack of Hillary Clinton's campaign manager's (John Podesta) email, alleged to have significantly impacted the United States election, resulted from a spear phishing attack. Podesta received an email that resembled a security alert from Google, encouraging him to change his password. Unbeknown to Podesta, the malicious email contained a Bitly link that redirected him to a fake Google login page, where his credentials were stolen. Guccifer 2.0 (the alleged mastermind), WikiLeaks and DCLeaks ultimately published more than 150,000 emails stolen from more than a dozen Democrats. Many have argued the leaks had material implications on the US presidential election.

If we borrow the lessons from *HBR's* 'Cybersecurity's Human Factor: Lessons from the Pentagon,' cyber leaders can accelerate their digital resilience at a fraction of the cost by relentlessly focusing on four high-reliability organisation (HROs) principles of integrity, deep expertise, procedural compliance, and forceful backup. This brings us to an important topic, focusing on the human elements to foster cyber resilience.

## Driving an effective enterprise-wide cyber-resilient culture

This chapter proposes a series of recommendations to drive an effective enterprise-wide cyber-resilient culture program through the following approaches:

- Putting people's hearts and minds, not technology, at the centre of the organisational cybersecurity strategies

- Developing a culture change program that uses a good mix of tactical and strategic initiatives to change workforce behaviour

- Creating the appropriate tone at the top to maximise a cyber-resilient culture program funding

- Using innovative data-driven techniques to gain insights into the risk profile of employees

- Extending the reach and maximising the impact of smaller cybersecurity teams

- Developing sustainable methods of measuring and continuously improving cyber-aware culture

**Through these recommendations, you can expect the following benefits:**

- Transforming employee attitudes and behaviours through compelling and contextualised messages and reinforcing good deeds for a positive security environment.

- Ensuring the C-suite and board remain steadfast and champion the security teams' efforts to drive culture change from the top down.

- Creating a workforce with deeply internalised beliefs that protecting the enterprise from cyber threats is everyone's responsibility.

- Having frontline employees who handle high-value transactions understand their role in defending the enterprise and proactively reporting suspicious behaviour. These include call centre staff handling sensitive customer financial data, healthcare workers managing life-critical patient records, engineers developing internet-connected heart monitoring devices, finance personnel approving high-risk invoices, and so forth.

Consider the analyses and recommmendations in this chapter to help scope an effective enterprise-wide cyber-resilient culture program. The top seven recommendations in *Table 3.1* are discussed in more detail under the Action Plan section:

*Table 3.1*

## Top Five Recommendations

1. **Develop a Tactical and Strategic Culture Change Program:** Security awareness and culture change need to be managed as a 'behaviour change initiative', and behaviour change needs to be viewed from a tactical and strategic lens. Develop a culture program that uses a combination of tactical and strategic initiatives in changing behaviour, with responsive governance and ongoing reviews.

2. **Set the Tone at the Top:** Effective leadership includes role modelling, active participation by C-level executives in defining the corporate culture and standards of behaviour. Any significant transformation program demands unwavering support from the chief executive officer (CEO), the C-suite and the board. Creating a cyber-savvy workforce is no different; sustained cultural shifts require the most senior officers to role model expected behaviours, uphold the virtues of the cyber risk appetite and, most importantly, proactively reward positive behaviours and hold wrongdoers accountable.

3. **Identify High-Risk Communities:** A consistent message from the Cyber Leadership Institute is security must be managed like other business risks. That means making deliberate choices and ruthlessly prioritising limited security budget on the most significant risks. To that end, we recommend the cyber leader to segment employees according to their risk profiles to deliver contextualised messages that emphasise specific threats employees face in their respective roles. Having a one-size-fits-all approach dilutes the effectiveness of limited resources and exerts untenable pressure on thinly resourced cybersecurity teams.

4. **Establish a Cyber Ambassador Program:** Extend the cyber team's reach by building a network of cyber resilience culture ambassadors throughout your organisation to engage the broader employee base while promoting cybersecurity best practices. That way, cyber resilience becomes everyone's responsibility, from the frontline staff to the board.

5. **Gamify to Engage Employees:** Eliminate boredom by leveraging concepts from the gaming world and apply them to cybersecurity awareness programs. That means use game incentives to engage and reward positive action, thus, transforming previously mundane activities into sticky and highly engaging events.

## MAJOR BUSINESS PAIN POINTS

As many large enterprises learn from their high-profile data breaches, cyber resilience is not about technology per se; it has more to do with patching the human brain. Social engineering – or hacking the mind – remains the preferred avenue for cyber threat actors, including well-resourced nation states, mainly because it targets the weakest link in any enterprise that cannot be patched with technical solutions.

However, several enterprises still mistakenly believe that cyber resilience is about investing in fancy tools or attaining multiple compliance seals, paying scant heed to the human factor. They invest intensively in technical solutions and lurch from one emerging technology to another, looking for a cure-all solution to their cybersecurity problems. Such over-reliance on technology is a strategic mistake that only creates a false sense of immunity. Any hope that some emerging technology will shield enterprises from social engineering attacks is hugely misguided.

Why does social engineering make a business vulnerable? There are five primary reasons why social engineering remains an enduring and effective tactic for cybercriminals to employ:

1. Well-crafted and highly targeted emails, such as business email compromise scams, can easily evade technical defences, including spam filters, email threat prevention, or antivirus software, as they don't contain embedded hyperlinks or attachments. As such, configuring systems to pick up targeted phishing emails is difficult.

2. Fundamentally, social engineering is designed for psychological manipulation. It exploits reckless risk-takers and emotionally vulnerable, arrogant, greedy or gullible victims.

3. Most social engineering attacks leave no audit trails, making it difficult for victims or law enforcement agents to attribute a cyberattack or fraud to a specific perpetrator.

4. Compared with technology-based attacks, such as using automated tools to crack passwords, impersonating a victim and requesting the help desk or call centre to reset their password is cheaper, faster and easier.

5. Threat actors develop custom hacking tools, based on the system or technology they wish to compromise. Social engineering, however, is technology agnostic and is equally effective across Linux, Mainframe, Windows, Android, iOS or any other platform.

## ACTION PLAN

Building a cyber-resilient culture requires long-term sustainable effort; it's not just a one-off initiative. Any change management program takes time to change behaviours and strengthen the cyber risk mindset in the organisation. A continuous and coordinated effort is required to increase the level of human-focused cyber-resilience; it can take at least 12 months to achieve any observable change. This action plan offers an approach to building a cyber-resilient culture program.

## 1. Develop a Tactical and Strategic Culture Change Program

To develop a culture change work program, first, recognise that behaviour change requires both tactical and strategic initiatives. Consider the following questions:

- Do regulatory bodies have any specific awareness and cultural requirements?

- What are the key security risks and threats to the business?

- Who are the high-risk user groups in the organisation?

- Are there other existing programs and functions that can be integrated?

- What are the metrics to communicate the effectiveness of cyber awareness programs to senior management and board?

The steps below answer these questions and show how you can develop a program that works in both ways:

### Tactical

- Identify secure behaviour requirements from standards and regulatory obligations.

- Identify top threats and security risks from external events and intel from security teams.

- Identify high-risk users while considering various factors like roles, types of personalities, beliefs, work dynamics, skills, visibility, and values. The challenge of cultural change is that every individual is different. There is no one-size-fits-all solution.

- Determine available channels that can be used to engage.

- Identify industry-wide and national cyber awareness and privacy-related events to get some good and quick wins at a low cost.

- Identify your advocates, influencers, challengers and end-users and design the program using the feedback from these groups. Note, however, that end-users are different for many reasons, so take the time to identify key personas that can help make the engagement with this group more effective. Behaviour changes and the complexity of dealing with different end-users mean that communicating policies through online learning programs alone will not be adequate, albeit necessary.

- Be prepared to respond to current news. With major brands falling victim to high profile cyber incidents, cybersecurity is becoming a dinner table conversation. Help your staff understand what the events were about and what they meant for them – but this needs to be done in real time for maximum impact.

## Strategic

- Establish program mission and goals and all support initiatives that can be shared with the business.

- Determine metrics and targets (see action point number eight – Measure the effectiveness of culture change) to know the behaviour the staff needs to perform and target key risk indicators.

- Build a mature and strong partnership with HR and communication teams. They have experience and resources in communicating and engaging creatively that will help get the cut-through needed. The use of layperson terms and real-life context versus technical terms will help make the story stick.

- Create an ambassador program (see action point number five – Establish a cyber ambassador program).

- Shift towards business cultural values instead of technology security needs.

- Build on the board's awareness by allotting time every quarter to update threats and what they mean for the organisation.

- Put yourself in the shoes of your staff and customers. Understand their processes and experiences to determine where the security value and challenge may be. Shift the discussion to enablement, which may involve a combination of education and redesign of the security approach.

## 2. Set the Tone at the Top

Long-term cultural shifts require senior business executives to role model expected attitudes, beliefs and practices. The executive leadership team must categorically signal that cybersecurity is of prime importance to the enterprise's mission and is everyone's responsibility.

The underlying premise is that whatever attitude senior executives exhibit (or set) will trickle down to the lower ranks of staff. If executives demonstrate eagerness and deep commitment to protecting high-value digital assets and upholding customer digital trust, making the cyber risk appetite an entrenched part of the enterprise's life, middle- and lower-ranking employees will naturally be inclined to enforce the same virtues.

On the contrary, if leaders pay lip service to cybersecurity by unnecessarily approving dozens of policy exemptions, plugging unmanaged personal devices into the corporate network, bypassing payment delegations of authority, travelling to high-risk countries with unencrypted devices or exporting sensitive data to unsanctioned cloud environments, their behaviour will also cascade down through the enterprise, exposing it to significant risk.

The following are the key actions enterprises can take to set the tone at the top:

- As part of their routine communications, the CEO must emphasise the significance of cybersecurity to the enterprise mission and solicit commitment from frontline staff by underscoring the critical role everyone plays in securing the enterprise. By categorically stressing the strategic importance of cyber resilience to the organisational mission during town hall sessions and through emails to all staff and publicly recognising cybersecurity heroes, the CEO, as the linchpin of management, can become the primary agent for cultural change.

- The chief risk officer should galvanise unwavering commitment from peers to uphold the cyber risk appetite statement's precepts and communicate those expectations to their teams.

- Business unit leaders should cascade the CEO's core messages to their wider teams, contextualising them to specific threats targeting their groups, and the different roles they play in securing the enterprise. At the same time, you must extend the same communication and education resources to the executives, explaining why their roles and profiles are easy and more desirable to be the target of a cyberattack.

- Senior leaders should actively participate in significant cybersecurity drills, such as regular cyber crisis simulations, including phishing, blue team/red team exercises, and external cyber stress testing. Have the leaders engage in games and simulations to help them understand the mind of a hacker and learn about cyber risks and defences.

- Senior executives should also send a strong message to others by rejecting requests that violate the policy, such as disabling security controls on servers, pushing back vital security patches or engaging with third parties that exhibit deplorable cybersecurity practices.

- Have a select number of executives and board members, including the CEO, participate in a digital footprinting exercise run by an experienced cyber consulting firm. This assessment looks at all the information about that person online, including social media, email accounts and anything on the dark web. A summary of the findings is then presented back to the executive in a private and confidential one-to-one consultation. They'll learn about what risks they pose to themselves and the company through poor cyber practices. Digital footprinting is a powerful way to raise executive awareness.

- Have the CEO champion the cyber ambassador program with a call to action via a short online video. The CEO should explain why security is essential and how staff can become cyber ambassadors and be part of the cyber resilience culture change program.

## 3. Educate Against Email Threats

The first step to combat the growing email scams is to provide employees with practical guidance to detect these threats early and protect the enterprise. Communicating some baseline messages to staff is essential.

The risk of employees being manipulated significantly reduces when the senior management ensures the following:

- Reassure employees that it's permissible to develop questioning attitudes and challenge high-risk requests, such as emailing sensitive information or processing payments, regardless of their origin – CEO, direct managers, customers, regulators or auditors.

- Make the cybersecurity message personal for employees by equipping them with the knowledge they need to protect their personal information, home devices, and families from common cybersecurity threats. When employees are proficient at defending themselves, they are inclined to adopt the same behaviours at work.

- Urge employees to exercise care when posting information online. Attackers troll social media sites to identify targets and use real data to craft deceptive emails.

- Educate employees on the use of hard-to-guess passwords and not to use the same passwords across multiple platforms. Hackers will attempt logging into work or banking systems using compromised social media or other credentials dumped on the internet.

- Enforce dual approval for all payment-out transactions. Tricking two individuals is harder than tricking one.

- Urge employees to manually type the email addresses of intended recipients instead of just hitting the reply button. This increases the possibility of only communicating with authorised parties.

- Encourage client-facing employees to acquaint themselves with the habits of their customers and payment patterns. This makes it easier to detect unusual requests.

- Purchase internet domains closely resembling yours, making it difficult for fraudsters to establish fictitious email accounts and websites.

- Ensure network security administrators correctly configure threat detection and spam filtering software.

- Require an additional method to verify payment requests, such as calling back customers or sending a one-time verification code to a mobile app.

- Assess employee behaviour patterns through routine social engineering tests, such as simulated phishing campaigns. These exercises highlight vulnerable segments, enabling the enterprise to redirect resources where they are most required.

## 4. Identify High-Risk Communities

Another critical step to ensure that cybersecurity messages stay is to deliver contextualised messages that emphasise specific threats employees face in their respective roles and provide appropriate guidance on detecting and thwarting those threats. Different departments, employees and third parties represent different risk groups and thus require different education methods, monitoring and reporting.

Segmentation allows the organisation to home in on the 'hot spots' of risk. It takes a targeted rather than a blanket approach to threat monitoring and mitigation, which improves prediction to identify and disrupt insider activities much earlier in the threat life cycle. To illustrate how these concepts work in practice, start by focusing on three of these high-risk segments: (1) software developers, (2) executive assistants, and (3) systems and database administrators.

- Software Developers: Charged with embedding security controls into critical business applications, software developers, if not adequately trained in secure coding, prioritise functionality over security, shipping vulnerable systems into live environments. The source code that developers produce is also an attractive target for cyber-related industrial espionage.

- Executive Assistants: These are often custodians of high-value corporate credit cards. They also have access to executive emails and a considerable volume of market-sensitive information, for example, initial public offering plans, unannounced revisions in financial forecasts, mergers and acquisition strategies, plans to expand into markets, the launch of new products, proposed business division spin-offs or proposed changes in leadership teams. Furthermore, an executive assistant can act within their boss's delegation of authority, approving high-value payments on their behalf.

- Systems and Database Administrators: Guardians of an enterprise's digital environment. These teams are charged with patching critical systems, hardening the digital environment, and administering user access across high-value systems. Consequently, mistakes or human error by systems administrators can leave the network exposed to critical vulnerabilities. Also, the privileged nature of their access makes systems administrators a lucrative target for threat actors.

Segmenting employees, according to their risk profiles, has three significant benefits:

a. Focused Training: Spend more resources on training employees exposed to higher levels of cyber risk, as determined by the sensitivity of the data they handle, the consequences of human error in respective roles and the attractiveness of related tasks to cybercriminals. Risk-based cybersecurity investment is a core tenet of a cyber-resilient enterprise.

b. Messaging Is More Audience Relevant: Custom cybersecurity messages stick when compared to generic guidance. For instance, citing case studies where hackers penetrated core banking systems by exploiting unpatched servers with a lack of multi-factor authentication will resonate with systems administrators. On the other hand, finance staff will relate more to cases where scammers tricked a chief financial officer at a similar enterprise into wiring millions of dollars to offshore accounts.

c. Two-Way Open Communication Channel: Facilitating closed-door sessions with specific groups promotes transparent conversations. Employees can openly ask questions without fear of supervisor backlash or sounding stupid. For instance, it's easier to advise payment staff to challenge payment requests that violate established processes in the absence of senior leaders, who often bypass procedures and send payment instructions via short message service or text messages.

## 5. Establish a Cyber Ambassador Program

A cyber ambassador program is where employees volunteer their time to train staff on core cybersecurity principles. They become ambassadors (also commonly called champions, advocates or sentinels). Even though it's a program that tends to be low-cost, it takes time and effort to get it done well. Organisations may need to allocate one person from the cyber department to manage the program. Here are some tips to get this right.

- Launch the Program Top-Down: The best way to engage and galvanise the entire organisation into action is to have the CEO record a video emphasising how serious leadership takes cybersecurity and encourage staff to volunteer their time to this important role.

- Ambassador Recruitment: Ambassadors should not be members of the information security team or in a leadership role. By drawing ambassadors from the frontline team instead of management, the culture of security is more likely to permeate through the organisation because the guidance is peer-to-peer versus top-down.

- Review and Select Applicants: When reviewing the applications and nominations, prioritise ambassadors representing a cross-section of locations, roles and service lines. Look for an attitude and a desire to learn about cybersecurity and take responsibility.

- Launch a Training and Advancement Program for Ambassadors: Ambassadors will require training and mentoring program and planning for at least three months to get your initial batch ready. Depending on the ambassador's cyber experience, it's helpful to segment them and allocate responsibilities accordingly. For example, each must have completed all cybersecurity modules already offered by the organisation to be a base level. As they move up the education curve, they are rewarded with more responsibility for security-related initiatives. Eventually, the ambassadors in the program will be able to train the next wave of ambassadors and even become cybersecurity professionals themselves.

- Host a Certification and Induction Ceremony: It's important to publicly acknowledge not only the first group of ambassadors but subsequent ones. Inviting a business executive to the ceremony further signifies leadership support.

- Maintain Ambassador Momentum: Once up and running, the cybersecurity team must continue to provide ongoing communication and resources to the ambassadors. Consider creating a forum for ambassadors to exchange ideas.

- Manage and Measure the Program: In addition to managing the program, measure its effectiveness. Track the number and types of inquiries or incidents submitted or reported by users to the ambassadors. Look at the number of queries submitted from ambassadors to the information security team. Tracking these incidents and reports could be done through web forms, social platforms or existing communications and ticketing tools. Where possible, have your ambassadors measure the time they spend on cybersecurity awareness training, presentations, and handling of incident reporting. Finally, look to see, after a predetermined period, if behaviour improvements are made as a result of the ambassador program (see action point number eight – Measure the effectiveness of culture change).

## 6.  Gamify to Engage Employees

In gamification, organisations use game incentives such as points, online badges and other rewards to motivate employees to embrace cybersecurity values proactively. Gamification is useful because it transforms mundane cybersecurity tasks into enjoyable, appealing and sticky activities. It's also a powerful mechanism to boost productivity as employees who the organisation publicly recognises for high performance are naturally inclined to repeat the same behaviours or aim higher. At the same time, it motivates peers to emulate strong performers, building a high-performance culture, shifting from 'I have to' to 'I want to' discretionary performance.

By deducting points from teams or individuals who consistently violate established procedures, such as emailing unencrypted sensitive information to external parties, gamification reveals employee segments that require additional training or targeted messages. CISOs can gamify cybersecurity in several ways. Here are a few examples:

- Software developers accumulate points by baking cybersecurity into new programs and consistently delivering bug-free code. Conversely, points are deducted from programmers who ship code with critical security vulnerabilities. Gamifying secure coding motivates programmers to learn and embrace the principles of secure coding by their own will, rather than treat it as a necessary evil. Knowing what's at stake also encourages project teams to proactively engage security testers and factor security requirements early into the project, including at the budgeting stage. It eliminates the cost of maintaining applications, as baking security controls into new digital platforms is significantly cheaper than retrofitting security into live programs.

- A system administration team that reliably deploys critical patches within required time frames is awarded points or earns badges. Points can be redeemed quarterly or half-yearly in the form of bowling or golf tickets or other modest rewards. In contrast, teams that short-circuit change management processes and compromise business stability through poorly tested patches will have significant deductions. Gamifying core system administration activities has two advantages: it motivates teams to maintain a hygienic security environment proactively and fosters discipline by discouraging groups from prioritising security at the expense of stability or vice versa. These two risks should be simultaneously managed.

- Customer-facing teams are awarded points for actively embracing the tenets of the enterprise's data classification and handling policy. For example, groups that encrypt sensitive data before sharing it with external parties are awarded points. On the other hand, those that send sensitive data in clear text via email, as informed by a data loss prevention tool, have points deducted.

- The blue team (defenders)/red team (attackers) operational technology cyber teams can be mobilised to simulate cyberattacks in a game called 'capture the flag'. This can be extended to the boardroom and executives at a less technical level, pitting themselves against each other and taking turns to play in small teams as attackers and defenders.

## Conclusion

Culture doesn't change overnight. It takes time for an employee to get into the mindset and understand the consequences of their actions or inactions. But when they do, they apply these practices at work, then at home, with their kids, and become part of the solution. Ultimately, the journey to building a cyber-resilient culture is a long-term commitment, but it will pay dividends when everyone takes personal responsibility.

# Chapter 5

# Developing High-Impact Cyber Resilience Strategies

## Clarity of Purpose and Superior Strategy Triumph Over Abundance of Resources

In December 1878, Sir Bartle Frere, the British high commissioner for South Africa, commanded Cetshwayo, the Zulu king, to dismantle his military system within 30 days. Cetshwayo quickly deployed emissaries to Natal to negotiate peace, but their pleas fell on deaf ears.[43] The Zulu refused to give in to the absurd demands of the British. This defiance would soon catalyse the chronicled battle of Isandlwana, the first significant battle of the Anglo-Zulu War in which a force of 20,000 Zulus annihilated a British contingent of 1,800 men. This unlikely victory, given the disparity of resources between the two foes and the inferiority of Zulu weapons, would remain an enduring symbol to native South Africans that white domination was not inevitable. But how did the Zulus pull such an improbable victory, given the inferiority of their weapons? Five key strategic factors came into play:

## 1. Discipline and Single Mindedness

The Zulu army boasted intense discipline and tactical organisation, using a regimental system called 'amabutho', which organised fighters according to age and experience, fostering cohesion and focus. Facing an existential threat, the Zulu King inspired his battle-hardened soldiers to fight for something way bigger than themselves, instructing them to go 'eat up the red soldiers'.

## 2. Superior Military Tactics

The Zulu employed a tactic established by Shaka Zulu called the 'horns of the beast', in which the main regiment delivered a frontal assault, while the other troops spread out to the flanks and delivered a secondary and often fatal attack in the enemy's rear. Cetshwayo soldiers also deployed numerous psychological tactics to intimidate their opponents – playing drums, chanting war cries as well as unexpected aggressive displays of fearlessness and unity to discourage the British. On the contrary, the British commanders greatly underestimated the resolve and skill of the Zulu army.

## 3. Concentration of Forces

By concentrating a large number of their soldiers at Isandlwana on a scale not seen before, the Zulu managed to significantly outnumber and overwhelm the British in spite of their advanced weaponry. On the other hand, the British split their forces across vast and unfamiliar terrain.

After a protracted battle, the Zulu managed to overrun the camp and kill most of the British and colonial contingent. This remains the greatest triumph in the Zulu nation's military history – and an ignominious defeat for the British Empire.

Granted, the Battle of Isandlwana took place more than 140 years ago, but as philosopher George Santayana once said, 'Those who cannot learn from history are doomed to repeat it.' Cyber leaders can certainly draw an important lesson from the Zulu fighters, who, despite having all odds stacked against them, vastly outwitted and defeated the British Army. In cybersecurity, as in war, clarity of purpose, clever tactics and strategic thinking always triumph over abundance of resources. This brings us to another important chapter – developing high-value strategies that optimise limited budgets to advance business goals and close critical business risks.

Faced with a barrage of high-profile data breaches, some crippling even the most resourced and complex of organisations, many business leaders now harbour deep-seated fears that cyber-threat actors are undeterrable and cyber resilience is unachievable. Inside boardrooms, there is a significant amount of justified frustration. Most leaders feel like passengers on a runaway train. But this ought not to be the case and that's why we have written this chapter.

**John Maxwell**, a famous leadership coach, once said, 'Everything rises and falls on leadership.'[44] Cyber resilience is no different – especially with the dozens of best practice frameworks, complex and overlapping regulatory requirements, and rapidly adaptive threat actors – a robust strategy is the bedrock of sustained cyber resilience.

In this chapter, we provide the key principles and actionable advice required to build a highly focused and adaptive cyber resilience strategy, an end-to-end view of cyber resilience, including:

- Conducting a comprehensive cyber risk assessment

- Linking cyber transformation to corporate strategy to enlist stakeholder buy-in and support

- Building a team to deliver and sustain change

- Agreeing on a target state

- Delivering on your promises

In the absence of a robust, business-aligned strategy, cyber resilience can easily become a slippery slope of endless expenditure, exerting untenable pressure on the business and fatiguing often poorly resourced cybersecurity teams.

Granted, every enterprise is different – there is no universally right, cybersecurity strategy. There is certainly no one-size-fits-all approach to cyber resilience, but the following framework provides a strong foundation for cyber leaders to prioritise security investments and optimise governance structures. But before we delve into the how, let's diagnose the problem.

## MAJOR BUSINESS PAIN POINTS

1. The majority of cyber leaders are hired to salvage serious problems: clean up data breaches, replace a fired cyber executive or respond to serious regulatory matters. Because they are thrown into the deep end from the start, cyber leaders barely have enough time to carefully forge their own agendas. Without clear-cut guidance on how to create high-impact cyber resilience strategies, amid crazy schedules, strategy design becomes an afterthought.

2. Behind the above problem is a deeper one. A consistent message from the cyber leadership community is that cyber resilience programs receive lip service from senior business leaders and boards. While this trend is changing thanks to tightening regulatory screws and external stakeholder demands, cyber programs remain underfunded initiatives, and very small teams are expected to play superheroes in the face of rising threats and a barrage of alerts.

3. Developing business-aligned cyber resilience strategies is a new domain. Strategy design concepts that have worked effectively in the military and business worlds for example, have not been successfully extrapolated to cyber leadership. Furthermore, the majority of cyber leaders hail from a solution engineering, operational or architecture background, with very minimal experience in strategy design, influencing, strategic communications and risk management. The absence

of these skills often spells disaster for a new cyber leader, leading to early frustrations, mental fatigue or complete failure to overcome inertia and drive change.

4. The cyber leader has to ruthlessly prioritise. But while it's clear that prioritisation is the prime difference between strategy success and failure, discipline is largely lacking within organisations. By attempting to manage all aspects of cyber risks proportionately, ignoring that each has differing business implications, cyber leaders are mired in urgent but not important matters. In the end, cyber resilience programs remain bottomless money pits, a constant stream of 'bleeding-edge technologies' that give a false sense of invulnerability.

Most cyber resilience strategies follow a tick-box approach against industry frameworks. This narrow compliance-based approach gives an exaggerated sense of invulnerability, leaving organisations exposed to serious blind spots. In addition, most of these frameworks, comprised of hundreds of controls, are not suited for smaller organisations. As Jim Collins wrote in his bestselling strategy book *Good to Great*,[45] consensus-based decisions are often at odds with intelligent decisions. The consensus-based industry frameworks are ill-suited to address one of the cyber leader's primary responsibilities: resource optimisation. In the section below, we provide an overview of the risk-based approach and highlight some of its limitations.

## The Old Approach –Risk-Based Cyber Resilience Strategy

Up until now, most organisations have adopted a risk-based approach to managing cyber risk. The premise of this approach is straightforward: cyber resilience is an extension of the traditional IT governance domain. That is, the cyber leader's primary responsibility is to reduce the firm's exposure to excessive cyber risks, specifically investing in additional controls to shift cyber risks sitting outside of the corporate risk profile to within appetite.

As illustrated by *Figure 4.1*, after a comprehensive, organisation-wide risk assessment, the cyber leader will prioritise transformation projects that, over a specified period, shift the high-rated risks (R3–R6) to 'at appetite' or 'within appetite'. If the cyber leader can prove to the cyber resilience governance committee and the board the rigour behind the risk assessment, and commit to a specific timeline, getting the go-ahead becomes more likely. R1 and R2 will not be prioritised as their likelihood of occurrence and potential business impacts have been assessed as immaterial.

The advantages of this traditional approach to cyber risk strategy design are clear: it follows a simple process. Risk assessments can be conducted swiftly. The approach is also easily understood by senior business stakeholders. But our experience on the front line, interaction with experienced cyber leaders, and study of strategy design, all highlight significant flaws with this model.

- First – the risk-based approach to cyber resilience strategy design treats risk mitigation activities in isolation, leading to needless waste and impacting business operations.

- Second – by sticking with the old-style approach, cyber leaders and their teams often overlook the sheer complexity and cost required to mitigate certain risks. For instance, immaturely committing to encrypting all core databases within the next six months, without a careful understanding of legacy technology, application performance, team capabilities and vendor perspectives can lead to failed projects, dispirited teams and severe loss of business confidence in the cyber leader.

- Third – the simplistic risk-based approach doesn't answer key questions of effective strategy design: Can we do it? Do we have the required skills to drive complex change, and if not, how can we leverage business partnerships?

- Last, and probably the most important – by solely focusing on risk, this simplistic model posits cyber resilience as a necessary evil, a cost centre or compliance function to senior stakeholders and the board. It fails to translate cyber resilience as a powerful business enabler that can anchor customer trust, drive business growth and improve share price performance. Consequently, cyber leaders who stick with this approach struggle to enlist the support of business stakeholders.

The Active Cyber Risk Profile (Figure 4.1) summarises prioritised cyber risks based on assessing the likelihood and potential impact of residual risk, given the controls currently in place to mitigate them.

Splitting the risk description, business drivers and business impacts clarifies the risk to the board, as well as informing management of the actions to bring risks within appetite.

*Figure 4.1*

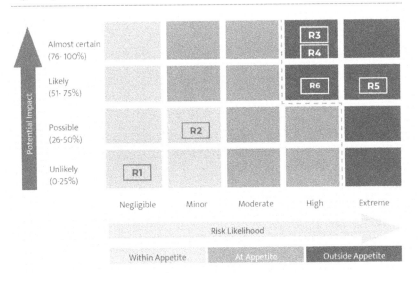

*Figure 4.2*

| Ref # | Key Risk Drivers | Business Impacts |
|---|---|---|
| R3 - Critical business service disruption | • Obsolete critical infrastructure no longer supported by vendors<br>• Lack of real time data replication procedures / offsite backup storage | • Loss of revenue<br>• Regulatory undertakings<br>• Brand damage impairing ability to retain or attract customers |
| R4 - Data breach by external parties | • Internet facing high-value digital assets with no multi-factor authentication<br>• Inadequate security monitoring over crown jewels<br>• Unencrypted critical database platforms<br>• Lack of privileged access management solution | Data breach leading to:<br>• Regulatory fines or undertakings<br>• Brand damage impairing ability to retain or attract customers<br>• Financial costs – rise in insurance premiums and data remediaton costs<br>• Impaired ability to attract talent |
| R5 - Data breach by malicious insiders or human error | • Lack of robust data loss prevention controls<br>• Rise in spear phising attacks targeting our industry<br>• Inadequate mobile device management<br>• Lack if formal security awareness program | • Loss of competitive advantage as IP is leaked to competitors<br>• Regulatory fines or undertakings<br>• Brand damage impairing ability to retain or attract customers |
| R6 - Supply chain cyber risk | • Poor visibility over critical third parties, especially shadow computing<br>• Lack of disciplined third-party assurance reviews | Data breach leading to:<br>• Regulatory fines or undertakings<br>• Financial costs – rise in insurance premium and data remediation costs |

# How to Develop a High-Value Cyber Resilience Strategy

First and foremost, bear in mind, it's not just about reducing cyber risk. To deliver value there are some questions you must consider:

1. What drives value in your business?

2. How do you measure that value?

3. How do you choose the most valuable strategies for cyber resilience?

4. How can you communicate the value you're planning to deliver?

5. How do you make sure that you deliver the value promised?

So, how can leading organisations develop high-impact strategies that accelerate their cyber resilience while maximising every dollar spent? We offer a different approach – one that borrows from agile and lean start-up methodologies to deliver flexibility, ease of implementation and rapid deployment.

We take a rough assessment of where we stand, determine where we want to be, quickly determine what the best way is for us to reach it and then start the process. One of the most critical elements of this accelerated process is being able to accurately measure along the way. To do so, you must answer the following important questions accurately:

a. What is going on? Only by understanding the major business risks, existing capabilities and external risk drivers can the cyber leader deliver effective and sustained change.

b. Who are the most important internal and external stakeholders? Is it the board, customers, regulators, suppliers or business partners?

c. Do I (the cyber leader) have the buy-in of the board, C-suite and other vital stakeholders to drive cultural change, secure funding and ongoing support?

d. How can I look beyond risk and compliance and position cyber resilience as a growth advantage or business enabler? How does the organisation deliver value to shareholders, and how does cyber resilience support that mission?

e. What are the top priorities after taking into consideration risk, business value, and cost/complexity of change? What are key dependencies and what initiatives can we bundle together to minimise business disruption?

f. What is the target state, and by what date do I intend to reach that state? Am I too conservative or too aggressive in my promises to the business and the board?

g. Can I deliver the promised transformation? What additional resources are required? Do I have strong external relationships and a program delivery team to execute change?

h. How do I measure success and demonstrate value back to my key stakeholders and the board?

## Measure, Measure, Measure

While there is a strong temptation to rush into execution mode, the first and foremost step in developing your cyber resilience strategy is to conduct a deep-dive assessment of your current state. You must assess the strength of your existing capabilities to protect against adversaries, and determine your areas of highest risk exposure. This includes painstakingly reviewing board papers, risk assessments, governance reports, incident registers, the IT road map, business strategies, the business value chain, and audit reports without being drawn into endless low-level reviews.

An honest assessment of your capabilities provides a strong foundation on which to build a cyber resilience strategy, as well as a benchmark to assess maturity as you ramp up capabilities. As the saying goes, 'You can't manage what you can't measure'.

Understanding the lay of the land also requires in-depth workshops with key stakeholders, IT teams, suppliers and vendors. Only when you fully comprehend the problem as well as the existing capabilities can your strategy achieve the maximum impact. This also sets a solid baseline for the cyber leader to demonstrate the impact of cybersecurity spend to the board of directors.

Here are some key questions to quickly determine your current state:

a. Does the organisation maintain an up-to-date and tight inventory of its high-value digital assets (crown jewels)?

b. Has the organisation mapped its list of non-negotiable controls against each crown jewel? For example, are there any crown jewels directly exposed to the internet that are not protected by MFA or have exploitable critical vulnerabilities?

c. What major assurance reviews (internal audits, external audits, deep-dives, threat hunting exercises, tabletop exercises) were conducted in the last 12 months? Are there any critical findings from these audits that are still open?

d. Are the board, directors and executive teams actively engaged in cyber strategy formulation and governance? What are the top concerns of upper management and the board?

e. What are the key external obligations (to regulators, institutional clients and other strategic external stakeholders)? How well is the organisation meeting these obligations?

f. Has the organisation been a victim of a sustained cyber intrusion? Was the cyber resilience strategy adapted to cater for key learnings that arose from previous attacks?

g. Does the organisation have full visibility of its internet-exposed footprint? Where is sensitive data stored? Are there any high-risk services (such as Active Directory) needlessly exposed to the internet?

h. Does the organisation maintain a comprehensive list of business partners and suppliers, segmented according to business risk? How tight is the cybersecurity assurance over high-risk suppliers?

i. What are the top five to ten cyber risks on the active risk profile? Does reliable data underpin these ratings or is the cyber risk profile based on highly subjective views?

j. Has cybersecurity risk management been integrated into the overall enterprise risk management framework?

A detailed diagnostic provides a good picture of the current state, enabling the cyber leader to measure ongoing maturity and demonstrate value back to the business. Conversely, cyber leaders who define a strategy without understanding the lay of the land often duplicate effort, spend money on the wrong priorities and frequently change course, which undermines credibility with the board.

## Get to Know Your Stakeholders

Cyber transformation is a complex undertaking that can only succeed when the cyber leader has gained the unwavering support and buy-in from critical stakeholders. Without the support of the CEO, the C-suite and the board, your strategy fails before it even takes off. To that end, the cyber leader must actively and proactively engage with key stakeholders.

Spend time at the formative stages developing strong rapport with your chief executive officer, chief operations officer, product development executives, chief information officer, chief customer officer, chief marketing officer and so on. Understand their key concerns and expectations and integrate their perspectives into your cyber resilience strategy – agree on mechanisms to measure success and report value back to them.

No matter how talented, no cyber leader can deliver an effective cyber resilience strategy in isolation. The key objective of a high-impact cyber resilience strategy is to advance the mission of the organisation and service its stakeholders. A key mistake we often see in our work training hundreds of cyber leaders is that most cyber leaders wait until the second or third draft before seeking stakeholder buy-in.

One virtual CISO we worked with during our intensive Cyber Leadership Program (CLP) made this strategic mistake. Engaged by the CIO to help define and implement a new cybersecurity strategy, the new CISO quickly rolled up their sleeves and got down to work. Using the strategy decks the CISO had successfully used in a previous/similar engagement, they quickly crafted an ambitious 12-month road map to uplift the organisation's capabilities from a scale of 1.5 to 3.5, using the CIS top 20 and NIST frameworks as benchmarks. (The current state of 1.5 was largely based on gut feel and quick consultations with technical teams.)

But the virtual CISO quickly ran into a brick wall. When they approached the chief financial officer to seek endorsement and funding, the finance chief quickly shot down the proposed strategy, highlighting to the CISO that the organisation had recently had its application for cyber insurance rejected due to several control deficiencies. The organisation was thus now in breach of its contractual obligations as its key institutional clients mandated this requirement. Failure to achieve this within the next six months would have material implications on the organisation's ability to underwrite new business as well as renew business relationships. The CISO was left with no other option but to completely ignore their 'best practice strategy' and redirect limited resources towards initiatives that mattered most to the board and broader organisational goals.

The lesson from this case study is that the cyber leader must always seek key stakeholder input early and get them on board, because without their support, the cyber leader won't deliver anything of significance. The majority of the cyber leader's planned initiatives will need resources, funding or active participation by stakeholders. So getting their buy-in is a must.

To succeed in this often-elusive task, you must move away from technical talk that posits cybersecurity as a function of threats and vulnerabilities, a mere business risk. The cyber leader must pitch cyber resilience as a growth advantage and explain how strong digital resilience will help push the business agendas forward, rather than position it as merely a risk reduction or compliance activity.

In reality, the cyber leader will not be able to directly match every cyber resilience initiative to strategic business goals. But each proposed initiative must be evaluated based on its ability to protect the organisation's core digital assets, and contribute to the business value chain, using the minimum possible set of resources.

Here are some practical examples of how you can position cyber resilience as a business enabler, rather than as a siloed technology project.

Business leaders now acknowledge that cyber resilience underpins product success. Corroborating this sentiment, 72% of CEOs polled by global consulting giant **KPMG**[46] in the US in 2019 agreed that 'strong cybersecurity is critical to engender trust with our stakeholders', compared with only 15% during the previous year. The scale has tilted: a growing number of customers now prefer **security over convenience**[47] and are **unwilling to do business**[48] with organisations that demonstrate lapses in cyber resilience. Therefore, explain how cyber resilience will help new products succeed in a hyper-competitive market, help attract new customers and retain existing ones.

Pitch cyber resilience transformation as key to de-risk the brand and buttress market trust, thus enabling the business to acquire and retain more customers. By taking away needless regulator, investor and market scrutiny, strong cyber resilience can underpin long-term brand success.

Position cyber transformation as an enabler of business agility. One CISO sought funding to replace all hardware-based, signature-based security appliances (internet security gateway, email filtering, firewalls and VPN appliances) with software as a service (SaaS) security solutions. By clearly articulating that the cloud-first security strategy would enable the business to support remote work, eliminate error-prone monthly patching routines, scale with business growth and boost security with advanced machine learning capabilities – the CISO turned the chief information officer, previously a detractor, into a vocal proponent of the cyber resilience strategy. Building critical controls early into products accelerates regulatory approvals, enhances the chances for new products to perform in new markets and significantly reduces costs associated with retrofitting security or product recalls.

a. Tie cyber resilience programs to regulatory requirements as a key to maintaining the licence to operate and avoiding regulatory undertakings and fines, especially for heavily regulated industries.

Here are some other practical ways to tie cyber transformation to business goals.

*Table 4.1*

| Strategic Business Objectives | How Can Cyber Resilience Add Value? (Examples) |
|---|---|
| Business Growth Strategy:<br><br>1. Acquiring new customers<br>2. Increasing sales to existing customers<br>3. Penetrating new markets<br>4. Launching new products and services<br>5. Preserving value in mergers and acquisitions | Enable the Business Strategies:<br><br>1. Boost the success of new products by baking cybersecurity during design<br>2. Accelerate new client due diligence by attaining a SOC 2 Type 2 attestation<br>3. Comply with data protection requirements for new jurisdictions the organisation plans to operate in, boosting trust and compliance<br>4. Ensuring that risk profiles for target acquisitions align with board-approved risk appetite and that hidden critical risks are uncovered before acquisitions<br>5. Simplify cybersecurity to delight customers with a smooth digital experience<br>6. Lower operational costs by significantly cutting down cyber fraud incidents |

| Strategic Business Objectives | How Can Cyber Resilience Add Value? (Examples) |
|---|---|
| Business Transformation:<br><br>1. Driving down costs through outsourcing and offshoring<br><br>2. Boosting business efficiency through automation | Transform Security Practices:<br><br>1. Reduce the cost of cybersecurity by carefully outsourcing activities that third parties can execute cheaper, faster and better<br><br>2. Supplant manual security tasks with advanced automation, reducing human error, lowering costs (in the long run), and boosting morale by redirecting the team to focus on strategic and innovative tasks |
| Risk Management:<br><br>1.Actively manage risk (assess, accept, treat, transfer) | Actively Manage Cyber Risk:<br><br>1. Mitigate all cyber risks that sit outside the board-approved cyber risk appetite<br><br>2. Acquire cyber insurance to insulate the business against probable high-impact incidents and meet external obligations |

| Strategic Business Objectives | How Can Cyber Resilience Add Value? (Examples) |
|---|---|
| Stakeholder Communications to Reduce Perceived Risk: <br><br> 1. Meet increasing investor/shareholder risk expectations <br><br> 2. Maintain compliance with tightening regulatory requirements | Boost Brand Equity: <br><br> 1. Comply with applicable regulations, e.g. privacy and mandatory data breach reporting requirements <br><br> 2. Preserve investor and shareholder wealth and actively maintain their trust through annual cyber risk reports |

The first stage is to agree on the current state, and perhaps offer a glimpse of what you want to do to address it, and then come back to your key stakeholders with the draft strategy. This gives stakeholders an opportunity to buy into the design, to agree, to disagree, to tell you what they think and to help you set the tone.

## Don't Forget the Basics

We have witnessed too many cyber leaders who assumed their executive roles with high expectations. They spend their first few months developing strategies, engaging with the stakeholders, getting their budgets approved and then starting to build their team, only for it all to go wrong.

It's always tempting to set your strategy on big-ticket items and bleeding-edge technologies. But cyber resilience is about laying very strong foundations and establishing disciplined, hygienic practices. Overlooking the basics could have some strategic implications for the CISO, for example:

- We have encountered situations where the internal audit team uncovers several policy non-compliances and report these to the board, throwing the CISO into defensive mode and dampening trust in their strategic road map.

- The organisation suffers an unexpected and debilitating cyberattack and the cybersecurity team is found woefully unprepared to respond or doesn't have any formal retainers with professional cyber incident response firms. As is often the case, it's discovered that the cyberattack was highly avoidable as the hackers exploited unpatched vulnerabilities, weak authentication, or an unknown third party with remote access to the network.

- A regulator conducts an audit and finds material breaches. By the time the new CISO has been in the role for six months, all trust and credibility has been lost, despite making the best efforts to get a good strategy in place.

Here are some practical ways to fix the basics while advancing your strategic initiatives:

- Ensure all remote access is protected by MFA, including SaaS-based business-critical applications.

- Conduct a password-cracking exercise and reduce the extent of guessable passwords.

- Address high-rated audit or regulator findings and implement mechanisms to track remediation of critical and high-rated matters via your cyber governance forums.

- Purchase an incident response retainer to gain prioritised access to skilled responders and forensics analysts in the event of a high-impact cyber incursion. Liaise with your cyber insurance provider to avoid duplicated services or engaging a provider that's not in the insurance provider's panel of experts.

- Run an automated data discovery exercise to identify confidential/sensitive data accessible to all staff and apply relevant protections. More often, IT teams dump entire databases of backup data for crown jewels for break-fix purposes and leave them exposed on poorly protected file shares for months, rendering layers of protection on high-value systems valueless.

- Remove all services needlessly exposed to the internet, especially high-risk applications like Active Directory, to minimise the attack surface.

- Significantly reduce the number of staff with global admin rights on your cloud environments, Office 365 or crown jewels. Implement just-in-time admin access using a privileged access management solution to prevent persistent, super-user access to critical systems.

- Ringfence network traffic and proactively block traffic from jurisdictions in which your organisation doesn't do business.

- Develop an inventory of crown jewels and determine if any of these high-value systems have serious control gaps, e.g. end-of-life, exposure to the internet without MFA, or troves of unencrypted sensitive data.

- Implement a disciplined server and endpoint vulnerability scanning regime and ensure access to aged applications with critical vulnerabilities is tight.

- Ensure all your crown jewels have daily offline backups, and the recoverability of this data is within business-approved recovery time objectives and is regularly tested.

- Facilitate a board and executive cyber crisis simulation tabletop exercise to align expectations, clarify critical responsibilities, determine external communication protocols and uncover key gaps before a real disaster strikes. As we say at CLI, you must know that you're ready when the inevitable happens.

## Focus on What Really Matters

First and foremost, strategy design is about making bold decisions and sticking with them. Only that way can you deliver deep and lasting change. Whether in business, military, IT or cyber resilience, the core tenet of strategy design remains the same – focus. Effectiveness requires focus – it's about muting noise and focusing limited resources on initiatives that yield the highest business impact per dollar invested. This enduring tenet was reinforced by management guru Michael Porter in a seminal *HBR* article when he wrote that 'the essence of strategy is choosing what not to do'.[49]

A key mistake we often cite is an attempt by cyber leaders to overcommit to senior business leadership views. They then attempt to squeeze their limited budget to mitigate every possible cyber threat across all digital assets, each of varying business significance. That creates noise, fatigues thinly resourced cyber resilience teams and leaves high-value digital assets woefully unprotected. Worse, by failing to deliver on their grand promises, their credibility suffers a great deal. Credibility is the fuel of leadership; without credibility it's virtually impossible to rally others to pursue a common goal.

To get this right, the cyber leader must muster the courage to ruthlessly prioritise what matters and have the nerve to say no to urgent but unimportant matters. That view was supported by Antonio Nieto-Rodriguez, a veteran in business strategy who emphasised the point: 'Prioritising increases the success rates of strategic projects, increases the alignment and focus of senior management teams around strategic goals, clears all doubts for the operational teams when faced with decisions, and, most important, builds an execution mindset and culture.'[50]

So, how do you prioritise cyber resilience initiatives?

An effective cyber resilience strategy at once mitigates critical risks and advances business goals. To get this right demands that the cyber leader breaks away from tradition and treats cyber resilience as a strategic business enabler – one which, if harnessed correctly, can assure business survival, drive growth, lower cost of capital and improve brand perception. Cyber risk mitigation will remain a core agenda item for any cyber leader but must not be their sole focus.

As we illustrate in *Figure 4.3*, cyber transformation activities must be selected based on their effectiveness in reducing business risk and their ability to improve business value, as well as the cost to implement them and maintain that control. This model provides an objective means to prioritise initiatives. It looks simple on the surface but is underpinned by rigorous work.

*Figure 4.3*

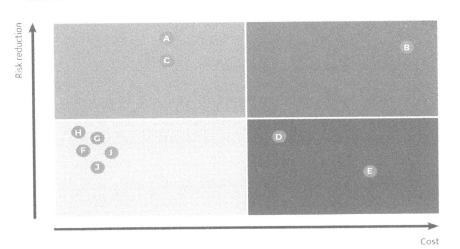

Figure 3 Business Value + Risk reduction lens

The mitigation activities are identified (A–J) and plotted as illustrated. This provides a comprehensive view of their effectiveness as well as their cost to implement. For instance, initiative A (deploying multi-factor authentication over an internet-facing core banking platform) delivers substantial risk reduction and business value. It should take precedence over initiative B (developing custom code to encrypt legacy databases) because of its complexity, high costs to implement and several unknown risk factors. Initiatives D and E naturally deselect themselves because they are way too complex and costly, and do not materially improve the risk position.

Strategic initiatives that deliver the highest business value must be prioritised. These reduce business risk by the highest margin (e.g. build customer trust thus drive sales) and have less complexity and fewer unknowns. The list of prioritised activities can be reached through collaborative workshops with key stakeholders.

The result is a combined set of high-impact, cost-effective initiatives that deliver business value the fastest way. Strategy is really about choices – not just about what you're going to do, but also what you're not going to do, and choosing which things need to come first. This model can effectively be used to identify projects that must be stopped or scrapped.

## Consider Key Dependencies

The cyber leader and their team must also explore synergies that can bundle projects up, delivering value in the quickest way and minimising business disruption. For example, if you plan to deploy privileged access management over your crown jewels, you should consider the other initiatives you can roll out at the same time to minimise business impacts.

To deliver value quickly, look at cyber resilience through the lens of the business value chain – building new strategic partnerships, securing new products, enhancing customer trust, increasing success in mergers and acquisitions, improving public perception, reducing perceived risks and enabling employee flexibility. To succeed, the cyber resilience strategy should carefully consider the digital transformation program and help the cyber leader securely deliver those initiatives in a scalable way.

Cybersecurity becomes an impediment to business agility and results in needless customer friction when it is built in isolation and from a compliance mindset. Another CISO we have worked with in the CLP is a case in point. The new CISO spent months building a comprehensive strategy to modernise cybersecurity capabilities for a subsidiary business unit, hiring expensive Big Four consultants to do this work. A few months later, however, the CISO learnt that the board had already approved a plan to divest the underperforming subsidiary, so the business could focus on their core areas of differentiation. Everyone was upset, especially senior executives who thought the CISO should have known better and consulted them before squandering precious resources and time. It's therefore important to understand the business and digital transformation road map before spending money.

Cybersecurity becomes a business enabler when built into the business strategy. Here are some examples of well-positioned cyber resilience strategies that we have identified through our work:

1. After consultations with the CIO, the CISO deferred an expensive and high-risk project of encrypting a core banking platform after understanding the platform was scheduled for migration into Amazon Web Services (AWB) during the next six months. This move eliminated the need to evaluate multiple third-party encryption tools as the confidential data would be encrypted using native AWS tools.

2. Another CISO joined a financial services firm and noted the organisation was about to launch a data loss prevention (DLP) project to meet data privacy requirements. However, when the CISO noted that the organisation didn't have an effective data classification and tagging process, he deferred DLP until these prerequisites were in place.

## Prioritise the Protection of Crown Jewels

Steer away from conventional, one-size-fits-all cybersecurity investment models and prioritise the protection of the crown jewels.

Crown jewels are the most critical information assets, those that if compromised could severely undermine the organisation's bottom line, competitive advantage, reputation or even threaten its survival. They include but are not limited to inventions, board deliberations, trade secrets, proprietary formulas and processes, prototypes and blueprints, technical designs, advanced research, confidential documents, manufacturing plans, software code, corporate and pricing strategies, and patented designs.

The protection of these high-value digital assets must take precedence over other ancillary systems. We have created a separate and comprehensive chapter on identifying and protecting crown jewels – see Chapter 5: 'Centre Your Cyber Strategy Around Your Crown Jewels'.

## Consider Regulatory Requirements

There will always be mandatory regulatory projects and external obligations you must deliver, especially if your industry is heavily regulated, such as in aviation or financial services, where compliance underpins your license to operate. So make sure these mandatory requirements are factored into the short- to medium-term road map and have adequate resourcing.

## Define the Target State

Like most things, unless you know what you're aiming for, you're probably never going to get there. Defining your target state is also a powerful way to reinforce credibility with key stakeholders as it lays a solid foundation to report the progress of your cyber transformation program back to the board and demonstrates the delivery of promises. What's more, clarity of vision creates a shared sense of purpose and reason to push through inevitable obstacles your team will face.

With dozens of industry frameworks out there, you must stay disciplined and determine what level of maturity you want to achieve in the next 12 to 36 months. The aspirational maturity level should be commensurate with your risk appetite, industry and, most importantly, the resources at your disposal to drive a transformation program. Furthermore, using industry standards as a benchmark makes your choices defendable in front of the board and regulators. Aim high, but don't exaggerate what you can achieve given known constraints.

As illustrated by *Figure 4.4*, you should spend Phase 1 addressing the low-hanging fruit, fixing critical risks, developing a comprehensive inventory of your crown jewels, tightening the supply chain and reducing the cyberattack surface. Any high-rated audit or regulatory matters should also be addressed during this phase.

Once these foundations are in place, in Phase 2 you should prioritise high-impact projects, based on their effectiveness in reducing business risk, complexity to execute and capacity to improve business value.

In Phase 3, you should then focus on advanced capabilities that are essential but more complex or costlier to execute than Phase 2 priorities.

The target state is not static. You must regularly adjust it in line with internal and external factors, such as mergers or acquisitions, new regulations, changes in contractual arrangements or, most importantly, strategic business direction.

*Figure 4.4*

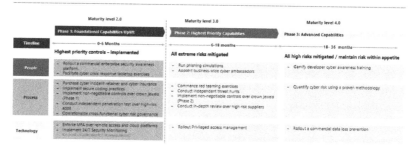

## Go Beyond the Generic Cyber Resilience Framework

While the conventional five-domain framework most organisations use is certainly a great starting point, don't take it as doctrine. Industry standards are based on consensus and never consider the nuances of individual organisations and their industry verticals. When designing a robust cyber resilience strategy, take a broader picture and consider your product road map, external obligations, technical debt, digital transformation strategy and risk appetite.

## Build Capability and Prioritise Quick Wins

Defining your strategic goals is the first step, but what's equally important is to carefully assess the existing capabilities and budget, then answer the questions: Am I able to execute the strategy within the agreed time frame? Is my target state too ambitious or too conservative?

This is a phase where we often see a lot of cyber leaders falter – they underestimate the complexity of cyber transformation projects and critical dependencies and ultimately overcommit to a raft of initiatives. When they eventually fail to deliver on the promises, their credibility suffers and their confidence tanks.

To accelerate cyber resilience, you need to focus on five areas:

- Assess the capabilities of the internal team versus the list of priorities, then determine additional resources required to drive the required change and manage new capabilities once they are implemented. The lack of skilled cybersecurity professionals is often the major obstacle to delivering change. Compounding matters, the CISO may find it difficult to attract the right talent in a competitive environment and doing so may take months. You must avoid prematurely hiring permanent staff. In the short term, you must tap into your consulting budget as much as you can and bring in experienced specialists to help implement your first 100-day goals, while figuring out budgeting processes and what your organisation really needs.

- Given the above challenge, it's important for the cyber leader to carefully assess what external resources can be leveraged to accelerate cyber resilience, instead of solely focusing on beefing up the internal team. This includes provisioning a requisite professional services budget, as well as outsourcing functions that can be delivered at scale and with higher quality by specialist firms. For example, some of our clients outsource the delivery of world-class, 24/7 incident detection and response capabilities, within their first six to eight weeks. If they had chosen to build such capabilities internally, the same process would have taken several months, cost several times more and delivered fewer superior capabilities. It's also likely that such initiatives could eventually fail if the organisation fails to attract the specific talent required to build a fully fledged security operations centre.

- Consider and prioritise quick wins that can accelerate your cyber resilience, such as purchasing cyber insurance cover. Cyber insurance can materially reduce your business risk by protecting your organisation against internal and external losses from cyber-related breaches, such as business disruption costs, replacement of impaired digital assets, legal expenses and regulatory fines, forensics and incident remediation, third-party damages, customer fraud protection, and customer communications. If your insurance cover or endpoint security vendor doesn't bundle cyber incident response capabilities, make sure you prioritise the purchase of an incident response retainer.

- Prioritise the reduction of your attack surface, for example, by removing the number of systems that needlessly communicate directly with the internet, thus quickly eliminating unnecessary risks.

- It's also tempting for the cyber leader to project manage the delivery of cyber transformation activities, but that takes away valuable time required to provide leadership, manage stakeholders and source funding. We recommend cyber leaders to establish a proper project delivery team, led by an experienced program manager, to instil rigorous project governance, change management and financial discipline. The project manager will set up a working group comprised of representatives from key departments, including enterprise architecture, customer success, procurement, legal, risk management and cybersecurity. To free up time for the cyber leader to manage upwards and outwards, the cyber executive must delegate key decision-making to the project manager and their leadership team.

It's also wise to get a formal cyber resilience program sponsor to drive change at the highest level of the organisation, helping you turn known detractors into supporters, influence key decision makers and drive the tone at the top. The CEO, who is the linchpin of management, is the ideal program sponsor, although another influential C-level executive with unobstructed access to the CEO can play this role. You will run into situations where the business needs to make serious trade-offs between security and efficiency – having a strong sponsor on your side will ensure security initiatives are not relegated to the back burner.

## Be Financially Frugal

Headline-generating hacks are helping to push the global cybersecurity spend, which **Gartner** forecasted to reach more than $215 billion in 2024.[51] However, through our extensive collaboration with hundreds of cyber leaders who go through our cyber leadership program, we have observed no direct correlation between cybersecurity spend and cyber resilience. Some business leaders feel like they are pouring money into a leaky bucket as threat actors keep outpacing cybersecurity teams. The answer lies in resource misallocation, in part. Here are three common ways cybersecurity teams waste money and how cyber leaders can avoid this.

## 1. Exaggerated Faith in Bleeding-Edge Technologies

Technical controls are a central piece of cyber resilience. Unfortunately, some cybersecurity teams keep lurching from one emerging technology to another, looking for a cure-all solution to their cybersecurity problems. This obsession with bleeding-edge technology piles up security tools beyond the capacity of teams to effectively configure and integrate and optimise them. According to **recent research**, the average enterprise manages 60 to 80 distinct security tools while large enterprises manage up to 140.[52]

But more is not necessarily better in cybersecurity. There is a risk of burnout as security teams spread themselves thinly across dozens of disjointed solutions. Complexity also breeds insecurity: as tools proliferate, security misconfigurations multiply, the attack surface expands and vulnerabilities pile up. These lauded solutions only provide a false sense of invulnerability in the end. For instance, investing millions in next-generation firewalls that allow unrestricted traffic movement across the network can be a waste of money.

These issues are well founded. According to **research**, organisations using more than 50 security tools are 8% less likely to mitigate threats and 7% less defensive than organisations using fewer security tools.[53]

To minimise cost and complexity, cybersecurity teams should consider leveraging native cloud security capabilities before purchasing disparate third-party security tools. Security teams can fast-track implementation while reducing complexity by tapping into native cloud security solutions (e.g. data encryption, privileged access management, mobile device management or security logging).

As these controls are integrated by default, the native cloud approach is often less expensive than third-party security solutions, which often require significant professional services to integrate and maintain. There are still several instances where these solutions are not fit for purpose. The idea, however, is to carefully evaluate the suitability of native cloud security tools before lurching to an entirely new toolset, which your team might not have the expertise to manage.

## 2. Hiring Permanent Staff Prematurely

It's common for some new cyber leaders to hire permanent staff too quickly before they've adequately evaluated their needs. But blindly attempting to build complex capabilities in-house is often a strategic mistake that blows budgets and exposes critical systems as the hiring process is prolonged.

Take security operations centres (SOCs), which some cybersecurity teams attempt to build in-house. An effective security detection and response function requires several complementary skills: researchers, malware analysts, incident managers and forensic examiners. These resources don't come cheap. Incident managers, for example, costs on average $120,000 per year, according to a **salary survey company.**[54] An alternative approach is to carefully consider the functions that can be cost-effectively outsourced to specialist firms.

## 3.  An Obsession with Security Audits

Tightening data protection laws have led to a flurry of cybersecurity audits. But some cybersecurity teams get bogged down in endless audits, uncovering too many issues beyond their capacity to address. These costly and duplicate audits often suck up a great deal of time, diverting teams from their primary mission of securing critical systems. They also create friction with IT teams, who feel that the loosely coordinated audit teams keep asking the same questions. As audit fatigue invariably kicks in, these reviews become worthless as the audit reports are archived and forgotten.

Don't get this wrong: carefully planned audits are integral to cyber resilience strategies. Here are three strategies cybersecurity teams can deploy to save money and relieve pressure on IT teams:

- Actively engage internal and external auditors to avoid redundant reviews and reduce pressure on IT teams.

- Rather than going superficially into many areas, prioritise reviewing high-value systems that underpin your competitive advantage, trade secrets or most profitable business lines.

- Start with the basics (e.g. high-risk supplier audits or privileged access reviews) before taking on complex assurance activities (such as red teaming or threat hunting).

More needs to be done, but it's reassuring to see business leaders allocating more resources towards cybersecurity. Sustained resilience, however, also demands that cyber leaders act with extreme frugality. The modern cyber leader is as much a transformational leader as a voice of financial prudence.

They must ruthlessly scrutinise every cybersecurity spend based on its ability to protect the organisation's core digital assets and contribute to stockholder value. Otherwise, they could find themselves with deeper pockets but weakened cyber resilience postures.

## CYBER LEADERS ON THE MOVE STORY 1

**Georges De Moura – Vice President and Group CISO at Edge and Head of Industry Solutions (Center for Cybersecurity) at the World Economic Forum (WEF) and graduate of the Cyber Leadership Institute.**

Georges De Moura, former head of industry solutions (Center for Cybersecurity) at the WEF and one of the most decorated global CISOs who has held executive and advisory roles at major global brands like Etihad Airways, Thales, IBM, and Airbus, De Moura certainly knows a thing or two about leadership.

It was refreshing to have De Moura in our April 2021 class of the Cyber Leadership Program, where he generously shared his leadership lessons with our global community of CISOs. We had to make this interview happen, knowing his lessons from lived experiences would prove invaluable to aspiring and experienced CISOs alike.

To understand what drives De Moura, I took him back to his childhood years. His parents escaped Portuguese dictatorship at the end of the 1960s and migrated to France to secure a brighter future for their children.

'My parents raised us in a family-oriented and caring environment,' De Moura opened the conversation from Geneva, Switzerland, where he lives. De Moura describes a modest childhood with very hard-working parents striving to give their kids a better life. During those early years, his parents instilled critical lessons about empathy, hard work and a continual quest for self-improvement. His parents' grit, determination and selflessness would prove invaluable lessons that would help him thrive in various global leadership roles.

'Those childhood learnings help me better empathise and connect with my team members,' De Moura explains. 'To succeed in any leadership role, your team must believe that you have their best interests at heart.' The impacts are tangible, especially in a highly dynamic market like cybersecurity. 'I have enjoyed strong retention in all my leadership roles. People stay, not for financial reasons, but because they feel safe, have clear visibility about career progression and where they fit in the big picture,' he explains. 'What does it mean for their personal development?'

De Moura graduated with an MSc, computer engineering from ESME-Sudria, France, in 1999. He soon faced a conundrum: either join the compulsory French military service or undertake a civil internship with a French company abroad. He chose the latter and flew across the Atlantic to start a new life in the US.

The risky move paid off. The turn of the century birthed digital transformation 1.0, internet adoption was rapidly accelerating, and Y2K fears sent shivers across boardrooms.

Armed with his computer engineering degree, De Moura interned at Thales, a global company that services defence, aeronautics, space, transportation and digital identity and security markets. 'It was pretty much just me in charge and figuring out how to do the job,' he recalls nostalgically. De Moura immersed himself in the intricacies of IT infrastructure, application support and service delivery, those formative years laying a strong foundation for his career.

He would stay at Thales for 15 years, rising through the ranks from an IT engineer to become the company's first-ever CISO in the US – a dual-hat role that combined IT infrastructure and security. In his early days, De Moura describes not being particularly attracted to cybersecurity. That said, because Thales was heavily focused on the defence industry, risk management was ingrained in the DNA of the organisation.

I wasn't surprised when De Moura highlighted friction between IT and security as one of the key challenges during that time. 'You want to be an enabler in IT,' he says. 'IT is a service-oriented function – your main goal is to keep customers satisfied.' As De Moura recalls, striking the right balance between security and service delivery remained a significant challenge during those early years.

When I asked about his most significant career highlight at Thales, De Moura doesn't hesitate, describing leading an ERP transformation program, replacing legacy applications with a complex SAP platform. The program carried significant strategic and financial implications. De Moura explained that cloud offerings were just starting to mature and were a clear no-go for many corporations – held back by security concerns.

The dual security and program delivery responsibilities forced De Moura to think outside the box. 'The situation required a paradigm shift,' De Moura explains. 'We carefully vetted suppliers, preferring strategic partners whose values aligned with ours to ensure long-term success. This was a risky move,' De Moura says, 'to host the country ERP in a private cloud. After careful planning, we landed on a hybrid cloud model, which was endorsed by the business.' While cloud benefits, such as increased agility and scalability, are widely understood today, De Moura took a significant risk on an emerging technology with minimal frameworks at the time.

Perhaps the most critical lesson De Moura got from the project is that 'You sometimes have to be a risk-taker,' he says. 'Being risk-averse can only get you so far.' A CISO must take emotion out of the equation and arm business leaders with advice to make calculated and risk-informed decisions. Businesses thrive by taking risks, not avoiding them. 'I presented something [with the ERP project] that looked high risk, but when the mitigation controls were considered, the residual risk was acceptable,' De Moura says, 'and I realised that the security function can actually be a business enabler.'

De Moura describes his time with Thales fondly. Yet, he knew that to remain relevant in a world of rapid digital transformation and dilapidating geographical boundaries, he had to reinvent constantly.

In 2014, he joined Golden State Foods (GSF), a multibillion-dollar privately-owned diversified food supplier. His tenure as director, enterprise technology services and security (CISO) only lasted one year but left an indelible mark on his professional journey. De Moura defined and executed a global cybersecurity and IT strategy covering hybrid cloud hosting, security transformation, and IT service delivery at a time when cyber threats were rising rapidly.

The secret to his success at GSF was largely because of the support from the CIO, who understood cyber risk. 'It was the first time I felt fully empowered as a CISO to establish the necessary policies, measures and capabilities to protect the digital assets,' De Moura explains.

De Moura notes that building trust with the CEO and executives in monthly meetings gave him the freedom to drive the cyber transformation program. 'You have to disseminate insightful and well-curated information to help decision makers make risk-informed decisions,' he explains.

At the beginning of Autumn 2015, De Moura's cyber executive career took another sharp and unexpected turn. In what De Moura describes as a pivotal moment in his career, he was headhunted to become the first-ever CISO for Etihad Aviation Group, the fastest-growing global commercial airline at that time.

De Moura took a leap of faith (with his family's blessings) and flew, family in tow, to the Persian Gulf to take up the new challenge. 'It was a tough decision,' he explains. 'My kids were born and raised in the USA.' This marked a new challenge at a professional level, too, with Etihad comprising over 35,000 employees. 'I jumped into a much bigger arena with a very diverse, complex and political environment,' De Moura says.

The environment, as De Moura explains, was highly dynamic, fast-paced, and 24/7. 'Safety, availability, and customer satisfaction were the most strategic indicators of success for the airline,' De Moura tells me, 'with security [later on] closely behind.' De Moura was hired as Etihad's first CISO and was tasked with helping his boss (group CIO and CTO) drive digital transformation securely. Etihad spun a project that replaced ageing infrastructure with several advanced technologies, including artificial intelligence, multi-cloud and omnichannel e-commerce platform, while at the same time embedding security, privacy and resilience deep into core business lines.

'I had to run multiple sprints in parallel, one sprint to define my [cyber resilience] strategy, one sprint to get my team in place all while developing a strategic partnership with a global technology firm,' De Moura recalls, at a time when the digital and threat landscapes were fast-changing and volatile. The attackers were as varied as they come – from opportunistic lone hackers to well-resourced nation states.

To succeed, he had to persuade a range of key stakeholders – senior executives, risk management, internal audit, technology, and suppliers to throw their total weight behind the transformation program. De Moura reiterates the necessity of viewing cybersecurity as a team sport. 'It requires collective and concerted action,' he underscores.

Like any successful leader, De Moura has also suffered his share of setbacks. He recalls giving an unconvincing response when an executive caught him off guard and fired the usual question, 'Are we secure?' The question was asked in his first month when he was still building situational awareness and strategies at that time. 'I did not necessarily answer as I would have liked,' De Moura says, grinning, though he made up for it in time, improving trust and communication.

After three years, De Moura and his family left the UAE for Geneva, Switzerland. There, he joined the World Economic Forum (WEF) as head of industry solutions (Center for Cybersecurity). The attractions to the WEF role were twofold. First, De Moura and his wife felt it was time they returned to Europe after more than two decades abroad. Second, De Moura thought that this new role – tasked with building executive cyber resilience awareness and driving deeper collaboration between the public and private sector – would help him give back to the global community in ways impossible to achieve within an enterprise environment.

I eagerly asked De Moura how he got his job at WEF, to which he replied, 'I followed the traditional process, which rarely worked for me, by the way, sending your résumé through an Indeed or LinkedIn post, but in this case, it worked.' When describing his move to Geneva, De Moura conveys the excitement of his family. 'They were dazzled by Lake Geneva, the mountains and the scenic views,' he exclaims, further cementing his decision to join WEF.

De Moura outlines his role at WEF as markedly different to his previous CISO roles. Here, soft skills are everything. 'You are interacting with world-class global CISOs, such as Darren Argyle (chairman of Cyber Leadership Institute); you cannot fluff your way with generic arguments and appeal to them,' De Moura elucidates. 'You need to bring substance, a compelling narrative, and value to the table.'

Throughout our discussion, De Moura was constantly imparting valuable lessons in leadership and life. He reinforces the skill of active listening, honing one's soft skills, and the importance of empathy and interpersonal awareness in leadership. Perhaps most powerful, however, were De Moura's closing remarks. 'You are constantly learning,' De Moura informs me. 'Don't think that the knowledge you have today is good enough for tomorrow.' He recommends keeping abreast and astute, developing your cybersecurity knowledge, soft skills and business acumen. Lastly, De Moura says, 'Check out your ego.' People can have very strong opinions, be very sure about their knowledge and be very stubborn,' he explains. 'Ultimately, it [ego] won't make you successful.'

# Chapter 6

# Centre Your Cyber Strategy Around Your Crown Jewels

### Why a Cyber Strategy Centred on Crown Jewels Matters Now More than Ever

These timeless principles have, however, been further refined considering our experience on the front lines of cyber leadership as well as ongoing collaboration with global leaders who go through our flagship Cyber Leadership Program.

The previous chapters underscored the incredible power of focus to accelerate cyber resilience at a fraction of the cost. There is always a temptation to mark every digital asset as high value, but that is a great miscalculation. As several high-profile data breaches have proved, bigger cybersecurity budgets don't necessarily translate to greater business resilience. Unfortunately, we come across too many cybersecurity teams attempting to spread themselves thinly across the entire digital ecosystem, each of varying business significance.

To be highly effective, however, cyber leaders must prioritise ruthlessly. Repivoting your cyber resilience strategy towards your crown jewels offers several distinct advantages:

- This is risk management 101. By disproportionately allocating a limited budget towards systems of the highest risk and the products customers most value, the cyber leader will naturally align the cyber strategy with critical business priorities.

- It significantly boosts cyber resilience without exerting additional pressure on cybersecurity teams. Conversely, attempting to apply the same protection levels across every asset depletes morale and leads to constant fatigue and costly mistakes.

- No enterprise has an unlimited security budget. A one-size-fits-all approach wastes shareholders' resources and diffuses the effectiveness of cybersecurity controls, leaving critical assets exposed to excessive levels of cyber risk. By focusing on what matters, business-savvy cyber leaders can accelerate cyber resilience and significantly lower security costs. By killing off strategic projects that don't advance the resilience of high-value digital assets and rechannelling the savings to beef up crown jewels protections, cyber leaders can improve cyber resilience without asking for more money, a concept called zero-based budgeting. This approach eliminates waste and maximises the value of every dollar invested in cybersecurity.

- Creates the optimum balance between security and convenience by eliminating controls that needlessly annoy customers.

- Strengthens executive oversight by measuring what matters and closing regulatory compliance loopholes. For instance, when running executive cyber crisis simulations, your scenario assumes a high-impact attack on your most important systems, e.g. a core banking application in finance or a patient record management system in healthcare.

We propose a series of recommendations from best practices and an approach to:

- Develop a comprehensive list of high-value digital assets, hereafter referred to as crown jewels, and implement a differentiated controls model.

- Institutionalise crown jewel assessment into business operational models, such as business process outsourcing, new systems development and a cyber assurance model, making it an inevitable and discrete part of strategic and operational decision-making.

At its core, crown jewel assessment is about instituting a disciplined approach to cyber risk management, enabling the business to focus resources on what really matters.

In *Table 5.1* are the top ten recommendations organisations can benefit and gain value from.

*Table 5.1*

## Top Nine Recommendations

1. **Link to Business Goals:** An enterprise cyber crown jewels strategy must be intricately linked to organisational goals and mission. Consequently, an effective crown jewel assessment requires a solid grasp of the organisation's mission, strategic objectives, intellectual property, value chain and key customer segments. In the end, crown jewels are the systems that support the organisation's competitive advantage, most profitable services and the licence to operate. So, nailing down the crown jewels assessment is the bedrock of a business-aligned cybersecurity strategy.

2. **Embed Regulatory and External Obligations into the Crown Jewel Assessment:** Develop a clear understanding of data privacy laws applicable to jurisdictions where your enterprise operates, as well as other external data protection obligations, such as the SWIFT mandatory security controls or PCI DSS. You should also engage your procurement team to understand major contractual obligations as well as insurance underwriters to determine minimum cyber insurance requirements.

3. **Engage Early:** Cyber resilience is a business matter, not just a technology issue. A holistic understanding of your crown jewels therefore requires early and ongoing engagement of key business process owners and senior stakeholders. This not only enhances the effectiveness of cyber resilience programs but also promotes transparency into cyber resilience spend, reinforcing business buy-in and support. Determining which systems constitute crown jewels requires early and ongoing engagement with senior business, risk and technology leaders.

4. **Be Highly Focused:** While there is a temptation to mark every system as 'high value', the reality is not all data or systems are created equal. A breach into an online merchant site that stores customer credit cards potentially has deeper and longer-lasting implications when compared to a breach of a back-office administration system. To be effective, maintain a tight list of crown jewels and be ruthless about the implementation of non-negotiable controls. It's better to start off with a small list and expand it over time; implementing non-negotiable controls across hundreds of systems is an impossible slog.

5. **Prioritise Intellectual Property:** The process of identifying crown jewels can be protracted, depending on the size and complexity of the enterprise. A prudent strategy is to start with your intellectual property assets, those digital assets that underpin your competitive advantage. These include, for example, inventions, board deliberations, trade secrets, proprietary formulas and processes, prototypes and blueprints, technical designs, advanced research, confidential documents, manufacturing plans, software code, corporate and pricing strategies. Once you tighten controls around these strategic systems, you can then extend your focus towards other business-critical systems.

6. **Understand Critical Dependencies:** Think beyond client-facing systems and consider critical IT infrastructure that support your mission-critical systems. Critical infrastructure – such as domain name service (DNS) servers, software-defined wide area networks (SD-WANs), authentication systems, cloud services console, and perimeter firewalls, all of which often present single points of catastrophic failure but are usually overlooked during crown jewel assessment. That said, the list of non-negotiable controls you implement across business-facing systems will be fundamentally different to the ones you apply on your infrastructure. For instance, your systems of record will require sensitive data at rest to be encrypted, but that control may be not applicable to your perimeter firewalls.

7. **Build into New Systems Design:** Institutionalise crown jewel assessment by ensuring high-value systems are identified during the design phase, and non-negotiable controls are built in from the onset, not bolted on later.

8. **Implement a Differentiated Cyber Assurance Model:** Implement a differentiated cyber assurance model, ensuring threats around your crown jewels are rigorously assessed, and high-risk vulnerabilities receive the highest priority. This is the essence of a crown jewels-centred strategy, beefing up controls on systems that matter the most.

9. **Continuously Adapt:** Many enterprises make crown jewel assessment a one-off exercise. Such a tick-box approach is short-sighted and ineffective. The revalidation of crown jewels should continuously adapt to changing data protection laws, business priorities and threat landscape. We recommend a formal assessment at least every six months, in consultation with senior business leaders.

## PROTECTING YOUR HIGH VALUE TARGETS

This chapter provides some practical guidelines for enterprises to identify and maintain a tight list of high-value digital assets and develop a highly focused cyber resilience program to maximise the value of cybersecurity investments and accelerate the strengthening of their cyber resilience posture.

Crown jewels are digital assets that underpin the future success or survival of an enterprise. These applications support business functions or processes whose failure would be so detrimental to an enterprise to significantly erode its competitive advantage, lead to significant regulatory fines or durably undermine brand equity.

The National Cybersecurity Alliance defines crown jewels as 'the data without which your business would have difficulty operating and/or the information that could be a high-value target for cybercriminals'.[55] When systems that define your market leadership are breached, this may jeopardise your going concern. In the end, you should be able to answer three vital questions: What are your most valuable digital assets, where do they reside, and are they adequately protected?

The infamous Equifax data breach, in which almost half of US citizens lost their confidential details to cyber thieves, provided a cautionary tale into the implications of a poorly managed inventory of IT assets. Equifax, according to the USA Government Root Cause Analysis Report, lacked a comprehensive IT asset inventory, meaning it lacked a complete understanding of the assets it owned. 'This made it difficult, if not impossible, for Equifax to know if vulnerabilities existed on its networks.'[56]

## MAJOR BUSINESS PAIN POINTS

But before we get down into action, let's discuss three top business challenges based on their impact and pervasiveness:

### Security teams under tremendous pressure

There is widely documented endemic shortage in cybersecurity personnel. This results in long hours, leading to stress and burnout, a top reason cyber professionals leave positions or the industry completely. Corroborating these studies, another **research found 84% of cybersecurity professionals** are experiencing burnout, and it's impeding their motivation.[57]

### Widespread resource misallocation

According to consulting giant **McKinsey**, strongly corroborated by our own experiences with clients, there is no direct correlation between spending on cybersecurity (as a proportion of total IT spending) and success of a company's cybersecurity program.[58] Enterprises keep pouring money into technical defences, but their defensive capabilities are not improving. In fact, most organisations feel like they are pouring money into a leaky bucket. They attempt to spread resources thinly across every cyber threat, leaving mission-critical systems severely exposed.

### Lack of focus complicates cyber incident detection and response

According to **Imperva**, a global data and application security solutions company, a 'staggering 27% of IT professionals confirmed that they received more than one million threats daily, while 55% received more than 10,000'.[59] Unsurprisingly, the same survey revealed that the majority of IT professionals (53%) conceded that they struggled to isolate bona fide security incidents amid all this noise.

Consequently, for most cybersecurity teams, searching for genuine threats amid this noise is like wading through oatmeal. Limited insight into crown jewels extends the amount of time threat actors go undetected, worsening impacts from data breaches.

Nailing down crown jewels enables the enterprise to strike the right balance between opportunity and cyber risk. Understanding which assets, for example, require multi-factor authentication and complex passwords reduces the constant friction between security and usability. Furthermore, this approach eliminates waste, focusing limited financial and human resources towards risks that really matter, maximising the value of every dollar spent on security.

## ACTION PLAN

This three-phase approach will help you identify and isolate your crown jewels and develop a sustainable and effective strategy to reduce their risk profile.

### 1. Ask Key Questions to Identify Cyber Crown Jewels

Identifying an enterprise's crown jewels is risk assessment at its core. To be effective, this assessment should start by asking simple but important questions:

- Which systems underpin the strategic mission and core competencies, or differentiate the enterprise from its competitors? This key question will immediately reveal digital assets that support major customer segments and revenue lines.

- Does the system support critical services or infrastructure such as mining, oil and gas, transportation, power supply or manufacturing plants, such as industrial control systems (ICS)?

What systems or algorithms represent your competitive advantage or intellectual property? This is especially important because, according to research, IP accounts for 70% of the value of a publicly traded corporation, though it may make up a small percentage of organisational data.[60] Subsequently, IP is extremely valuable to hostile forces – whether company insiders or sophisticated attackers.

How many sensitive or personally identifiable customer records does the application hold, transmit or process? Systems that hold millions of sensitive customer records, medical information or payment card information demand higher levels of protection. A breach of any of these platforms could also, aside from a breach of privacy regulations, result in significant reputational damage or customer backlash.

Does the system process high-value transactions or does it just hold static data? Poorly secured high-value payment platforms, such as SWIFT platforms, could expose the enterprise to significant risk of financial fraud. A case in point came from the Bank of Bangladesh, which, in 2016, suffered a $81 million loss when cybercriminals compromised its poorly secured high-value payment systems. In fact, the hackers were prevented by a human error from stealing the entire $1 billion they were after.[61] Similarly, online investment management platforms, where customers can withdraw high-value retirement income, represent higher levels of risk compared with systems that offer read-only access.

What are our regulatory and other external data protection / cybersecurity obligations? For instance, companies that store, process or transmit payment card details may need to comply with PCI DSS requirements. Enterprises that use the SWIFT network to process interbank transactions may require to comply with the new SWIFT mandatory security requirements. It's vitally important to understand data privacy laws and mandatory data breach requirements for countries your organisation does business in, and ensure relevant systems have minimum level controls to comply with the law.

- What underlying IT infrastructure underpin network resilience? For example, an Active Directory that provides single sign-on capability to dozens of applications inevitably becomes one of the most vital systems.

## 2. Crown Jewel Risk Assessment Process

Identifying, assessing and protecting your crown jewels requires a disciplined and repeatable process. It's never a one-off exercise, but one that must be institutionalised into the bloodstream of your operational processes. Here are some practical steps:

- Facilitate workshops with senior business stakeholders to understand mission-critical processes and map these to underlying digital assets. These should include the CEO, COO, CRO, head of HR, general counsel, representatives from new product development, M&A, customer retention, marketing, etc.

- These workshops will further reinforce an important message, that cyber transformation is a shared responsibility, not a technology problem, soliciting their buy-in into programs to protect those assets.

- It is often impractical to engage these executives at granular level. Each executive must nominate a business owner, a delegate to make key decisions without creating unnecessary bottlenecks.

- Once the critical business processes have been identified, map these to applications and technologies that support these critical business processes.

- Capture pertinent information relating to each key system-related business process, system description, underlying infrastructure (operating system and database technologies), business owner, where the system is hosted (onsite, public cloud, private cloud, etc.), system owner (custodian), known issues, previous breaches, known regulatory or external obligations, nature of data held or processed (customer PII, intellectual property, payment card details, etc.), any high-value payments processed, etc.

Business processes and threats are dynamic, so this information needs to be assessed and updated regularly. Ongoing validation of your crown jewels is so important that the US government requires agencies to 'review their high-value assets (HVA) list on a quarterly basis and provide updates and modifications via the Homeland Security Information Network'.[62]

During this mapping exercise, you should also determine the system's threat profile. This is important because not all high-value digital assets will be exposed to the same risk. For instance, high-value digital systems exposed to the internet, hosted in the public cloud, joint venture or outsourced environments represent higher risk compared to low-value systems sitting behind layers of defences. To do so, ask these five questions:

1. Where is the crown jewel hosted (on-premise, public cloud, private cloud, hybrid or outsourced physical data centres)?

2. Who has access to the crown jewels? Place emphasis on remote access by contractors and privileged system access.

3. Is the crown jewel exposed to the internet, or is it protected by layered defences?

4. Does the system process high-value transactions?

5. Do we have adequate protections around the crown jewels, such as multi-factor authentication or data encryption?

Not all systems are created equal. Resist the temptation of classifying every system as a crown jewel, as one expert underscored. Without enough discretion, this can raise operational costs and promote operational efficiencies, undermining the entire process.

# Crown Jewel Risk Assessment: Illustrative Process

*Figure 5.1* provides an illustrative example of how you can identify, assess, classify and apply differentiated controls over your crown jewels.

*Figure 5.1*

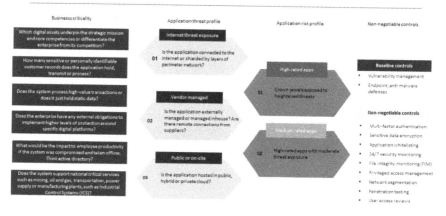

## 3. Develop a Set of Non-Negotiable Controls

Once you have identified your high-risk applications, the next step involves implementing a set of non-negotiable cybersecurity controls that, if designed, implemented and operated effectively, will significantly reduce your cyber risk profile. These controls are designed to maximise the effectiveness of cybersecurity investment and teams. There is no one-size-fits-all set of mandatory controls; each set will be driven by the enterprise's risk appetite, customer expectations and regulatory environment – the examples provided here are for illustrative purposes only. Several frameworks exist to provide more detailed guidance on security controls. These include:

- The NIST Framework for Improving Critical Infrastructure Cybersecurity is produced by the National Institute of Standards and Technology of the US Department of Commerce. This framework enables organisations – regardless of size, degree of cybersecurity risk or cybersecurity sophistication – to apply the principles and best practices of risk management to improve the security and resilience of critical infrastructure.

- The Center for Internet Security Critical Security Controls produced by SANS is a recommended set of actions for cyber defence that provide specific and actionable ways to stop today's most pervasive and dangerous attacks.

- The ISO 27000 series – The International Organization for Standardization (ISO) 27000 series enables organisations to implement processes and controls that support the principles of information security.

*Table 5.3* provides an example of high-impact cybersecurity controls we have helped multiple clients deploy. These can provide a good base to define a set of your non-negotiable controls over crown jewels.

*Table 5.3*

| Essential Control | Control Description |
|---|---|
| 1. **Multi-Factor Authentication** | Mandate multi-factor authentication (MFA) for access to high-value applications, transactions or users accessing the enterprise network from remote locations. MFA requires a combination of something a user knows (such as username and password) with something a user has, such as physical token or a one-time password (OTP) or something a user is (facial or fingerprint recognition). MFA is inherently harder to crack when compared to the traditional username and password combination. |
| 2. **Network Segmentation** | Design a network infrastructure to isolate your digital assets into different segments based on risk. A segmented network makes it significantly harder for an attacker to compromise one system and hop on to others, a concept referred to as 'lateral movement'. Once this is achieved, restrict access to high-risk network zones based on a strict need-to-do/know basis, opening connections only to those systems and users that absolutely need to connect with the enterprise's high-value systems. |
| | Once the hackers had infiltrated Equifax's system via the **ACIS portal**, they were able to move freely across its network 'to any other device, database, or server ... globally', because the servers that hosted the ACIS system were not segmented from the rest of Equifax's network.[63] |

| Essential Control | Control Description |
|---|---|
| 3. **Application Safelisting** | Deploy commercial tools to prevent unverified or unauthorised applications from executing on all high-value systems. When properly configured, application safelisting can significantly boost system security and stability, as well as mitigate software licensing issues. Application safelisting is a key control to block malicious code, a key threat to production workloads. |
| 4. **Privileged Access Management** | Tighten controls around privileged accounts to mitigate against malicious insiders and external attackers. Privileged accounts present the proverbial 'keys to the kingdom' and are a preferred target by cybercriminals as they provide deeper and wider access across systems without the need to escalate privileges. A proper privileged access management (PAM) solution delivers a number of modules that make this harder for threat actors, such as automated privileged access discovery, workflow for temporary privileged access requests and automated revocation, storing privileged account passwords securely in an encrypted vault and automated password rotation, recording privileged access sessions for audit and forensic purposes. |

| Essential Control | Control Description |
|---|---|
| 5. Data Encryption | Encryption scrambles data, making it unreadable without presenting the associated private key or password. High-value data, such as health records, passwords and board papers, must be encrypted at rest and in transit using industry-grade encryption tools. Admittedly, data encryption is both complex and costly, but in the face of rising cyber threats, sensitive-data encryption is a baseline customer and regulator expectation. Encrypting data without effective strategy to manage associated keys could, however, lead to significant availability issues. |
| 6. User Access Validations | All user access to high-value systems must be validated frequently – at least quarterly. The review should confirm that user access is aligned with job roles and eliminate excessive access or conflicting accesses. Excessive access or inappropriate segregation of duties must be identified and promptly rectified as they can expose the enterprise to significant operational or fraud risk. **ING Australia,**[64] part of a multinational insurance and finance group, suffered an A$30 million loss in 2012 when one of its accountants exploited excessive system access rights and processed 200 illegal transfers. The accountant later admitted to using logins for terminated employees to delete or alter illegal transactions to make them appear legitimate, claiming her manager didn't show any concern about her excessive access. |

| Essential Control | Control Description |
|---|---|
| 7. Security Monitoring | Deploy logging and monitoring tools over your high-value digital assets to alert the security operations team of any suspicious activities, such as addition or usage of privileged accounts or exfiltration of sensitive data. Security tools should ideally ship logs to a 24/7 security operations centre to enable automated log correlation, filtering, and rapid notifications. |
| | Logging security events without actively monitoring them wastes computing resources. A stark example of this was seen in 2013 when **Target's**[65] US security team ignored security warnings sent by their security operations team in India, giving hackers a window to pilfer more than 40 million payment card details. |
| 8. File Integrity Monitoring | File integrity monitoring (FIM) automatically detects any changes to critical files and alerts on any suspicious activity. FIM, which is a type of change auditing, verifies and validates these files by comparing the latest versions of them to a known, trusted 'baseline'. If FIM detects that files have been altered, updated or compromised, FIM can generate alerts to ensure further investigation, and if necessary, remediation, takes place. A post-mortem review of the Equifax hack revealed that the company's failure to implement basic security protocols, including file integrity monitoring and network segmentation, allowed the attackers to access and remove large amounts of data. FIM, the investigation concluded, could have detected the **Equifax**[66] hack. |

| Essential Control | Control Description |
|---|---|
| 9. Security Assurance | No matter how many defences you deploy, there is always a possibility that your systems will have flaws for threat actors to exploit. Implement a differentiated security assurance model, ensuring that all crown jewels exposed to the internet are assessed for vulnerabilities by suitably qualified internal or external resources at least annually. All high and critical vulnerabilities on your crown jewels must be prioritised for remediation. More importantly, engage experienced cybercrime experts to conduct targeted threat hunting on systems that host your IP assets and the network. During this threat hunting exercise, elite cybercrime investigators conduct a detailed review of systems against bona fide threats targeting your specific industry to identify indications of hidden adversaries. |
| 10. Security Patching | Despite overwhelming evidence confirming that unpatched systems are a major avenue for cyberattacks, several IT teams remain slack at patching vulnerabilities. Most cyberattacks exploit unpatched systems. A primary defence measure is to prioritise the patching of all your crown jewels, embracing a zero-tolerance policy for needless security exemptions over critical systems. When critical vulnerabilities are announced, crown jewels must have top patching priority. |

## Reducing Cyber Risk on Intellectual Property

Developing a comprehensive list of your crown jewels can be daunting, as many enterprises maintain hundreds or even thousands of unique applications. An effective approach to tackle this challenge is to start with those systems that hold your intellectual property (IP). This includes but is not limited to inventions, board deliberations, trade secrets, proprietary formulas and processes, prototypes and blueprints, technical designs, advanced research, confidential documents, manufacturing plans, software code, corporate and pricing strategies, and patented designs.

The World Intellectual Property Organization (WIPO) defines IP as creations of the mind – inventions, literary and artistic works, symbols, names, images and designs used in commerce.[67] IP is protected in law by patents, copyrights and trademarks, in order to motivate individuals and companies to profit from ingenuity.

IP has become a lucrative target for sophisticated cybercrime syndicates, and nation states and their proxies. IP theft is broad: counterfeiting pharmaceuticals or product designs, stealing and reverse engineering proprietary technology, patent infringement and stealing trade secrets (proprietary systems, devices, algorithms and strategies). Arguably, IP assets represent some of the most vital digital assets. The IP Commission Report asserts that the IP of a publicly traded company accounts for an estimated 70% of its value.[68]

Given such significance, it's therefore unsurprising that IP theft costs the US up to $600 billion a year, now considered to be the greatest transfer of wealth in history. This number according to the IP Commission Report 'is still difficult to assess because companies may not even be aware that their IP has been stolen, nor are firms incentivised to report their losses once discovered'.[69] Once this information falls into the wrong hands, its value is significantly diminished, counterfeit products hit the market, companies lose substantial revenue to counterfeited goods, and this, in turn, stifles innovation.

Of all the threat actors, insiders pose the greatest threat to IP assets. According to a study conducted of 120 prosecutions the US government has brought for theft of trade secrets, in more than 90% of the prosecutions, the defendant was an insider and had access to the trade secrets: they were either an employee of the victim or they worked for a vendor or contractor of the victim.[70] Here are some key considerations to tighten control over IP assets:

- Conduct a detailed assessment of the enterprise mission to determine intellectual property, trade secrets, and patents that underlie your market advantage. Product development and legal teams are good sources of such information.

- Understand where these IP assets reside and create a detailed inventory. This information is often held away from the enterprise networks (private contractors and their subcontractors, research firms and laboratories, offshore software development firms, etc.).

A good understanding of the jurisdictions you operate from is also essential, as this can determine the difficulty of protecting these high-value assets. A good example is the Chinese cybersecurity law, which forces companies operating in China to disclose critical intellectual property to the government and requires that they store data locally.[71] That can significantly complicate measures to preserve the confidentiality of this information.

Review the existing controls to preserve the confidentiality, integrity and availability of your IP assets, and formulate action plans to address deficiencies.

Conduct comprehensive security due diligence on new suppliers involved in the development, storage or handling of IP assets, and ensure they have robust preventative and detective controls, including managing insider cyber-threat risks.

Embed IP protection clauses in relevant third-party or supplier contracts and ensure there are adequate security assurance processes over the protection of those assets. Ensure no supplier will further engage subcontractors to handle your IP without your explicit written permission.

Require staff and contractors to sign non-disclosure agreements before accessing IP assets and disclose conflicts of interest. Conduct exit interviews and request terminated staff to formally attest that they are not taking IP assets with them.

Have clearly documented and communicated IP protection security policies.

Lock down systems that hold IP (disable USB access, host systems within segmented networks, and when exported to end-user devices, such as laptops, deploy robust encryption and endpoint security).

Implement robust data loss prevention controls to reduce the likelihood of both malicious and unintentional leakage.

Log access to IP assets and automate alerts when suspicious activity is detected. Educate employees on your data loss prevention and security monitoring controls. When staff and contractors know their actions are monitored, that becomes a strong deterrence.

Regularly reinforce the significance of intellectual property protection to product development teams and educate high-risk communities on spotting targeted phishing attacks.

The US-China Business Council recommends incorporating IP protection into facility design. Some companies, for example, limit IP exposure by ensuring that sensitive information is kept in low employee traffic areas or behind unmarked doors.[72] The same guidelines further recommend companies to closely monitor or prohibit the use of flash disks, portable hard drives, laptops, cell phone cameras and other devices that could be used to capture and transmit sensitive information.

The FBI, on the other hand, recommends that IP assets should be stored on digital assets disconnected from the internet.[73]

Restrict executives travelling to high-risk countries from carrying laptops or other devices that contain IP assets. Create guidelines to harden these assets should it be necessary to travel with them to high-risk countries.

# Chapter 7

# Transforming Mashonaland Health Cyber Function – A Fictional Case Study

### Executive Influence a Better Predictor of Cyber Transformation Success than Technical Proficiency

In July 2022, Elizabeth Johnson, 46 years old, was hired as the new CISO for Mashonaland Health, the largest and oldest private healthcare provider in the Kingdom of Mutapa, a country characterised by jagged mountains, deep valleys, large mineral deposits and breathtaking streams. Mashonaland Health is one of Mutapa's emblematic institutions. Established in 1967, it runs 77 hospitals (1,200 beds) and 37 aged care homes spread across the country, servicing about 3 million patients per year. The chain of hospitals provides a range of services, including acute medical and surgical services, emergency care, aged care, rehabilitation, and specialist clinics. Mashonaland Health boasts more than 10,000 staff geographically dispersed across the country.

### The imperative for change

In January 2022, Matebele Health, a smaller competitor running ten hospitals in Mutapa, was forced to divert patients from some of its emergency rooms to other hospitals and postpone high-risk surgeries when hackers used stolen administrative accounts to burrow deeply into its network and cripple core systems using ransomware. The

Matebele Health hack served as a wake-up call for the Mashonaland board, which had long ignored calls to boost its cyber resilience and hire an experienced CISO to lead the charge. Two other factors were also in play:

a. The rising demand for medical healthcare information on the darknet when compared with other classes of stolen information was motivating cybercriminals to target the poorly secured healthcare sector. Hospitals were easy to hack and more likely to pay. Without quick access to patient histories and other pertinent information, hospitals can't engage in high-risk procedures without exposing themselves to serious legal risks.

b. Citing mounting geopolitical tensions, the Mutapa government had already started formulating a comprehensive Critical Infrastructure Resilience Bill, which would mandate ISO 27001 certification, among other requirements, across all organisations deemed pivotal to citizens' well-being and national security. Once it received royal assent, the bill was set to become law in July 2024.

When Elizabeth Johnson landed in Mutapa in July 2022 she quickly got down to work, exuding an intense zeal for transformation. Elizabeth was headhunted from Mauritius, a resort country tucked 1,800 kilometres off the east coast of Africa. Back in her home country, she had held several technology risk and cybersecurity leadership roles for more than a decade, most recently working as the head of cybersecurity at a large bank.

## Stakeholder Consultations

As soon as Elizabeth Johnson settled into the role, she quickly organised meetings with key stakeholders to understand the lay of the land (top business priorities, potential roadblocks) as well as to build rapport. The chief executive officer, the chief information officer and the chief risk officer were at the top of her list.

## Chief Executive Officer

First was Joseph Thomas, the faintly aloof CEO and executive director who wore charcoal double-breasted suits almost daily. JT, as he was widely referred to, rose through the ranks and had been with Mashonaland Health for 23 years. Once they had established some rapport and talked about family and passions and the challenges of moving countries, Elizabeth asked a few probing questions, and carefully listened as the CEO articulated the company's vision, strategic goals and expectations:

'With a history dating back to Mutapa's independence in 1967, we are proud to be recognised as a leading research and healthcare provider of international standing. Our impact transcends our geographical borders. We are seeing an influx of patients from the greater sub-Saharan countries, attracted by our state-of-the-art medical equipment and highly skilled physicians. Our mission is anchored by three core values: to lead with empathy, constantly strive for excellence, and uphold the highest ethical standards. Our purpose gets clearer every day: we exist to provide an equitable and innovative healthcare ecosystem that enables all of Mutapa's citizens to live healthy, fulfilling and long lives. Our expansive and interconnected networks of hospitals service more than 80% of Mutapa. We have many strategic projects, but three matter the most:

1. To improve patient care through innovative, highly secure and easy-to-use digital platforms. By securely embracing digital transformation, we will tap into digital technology's potential to fundamentally create new experiences for our patients, staff and business partners.

2. To grow our operating income by 30% by positioning Mutapa as the top and most preferred medical destination in sub-

Saharan Africa (expanding medical tourism). We are also midway through the acquisition of Manica Health, so we can expand our impact further east.

3. To deliver $20 million cost efficiencies by fixing broken processes, eliminating activities that don't add value to our patients, and outsourcing activities that can be delivered cheaper and more efficiently by third parties. We will reinvest these savings to provide safe and high-quality healthcare for our patients. We should never lose sight that while Mashonaland Health is a national pride, we are a privately held organisation with owners committed to long-term profitability and sustainability.

'We are being pressured from all directions. Our patients want more personalised and easy-to-access healthcare. Regulations are tightening. Hospitals, as we saw with the Matebele Health hack, are under siege. If we suffer the same attack, our credibility and reliability would be permanently undermined. Because Matebele capitulated to ransom demands, the emboldened and enriched crooks will likely strike again, and we make a logical target.

'That's why digital transformation sits at the top of everything we aim to achieve. But to do so we must radically change the way we do things and recreate Mashonaland Heath into an agile business where our staff feel empowered to experiment with innovation, challenge the old ways of doing things and move at the speed of thought.'

Seeing the clock tick towards the top of the hour, Elizabeth asked a closing question: 'What keeps you awake at night, and if you were in my shoes what would you prioritise?'

'The Matebele Health hack reminded that hackers are not going to spare us because targeting hospitals is morally irreprehensible. They are cold-hearted. I'm not sure if the crooks spared us because we have good defences, but my gut tells me we were just lucky. We don't know what we don't know, and that's exactly why we brought you in as a senior executive to give the board assurance that we are investing in the right things. Last year we spent $5 million in cybersecurity, but all I got was long-winded PDF reports with red and amber issues I couldn't make sense of. I keep signing off huge consulting invoices, yet all this effort is proving incapable of assuring the board that we are doing the right things. I feel these dark-suited consultants pocketed our money and took us down the wrong road. We have a board meeting in September, and it would be great if we can slot you on to the agenda to inform the board of what our most material gaps are and our investment priorities. Remember that securing our networks is not simply a commercial goal, but also, an important moral obligation to the nation.'

## Chief Information Officer

During the next few days, Elizabeth had a two-hour meeting with the CIO, Jennifer Jones, to whom she also reported. The conversation uncovered four pillars of the digital transformation program:

1. To aggressively embrace artificial intelligence and big data to automate patient diagnosis and provide prescriptions with the same accuracy as a trained physician. Mashonaland Health was ripe for this change because the amount of medical data it held across its ecosystem was staggering.

2. To modernise IT infrastructure by migrating 60% of mission-critical systems to Microsoft Cloud to enable greater financial flexibility, agility and business resilience. As workloads are migrated to the cloud, Mashonaland Health also needed to ensure security could flexibly accommodate changing business needs.

3. To create an open architecture to interconnect Mashonaland Health to Mutapa Digital Health Platform, providing physicians with instant access to patient medical history, allergies and laboratory test results. Doing so would eliminate

redundant tests, avoid adverse medication reactions, as well as accelerate diagnosis and prescription.

4. To replace phone calls, text messages and spreadsheets with a web- and mobile-based staff rostering system to improve nurse shift predictability, cut costs and improve staff digital experience.

'Our infrastructure is a Balkanised mix of bespoke applications, too dated to meet business demands. Some of those can't be protected by modern cybersecurity solutions without breaking them. So, we must move fast and create a digital platform that can not only foster digital resilience, but also scale with our growth agenda,' the CIO reiterated.

## Chief Risk Officer

Next in line was Bernadette Mlilo, the chief risk officer, who had joined Mashonaland Health two to three years ago from one of Mutapa's platinum mines, where she held the chief audit officer role for six years. After a few pleasantries, Elizabeth and Bernadette discussed several matters including the enterprise risk management model, governance structure and the culture at large. Elizabeth jotted down a few important points:

1. While Mashonaland Health had a relatively mature enterprise risk management process and culture, cyber was barely covered at the bimonthly executive risk and compliance meetings and six-monthly board meetings.

2. The enterprise risk profile tracked the top twelve risks at the executive risk and compliance meetings and only eight at the board level. A consolidated 'IT systems resilience and security' risk marked as red was tracked at both executive and board levels but lacked sufficient granularity on key risk drivers and related mitigations.

3. On a scale of 1 to 10, the CRO rated Mashonaland's Health a solid 6 in terms of risk culture. While there was a new push by the board to embed risk management deep into business processes, the process was still disjointed and often impeded by the command style structure that characterised Mashonaland Health.

4. While the CRO had recently completed the CERT Certificate in Cyber Risk Oversight Program offered by the National Association of Company Directors, she was still struggling to produce insightful cyber risk reporting to the board, hampered by the complexity of the subject and the organisation's networks.

'We had a couple of fractional CISOs join Mashonaland Health in the last year, but none of them made a dent. To get things done in Mutapa, you need the right people on your side. These suited consultants brought in so-called best practice, tick-box cyber risk models and tried to push us towards ISO certification, but the reality is that Mashonaland Health was simply not prepared to take such drastic steps. They failed to build an informal network of relationships with key executives and couldn't shake the stereotype that they were consultants, with a utopian view and limited understanding of how the corporate decisions are made,' the CRO said.

Elizabeth quickly moved in to interview other pertinent stakeholders and gather key insights into the organisation's operating model, key business partners, technology stack, and potential roadblocks. She sat down with the enterprise IT architect, the chief financial officer, the chief strategy officer, the company secretary and select members of the cybersecurity team that she was hired to revamp. She spent weekends studying board papers, internal audit reports, IT strategies and financial statements.

## From Analysis to Execution

Elizabeth came to the following conclusions after immersing herself in the organisational culture, its sources of revenue, digital transformation and corporate goals:

1. Mashonaland Health had not materially improved its risk profile mostly because the so-called strategy (a list of controls emanating from a substandard ISO 27001 gap assessment) was no strategy at all. It not only lacked a clear set of coherent choices but there was also no clear-cut and compelling logic behind prioritised initiatives and related trade-offs. To quickly demonstrate value and shake off the stereotype that weighed heavily on the cybersecurity team, she needed to carefully choose a small set of high-impact projects and explain the logic behind her choices and the residual risk associated with difficult trade-offs Mashonaland Health would make.

2. She acknowledged that Mashonaland Health was coming late to the party – her team could not afford to cruise at 30 kilometres per hour and change the entrenched view that cyber was a bottomless money pit. To quickly build rapport, she had to make bold choices. After workshops with key stakeholders, she identified a small set of sacred cow projects to either kill or pause indefinitely. Chief among these was data loss prevention, a year-long project with loosely defined end goals and a complex business case. While the significance of this project in the healthcare sector was indisputable, it was sucking a disproportionate number of resources that would be redirected to areas of higher risk – primarily rolling out MFA on 16 internet-facing applications, assessing the efficacy of backups, and laying the foundations for imminent critical infrastructure regulations. Furthermore, it was prudent to replace Mashonaland Health's hardware-based internet and email security gateways with cloud-based solutions before implementing data loss prevention – a key dependent that wasn't considered by the previous strategy.

3. Phase One of the Cyber Resilience Strategy would focus on three high-priority areas: (a) Forming an informed view of the organisation's ransomware defence readiness as this is the board's top concern, (b) Creating a detailed cybersecurity risk profile to highlight material gaps and prioritise remediation, and (c) Moving in quickly to mitigate known high-risk areas and raise the bar for attackers: implementing MFA on internet-facing high-risk workloads, creating offline backups for high-value systems, getting a cybersecurity incident response retainer, and a range of cybersecurity hygienic practices (such as, clearing up a backlog of high and critical vulnerabilities, extending security controls across endpoint devices, and tightening privileged access across crown jewels).

4. One message had sunk in deeply through her consultative process. Management at Mashonaland Health hated being told what to do, a culture that permeated across Mutapa. To drive change, it was important for Elizabeth to constantly engage these stakeholders before drafting her strategy: after first drafts and throughout execution. To break the impasse, she proposed the implementation of a cross-functional cyber risk management committee. This group, comprising the CEO, CIO, CFO, COO, CISO and product development team, would provide executive-level support to cyber transformation, send important signals across the business that cyber was key to Mashonaland's Health existence, and act as a conduit between the cyber function and the board. When the CRO insisted that cyber risk be added to the existing executive risk and compliance meeting to avoid reinventing the wheel, Elizabeth stood her ground and persuaded them that doing so would greatly dilute cybersecurity, by squeezing it into an already busy agenda. By creating a governance model that was based on common sense and genuinely consultative, translating cybersecurity into vivid, everyday language, she made cyber risk accessible to a broader audience. Everyone

in the cybersecurity governance committee could now see, for the first time, how their efforts contributed to the organisation's resilience, and why change mattered.

5. Elizabeth convinced the CFO and CIO to tap into IT discretionary spend and bring in experienced outsiders to help execute immediate priorities, while giving her time to draft a comprehensive road map. But to avoid her predecessor's mistakes, she would pair them with internal team members to ensure their expertise was concentrated on critical goals – not some 'external best practice'.

6. In defining her strategy, Elizabeth was careful not to set unrealistic or overly zealous goals, while at the same time acknowledging that irrational pessimism wouldn't fly given the glaring gaps and board concerns. The next step was to define Phase One, which consisted of six key themes:

   i.  Work with the managed service provider to clear a backlog of critical vulnerabilities. But Elizabeth's team would take a risk-based approach, prioritising vulnerabilities that were actually exploitable and systems exposed to the internet. (Elizabeth also noted that the vulnerability service level agreement [SLA] clause signed years ago was dated and renegotiated with the key vendor to further tighten them from 30 to 14 days. The vendor relented, noting that the contract was up for renewal within nine months.)

   j.  Engage a suitably qualified and independent team of experts to conduct a ransomware defence assessment. Further project work would be informed by the number of critical findings identified by the assessment.

   k.  Phase One of the digital transformation program (driven by the CIO) was already underway, which included the migration of some mission-critical systems (those classified as cloud-able). Given some of these systems contained sensitive healthcare information, the new CISO prioritised the rollout of a cloud security posture management tool to automate the discovery and remediation of vulnerabilities and misconfigurations across Microsoft and Oracle clouds. Bolting on security early would lower its cost and advance Mashonaland Health's goal to embrace innovation securely.

l.   Elizabeth ordered a swift and targeted review of all third-party organisations with remote access to Mashonaland Health's network to ensure unrequired access was removed, the remaining vendors had MFA enforced, and access was channelled via encrypted virtual private network (VPN) sessions. She deferred a project to ensure all third parties logged into a segmented network zone to Phase Two – citing complexity and cost.

m.  She persuaded the CFO that while it was understandable to apply for cyber insurance cover, the timing didn't make sense. It would be more prudent to aim for that six months later, when Mashonaland Health has formed a view on its risk profile, improved its cyber hygiene and reduced the attack surface. That way, the insurance would stand a higher chance of approval and come at lower premiums.

n.   One key lesson she had learnt from her long cyber leadership career was that while technical controls were central, creating a shared sense of purpose and rallying everyone behind Mashonaland Health's cyber transformation was even more crucial. The cybersecurity team would roll out a cloud-based cyber awareness program to educate staff on the latest threats and defences through bite-sized, highly engaging videos; and run quarterly phishing simulations, as well as opt-in Microsoft Teams sessions on specific, deep-dive topics. During Phase Three, the cybersecurity team would enlist frontline staff as cybersecurity ambassadors to foster grassroots input and participation.

To remove the disconnect between senior business stakeholders and the cybersecurity function, Elizabeth used a simple table that linked core security projects to each of Mashonaland Health's four strategic business goals. This is illustrated in *Table 6.1*.

*Table 6.1*

| Improve Patient Care Through Innovation | To Grow Our Operating Income by 30% |
|---|---|
| 1. Develop and operationalise an API security policy to ensure Mashonaland securely integrate Mutapa Digital Health Platform. | 1. Work collaboratively with the legal team to develop a cross-jurisdictional data privacy and breach response plan, prioritising countries targeted for medical tourism growth. |
| 2. Roll out a cloud-based and hands-on learning platform to empower developers with practical skills to build secure applications throughout the development life cycle. | 2. Develop a detailed cybersecurity framework to proactively showcase Mashonaland Health's data privacy and security capabilities, positioning cybersecurity as a key business enabler. |
| 3. Roll out single sign-on to improve staff and patient digital experience, significantly cut off password reset tickets, and simplify integration with third parties. | 3. Identify opportunities to unify security controls with Manica Health (targeted for acquisition FY25) and mitigate risks outside of appetite. |

## Deliver $20 million cost efficiencies by fixing broken processes

1. Replace the poorly tuned internal security information and event management (SIEM) platform with a completely outsourced end-to-end threat intelligence and 24/7 security operation centre (SOC) – cutting down OPEX by 30% and boosting visibility across high-value systems.

2. Replace a range of hardware-based security appliances with next-generation software as a service (SaaS) systems – improving cyber defence and reducing OPEX by 20%.

3. Recentering time-consuming third-party security audits on high-risk vendors and outsourcing the reviews to a suitably qualified third party that can execute at scale and lower costs.

## Build a digitally resilient business

1. Revamp and test the disaster recovery plan to ensure crown jewels can be promptly recovered within business-agreed recovery time objectives.

2. Roll out a multifaceted security cultural uplift program to embed positive security culture deep into business operations.

> **Deliver $20 million cost efficiencies by fixing broken processes**

4. Restructure the cybersecurity team to align skill sets with business goals and outsource commoditised services.

## Transforming the Cybersecurity Function

Elizabeth knew that for her to deliver impact, she had to take bold moves right away. She resisted the allure of hiring direct reports who would say, 'Yes, boss,' to all her suggestions. Her aim was to create a dynamic culture where staff ruthlessly challenged ideas that were misaligned with business goals, meaningless workgroups and redundant controls. Because her background was in technology risk governance and control, she prioritised hiring three key people in roles that would cover her blind spots and quickly boost momentum:

a. **Director of Cybersecurity Strategy and Architecture:** This strategic role (and Elizabeth's second in charge) would work closely with enterprise architecture, product development, infrastructure and other cybersecurity functions to understand strategic priorities, and ensure cybersecurity was positioned to advance business goals. This role would lead the design and implementation of strategic cybersecurity solutions.

b. **Cybersecurity Program Director:** She sought an experienced program manager with solid understanding of technology and cybersecurity solutions to coordinate and oversee the planning, execution and delivery of cybersecurity strategic initiatives. Doubling up as the chief of staff for the CISO, this function would also look after change management, cost control, project governance and reporting, as well as maintain active collaboration with the architecture, infrastructure, development and application teams.

c. **Director of Cybersecurity Vendor Governance:** An aggressive outsourcing strategy was pivotal to help Mashonaland Health meet its cost savings targets, scale automation and accelerate digital transformation. The renewed focus dictated that Elizabeth hire this dedicated director. In collaboration with the cybersecurity program director, the new hire would drive vendor contract negotiations, streamline vendor governance, implement an effective control monitoring regime and manage strategic vendor relationships.

There were some key cultural philosophies at the heart of her cybersecurity team transformation. She sent an unequivocal message that the new cybersecurity function would be characterised by psychological safety – a deep-rooted belief that the team was allowed to experiment, make mistakes and learn from them without fearing for their jobs or other repercussions – behaviours underscored by the CEO during her initial briefings.

She knew that it was one thing to draft a compelling cybersecurity strategy but executing it was another thing. That required a highly motivated team who stuck together during difficult moments. While individual successes were celebrated, she redrafted departmental and individual key performance indicators (KPIs) to promote teamwork and collaboration; to recognise staff who lived Mashonaland Health's values of empathy, integrity and constant quest for excellence.

Elizabeth was inheriting one of the least engaged teams across Mashonaland Health. She knew that left unchecked, the disengaged workforce could negate her efforts to transform the organisation. Quick survey results from her team yielded consistent themes: they wanted to feel seen, understood and recognised, as well as work flexibly. Boosting team engagement would boil down to five things:

a.  Simplifying cybersecurity goals in the language of the business, reiterating the bigger *why*, and tying individual and team KPIs to business goals. For example, changing fuzzy KPIs for the IT security manager from 'Facilitating penetration testing on all new APIs before go-live' to 'Creating a detailed inventory of APIs and enforcing non-negotiable controls across 100% of APIs to ensure physicians have timely and secure access to patients' healthcare information.' Not only did this provide a measurable goal; it also gave the IT security manager a stronger sense of purpose.

b.  She circulated the draft strategies with her leadership team, who in turn cascaded core messages across their broader teams. In Elizabeth's case, she did this with a genuine mindset to solicit feedback and ensure the team felt they owned the strategies, that it wasn't superimposed on them (a mistake that sank the previous management consultants). For example, when one junior security analyst admitted that it would be difficult to develop and operationalise an application programming interface (API) security strategy when the team had shallow domain knowledge, she allocated some budget to enrol the team into a globally recognised, hands-on application, training program on APIs and microservices.

c.  But to sustain change, Elizabeth knew that she had to go way deeper than PowerPoint slides, and walk the talk. She routinely walked up to staff's desks, greeted them by name, genuinely enquired about their lives outside of work and openly asked if there was anything the team could do better. The feedback was retrofitted into tactical plans. She encouraged her team to tell her exactly what they thought and created a simple intranet site where cybersecurity staff could suggest improvements. To gain trust, she moved her desk from the executive level to the same floor as her team, enabling them to walk over and ask key questions, thus breaking the needless formalities that characterised the previous era.

d. She replaced the proverbial stick (negative messages that threatened staff with a series of repercussions if they violated work policies) with the carrot. She implemented the monthly Cyber Hero awards where staff nominated peers who had gone beyond the call of duty to uphold the virtues of the cyber transformation program. She tactfully delegated her architecture and program directors to present during company-wide town hall events, elevating their visibility and carefully rejecting the notion that she was the saviour brought in to shake things up. She rarely used the word 'I' – sending a clear message that any material success resulted from a shared vision, not siloed efforts.

e. She convinced her boss, the CIO, the departmental policy that mandated employees be in the office at least four days a week was misaligned with Mashonaland Health's ambition to become the best place to work in Mutapa. There was really no need for most technical staff to spend hours commuting to work only to be stuck on their screens resolving Service Now tickets when they could be equally effective at home. In response to her quick poll, cybersecurity staff had unanimously agreed that three days in the office was ideal. With her boss's blessing, she quickly relaxed the policy in line with her staff's needs. The new flexibility, combined with fortnightly team activities, catalysed her team's morale and well-being.

## Anticipating Major Pitfalls

Once Elizabeth outlined her three-year road map, the next stage involved anticipating key risks that could significantly impact the achievements of those goals, and working with the project team and stakeholders to identify targeted mitigations. The collaborative approach identified three potential pitfalls, as outlined in *Table 6.2*.

*Table 6.2*

**Antiquated mission-critical systems not readily migrated to the cloud or secured with modern technologies**

a. Implement a tight set of mitigating controls (e.g. remove internet access or move to a segmented secure zone) to reduce risk until the systems are decommissioned.

b. Conduct a deep-dive assessment of vulnerable and aged systems for board-level risk acceptance.

**Misalignment of priorities with IT and product development teams leading to de-prioritisation of cyber initiatives**

c. Ongoing collaboration with the risk management office, external auditors and internal audit function to streamline assurance reviews, avoid duplication of effort, centre reviews on unknown areas of high risk and eliminate waste that emanated from audits beyond the ability of the cybersecurity team to mitigate.

d. After consultations with the cyber risk governance committee, three initiatives – securing a hospital chain targeted for acquisition, improving patient digital experience through simplified security and enabling secure integration with Mutapa Digital Health Platform – were elevated to corporate KPIs, securing undivided attention from the leadership team and the CEO.

e. The CIO had already successfully sponsored monthly one-day hackathons where teams across solution engineering, big data, development and architecture unleashed their ingenuity and rigorously debated better ways to embrace advanced technologies. This was low-hanging fruit, and with the CIO's blessing, Elizabeth quickly embedded her cybersecurity team into the hackathons, fostering a secure-by-design culture, and breaking silos between the cyber team and its peers.

**Project cost and schedule overruns**

    f.  By the time the new CISO took over, Mashonaland Health was overburdened with sacred cow projects – a dozen or so projects that had outlived their relevance and were over budget and behind schedule. She set out a 30% provision in her transformation budget and established a disciplined project that leveraged PMO tools, best practices, rigorous cost tracking, quality assurance and a good mix of internal and external expertise. Most importantly, she courageously eliminated fuzzy security projects (like 'to achieve zero trust by 2024'), freeing up her team to work on specific and high-impact projects with measurable outcomes.

## In conclusion

The case study highlights that successful cyber transformations are less about bleeding-edge technologies and more about creating a multifaceted program that comprises setting the right tone at the top, a culture of constant and genuine collaboration, fostering team spirit, acting with extreme frugality, making bold choices, and ultimately, common sense.

By the end of 12 months, Elizabeth's team had delivered 90% of the initiatives on their road map and reduced operational costs by 25%. This was achieved, for example, by embracing cloud-first strategy, renegotiating vendor contracts, cleaning up unrequired licenses, and cancelling duplicate and aimless assurance reviews.

Elizabeth recentred her team on strategy execution, secure application development and architecture, bringing a deeper sense of purpose to their work. This was achieved, for example, by outsourcing security operations, third-party reviews, and penetration testing. By transforming her role from a leadership one to more of a facilitator of cyber risk management, and an enabler of transformation,

Elizabeth got everyone excited about cyber transformation. She permanently replaced the view that the cyber team was a 'bunch of rigid, compliance-focused professionals' with a respected and commercially minded team whose input the business now proactively sought before making consequential decisions.

Elizabeth understood that to drive lasting change, she needed to change the culture first. But doing so required her to carefully preserve the good aspects of the old culture, cutting off the toxic bits and unleashing her emotional intelligence to navigate a complex web of stakeholders.

She was delighted that she had stepped out of her comfort zone, migrating to a new country with two teenage daughters. 'I married right. When the opportunity came, my supportive husband didn't even blink. It took him a while to land a corporate finance role in Mutapa, but he was clear we were on this journey together. I am glad I took the risk. How many people get the opportunity to turn around a cyber function for an organisation so pivotal to the future of a nation?'

As in any leadership journey, Elizabeth made some miscalculations and missed some targets. But she was ruthlessly honest with the cyber risk governance committee and the board, highlighting any potential slippages, and finding alternative ways to manage risk. In a vote of confidence, the board approved an additional $2 million to expand the team and fuel digital resilience.

## CYBER LEADERS ON THE MOVE STORY 2

### Noureen Njoroge – Director of Global Cyber Threat Intelligence at Nike and a graduate of the Cyber Leadership Institute.

Noureen's awe-inspiring story began in Nairobi, one of Africa's most influential cities, where she was born and educated. Nairobi, also known as the Green City under the Sun, means 'the place of cool waters' in Maasai.

'I had a good upbringing, and I am grateful for that. My parents, both qualified engineers by profession, invested a lot in our education and instilled a never-ending quest for self-discovery and learning. Those ideals stuck with me and continue to serve me well,' the charismatic Noureen opened the conversation.

At the tender age of 14, Noureen stripped her home PC down, carefully studied dozens of individual components, and then rebuilt the PC. From that moment, her tech career started. When other Nairobi teenagers were receiving frivolous Christmas gifts, Noureen petitioned her parents to buy her computer parts. She eventually assembled a few computers from scratch and donated to local schools and hospitals in need. 'I am passionate about helping others and find great fulfilment in doing so,' explained Noureen.

Soon after high school, Noureen left Kenya to pursue her university studies in the US. She recalls having mixed feelings. 'I was elated about my new adventure and nervous at the same time since I did not know what to expect in a foreign country. This was my first time living away from home, and I was still very young. Fortunately, I had a large extended family across the US, which gave me a softer landing.'

Noureen was soon accepted by three universities, thanks to her early community engagement – coaching and supporting young girls. Her first pick was a four-year university, but the first year of school was not easy. She sought advice from one of her college professors, embraced the advice and transferred to a community college. There, Noureen was able to focus better as the college offered more options and lots of support, especially to international students.

She later joined the University of Massachusetts Lowell (UML) soon after graduating from MassBay Community College with a computer science degree. While still in college, Noureen was accepted into an internship program at Intel Corporation, the global manufacturer of semiconductor computer circuits. That internship set strong career foundations and soon opened successive technical and product development roles at Monster (an international online recruitment firm). Upon graduation from (UML) she joined Bose Corporation (audio equipment giant) as a systems analyst.

As we collaborated with Noureen during the eight-week Cyber Leadership Program, her rare combination of deep technical expertise and business acumen stood out. There is a reason why. She explains, 'I have always lived by the mantra, 'Preparation meets opportunity!' My mum also reminds me to always be prepared for an opportunity that I may not have than have an opportunity and am not ready.

'I tackled each of my earlier technology roles with a near-obsessive level of intent. Bose gave me tremendous opportunities, and I stepped up to the challenge. I rolled up my sleeves and spent countless hours in the data centre. I built critical applications in the cloud, set up demilitarised zones (DMZs) and any other technical work I could lay my hands on.'

Noureen's narrative again proves that the journey to cyber leadership roles rarely takes a predictable path. One day, an internal presentation on malicious code intrigued her curiosity. She promptly leveraged her internal networks and jumped ship into the brighter side of cybersecurity. 'That remains one of my best career decisions. Look where we are now; cybersecurity has zoomed to the top of every corporate risk profile.'

Fortuitously, during the same year, the Massachusetts Institute of Technology (MIT) launched an intensive cybersecurity program in technology, application & policy. Noureen enrolled in the inaugural class, further solidifying her technical expertise and broadening her network.

A few years later, CISCO, the world's largest networking and communications company, came knocking. In the spring of 2016, Noureen joined CISCO as a cybersecurity engineer. During her tenure, she stepped up to leadership, leading a cyber threat analytics team, which she grew from a team of one (herself) to a fully fledged department by the time she left, almost five years later.

'My secret weapon has been and will always continue to be investing and nurturing those meaningful connections I establish along this career journey. I still stay in touch with my elementary school teachers, previous managers, and university professors. At CISCO, I was lucky to meet so many great mentors, like Omar Santos, whose wisdom helped me a lot in my security journey, understand the company culture and avoid career-derailing mistakes.'

As Noureen rose through the ranks, one thing became glaringly apparent – women were grossly underrepresented in technology. During her time at CISCO, she decided to turn those lemons into lemonade, founding North Carolina Women in Cybersecurity Network. This organisation has inspired young women from dozens of countries to pursue careers in cybersecurity. In addition, Noureen founded the Global Cybersecurity mentoring program, which has been running since 2019, with global representation from around 30 to 38 countries. Her goal is to inspire, motivate and mentor others in the industry of cybersecurity. (Check out more here **cybersecmentorship. org**). 'We need more mentors in this industry,' Noureen emphasised. 'As a leader, I aim at raising other leaders and NOT followers as there's no success without a successor. Success always leaves clues!'

Noureen is a global keynote speaker, has received multiple industry accolades for her courage to lead, most notably listed among 2024 and 2023 top 40 under 40 Women Cyber leaders, ranked among the Top 50 Cybersecurity Influencers & Ambassador in the industry, award winner of both 2020 and 2021 Cybersecurity Woman of the year, and CISCO 2019 Cybersecurity Champion.

Noureen, together with two other change-makers, Diana Waithanji and Vandana Verma, received a scholarship to join a cohort of cyber leaders/CISOs at the Cyber Leadership Institute, where their brilliance shone through. She sets an example for others to follow in her hard work to keep ahead of the pack in a rapidly changing industry, her commitment to generously share insights with others, and her unquestionable desire to help enterprises protect their business and their data in a complex and uncertain world.

Noureen holds a bachelor's degree in information technology from the University of Massachusetts, an executive MBA from Harvard Square, and a cybersecurity diploma from MIT. Noureen also sits on several corporate executive boards where she's keen to offer strategic guidance and advice on key business decisions that enable the company's growth and success.

Noureen's boundless humility and bare-knuckled approach to big problems strongly reflect our ideals at the Cyber Leadership Institute. We are very proud to have her join our recently formed Community Advisory Board, helping us infuse CISO perspectives into our road map. When I asked Noureen to share her parting advice to aspiring cyber leaders, she spontaneously replied, 'Just DO IT.'

# Chapter 8

# Delivering Successful Cyber Transformation Programs

This chapter was a collaboration between Cyber Leadership Institute and Natasha Passley, a senior cyber security and technology executive. Natasha is also the 2020 CLI cyber strategy design competition winner. She is reachable via LinkedIn - https://www.linkedin.com/in/natashapassley/

## The Rising Need for Agile and Business Centred Cyber Transformation Projects

If the recent hacks at high-profile companies like SolarWinds, FireEye, Microsoft and Facebook have confirmed anything, it is this: the menace of cybercrime will only become grislier. These non-stop incidents are instilling a lesson into corporate directors and executives – one they have long ignored. Turning a blind eye to cyber risk will badly dent their legacies or force their enterprises into bankruptcy. The immediate implications of this awakening are clear. Organisations are now pouring billions of dollars into cyber transformation programs and hiring new CISOs to clean up messes and accelerate cyber transformation.

Many organisations still embark on three-year cyber transformation programs to take them to a level of acceptable maturity and reasonable resilience. The reality, however, is that not many enterprises ever realise the benefits promised. Based on our in-depth collaboration with cyber leaders from dozens of countries that go through the Cyber Leadership Program, most cyber transformation programs are delivered after four, five or six years. In some cases, the programs fail entirely.

When we dig deeper, several root causes emerge, particularly underestimation of resourcing needs, technological constraints, and initiatives misaligned with business priorities. Further compounding matters, most troubled or failed transformation programs are never publicised, leaving cyber leaders with few case studies to learn from. Alan Cane agrees: 'The gory details (around project failure) are rarely publicised ... both supplier and supplied have too much at stake in terms of reputation and customer confidence to want to wash their dirty linen in public.'[74]

While the cyber transformation discipline is still in its relative infancy, cyber leaders must recognise that the underlying challenges are neither new nor unique to cybersecurity. A decade ago (2011), Bent Flyvbjerg and Alexander Budzier at the University of Oxford's Saïd Business School examined 1,471 IT projects against their forecast costs and overruns. They concluded that the projects exceeded their budgets by an average of one-quarter. Furthermore, the research found that businesses consistently underestimated the costs while at the same time overestimating the benefits of IT projects.[75]

Cybersecurity has since rapidly evolved into broader business risk. Cloud-based appliances have supplanted hardware-based firewalls, but program failures remain rooted in the same causes. These failures directly implicate the cyber leader, who often loses credibility as programs tank and businesses feel like they are pouring money into a leaky bucket. As we say at the Cyber Leadership Institute – credibility is the currency of the CISO; once lost, the CISO's job becomes untenable.

Further compounding matters, the traditional three-year road map does not work anymore. As program teams are stuck in endless planning, cyber-attackers are busy sharpening their weapons and infiltrating networks. By the end of those three years, many planned initiatives are already dated and no longer equipped to address new threats. As most cyber leaders have learnt the hard way, a devastating cyberattack can happen during the start or middle of the transformation journey, throwing the entire program into rough waters.

This is not a counsel of despair, however. This chapter provides proven and practical strategies cyber leaders can rapidly deploy to fast-track cyber resilience, deliver value fast, and achieve the fragile balance between rapid transformation, risk reduction and business stability.

## Top Thirteen Recommendations for Cyber Leaders

We provide a summary of top recommendations for cyber leaders to accelerate their cyber transformation programs in the following section.

1. **Risk-Prioritise Relentlessly** The primary responsibility of most cyber leaders is to reduce the cyber risk profile of their enterprises. As such, the cyber transformation strategy must prioritise areas of the highest risk. Sometimes, this requires re-engineering processes, educating people and identifying mitigating controls – not necessarily buying new technology. Every dollar spent on cybersecurity represents an opportunity cost to the business. The cyber leader must, therefore, strike the right balance between risk reduction and business value.

2. **Aim for Cyber Resilience, Not Just Security** Leading cyber leaders have long changed the narrative from cybersecurity to cyber resilience, knowing that solely investing in defence measures is a dated approach. A cyber transformation program must strike the right balance between defensive measures and resilience – the ability of an organisation to prepare, respond and recover when cyberattacks happen.

An enterprise is cyber resilient if it can defend itself against these attacks, limit the effects of a cybersecurity incident, and guarantee the continuity of its most important business lines during and after the attacks. The traditional cybersecurity strategy focuses on protecting digital assets, but resilience takes a more holistic approach – ensuring the business can absorb inevitable attacks and minimise the impacts on its most vital customer segments in the event of an attack.

3. **Build Sustainable Capability, Don't Just Implement Technology** Cybersecurity programs often fail to deliver sustainable cyber resilience because they place a disproportionate focus on technical capabilities rather than taking a holistic view. The latter delivers pillars that make cyber resilience robust and sustainable, such as cross-functional governance forums, strong cyber-savvy culture, high-performing teams, an efficient operating model, repeatable processes, business-centred metrics, and a robust assurance program.[76] Such a holistic view into cyber capability development and transformation eliminates waste, addresses critical blind spots and maximises the value of cybersecurity investments.

4. **Obtain Board and Executive Management Buy-In** Most cyber leaders are frustrated that cyber transformation budgets take months to approve, after endless iterations and needless challenges from senior executives. By the time they move to the design phase, the risk landscape has changed. Leading organisations, however, rely on robust program governance structures comprised of an empowered steering committee and clear-cut reporting to the executive committee and the board. Active executive engagement fosters rapid transformation and accountability and helps prioritise the cyber transformation program as it competes with other change initiatives across the business.

5. **Establish a Funded, Dedicated Cyber Transformation Program** It goes without saying that to drive change, the cyber leader must have a dedicated and well-funded budget to acquire new solutions and build a high-performing team. The budget must be controlled by an experienced program manager, with oversight from a cross-functional program steering committee. This ensures that the budget is spent on areas of the highest value and most significant risks.

   Giving complete visibility of cybersecurity spend to the cross-functional program steering committee corrects (positively) the growing narrative that businesses are spending millions on cybersecurity, with little to show for it. It is also equally important to assemble an experienced program delivery team with a track record of delivering programs of equal or greater complexity. The stakes are too high to learn on the job.

6. **Get an Influential Member of the C-suite to Sponsor the Cyber Transformation Program** As many cyber leaders have learned the hard way, no matter how advanced your technologies are, or how motivated and experienced your program delivery team is, your chances of success are very slim if you cannot influence power brokers.

   A proven way to neutralise this risk is to have a high-ranking business executive act as the cyber transformation program sponsor. Ideally, the sponsor should have organisational influence, deep awareness of political dynamics, unobstructed access to the CEO and a proven ability to galvanise essential resources towards critical programs.

   The sponsor can also act as a conduit between the program and the executive team, approving decisions on the fly and filtering noise from the other executives. It is also important that the program sponsor has significant skin in the game, sitting within the high-influence/high-interest quadrant. (Refer to Chapter 2: 'Driving Change Through Persuasion and Influence' for more information on the stakeholder analysis quadrant.)

7. **Clearly Align the Delivery Roadmap with Your Cyber Resilience Strategy** The cyber transformation program must centre cyber resilience strategy, which, in turn, must be anchored in key business priorities. That way, the program can deliver maximum benefits and reduce business risk. While cyber leaders must actively resist the temptation to chase every flashy object and succumb to vendors' fearmongering tactics, it is also equally important that no cyber transformation program is carved in stone. The road map must be reviewed and revised regularly to align with changing business needs, tightening regulatory screws, and emerging threats.

   An effective cyber transformation program prioritises quick wins to build confidence and turn the proverbial flywheel quickly. The road map, which becomes the basis of reporting progress back to the steering committee and the board, must clearly state short-, medium- and long-term deliverables.

8. **Deliver Incrementally and with Agility** Your cyber transformation program must be flexible and adapt to the changing threat landscape and enterprise goals. Leading cyber leaders are shifting away from traditional waterfall project delivery models towards agile methodology, gaining rapid implementation cycles, constant learning, active collaboration and ongoing iterations. While the traditional approach's advantages of predictability and compliance are unquestionable, the benefits of agile methodology (such as higher productivity, shared learning and higher team collaboration) are better suited to deal with the uncertainties that characterise the cyber-threat environment and today's digital enterprise.

9. **Start from a Solid Baseline** Resist the urge to rush into execution mode and instead conduct a benchmarking exercise against an established cybersecurity framework to measure the current state before you lock in a delivery road map. With a solid baseline, the results of your transformation program – high-rated risks reduced to within appetite, key milestones delivered, or improved customer experience – will speak for themselves. Basing your transformation program on industry frameworks helps the cyber leader avoid overlooking fundamentals while providing reasonable assurance to the board that the program aligns with good practice.

10. **Focus on the Crown Jewels** Ditch the one-size-fits-all cyber transformation program and prioritise the protection of your crown jewels. Attempting to protect every digital asset drags change, adds needless complexity and dilutes the value of cybersecurity investments. An effective cyber transformation program reduces the attack surface on crown jewels, hardens their underlying infrastructure and focuses a limited cybersecurity budget on where it is needed most. (Refer to Chapter 5: 'Centre Your Cyber Strategy Around Your Crown Jewels'.)

11. **Understand What Can Go Wrong and Be Ready for It** With millions of dollars and also careers at stake, cyber leaders must confront the painful reality that any complex transformation program has several hidden blind spots. To do so, the program must detail critical risks that could derail or impede success, and identify resolute measures to reduce their likelihood and impact. These include lack of skilled technical resources, unanticipated integration issues, constraints exerted by legacy applications, and entrenched cultural hurdles.

An experienced program manager will assess these considerations, balancing program needs with keeping to timelines, controlling the budget and delivering the cyber risk reduction objectives. In the end, a firm grasp of budget control and program management disciplines are better predictors of success than in-depth technical knowledge of the solution.

12. **Manage the People and Change Impact of the Program** Some of the solutions you'll be delivering will be complex and will require a skills uplift for the people supporting these solutions. Any cyber transformation program that is sustainable proactively addresses required business process changes and user training needs. This requires the early engagement of a skilled change manager who can translate technical matters into business-relatable benefits, constantly sell the vision across the organisation, and slowly alter the 'we have always done it this way' mindset.

Business teams have often perceived cybersecurity as a necessary evil. A skilled change manager changes this narrative by working hand in hand with the cyber leader to pitch cyber transformation as a growth enabler, a market differentiator that undergirds long-term brand success.

13. **Setting Up Your Cyber Transformation Program to Deliver Value** According to Cybersecurity Ventures, in just over a decade, the global cybersecurity market grew by approximately 35 times, rising from $3.5 billion in 2004 to roughly $120 billion in 2017.[77] But despite the exponential rise in cybersecurity spend, cybercriminals keep outsmarting enterprises, pilfering billions of sensitive customer records, wiping bank accounts, manipulating financial markets, stealing intellectual property, causing massive operational disruption and committing other damaging acts.

The scale of the cybersecurity threats businesses face is well documented, and in recent years there has been a much greater awareness of cybersecurity and risk among company boards. Most board members now realise that securing an organisation's data, assets and people is vital to long-term success. As a result, investment funding for cybersecurity solutions globally is increasing.

The pandemic also stirred a rise in ransomware and phishing attacks. Heavy emphasis on digital transformation further complicates things and increases opportunities for exploitation. Cyber leaders no longer need to prepare lengthy slides to convince the board that cybersecurity requires their attention; every data breach paints a clear and indisputable picture regarding the significance of this risk. To succeed in their roles, CISOs must actively demonstrate that every dollar spent on cybersecurity is delivering value and constantly reinforce that message.

A key starting point is locking in a business-centred, cyber transformation road map supported by critical decision makers. A formal and disciplined program governance structure provides ongoing visibility to senior executives and the board on the organisation's investment in cybersecurity and resilience. A recent report by Oliver Wyman agrees: 'A funding strategy with checks and controls [is necessary], for example, the extent to which investments have changed the nature of cyber risk for enterprise.'[78]

Without a cohesive and governed method for budget control, investments are often spent on the latest 'silver bullet' security solutions that either do not meet the organisation's needs or fail to integrate with legacy systems and infrastructure. Some programs establish three-year objectives for cyber risk and cybersecurity capability maturity at the outset, and then never deviate from these original goals.

A rigid program quickly becomes dated and loses relevancy. The results are predictable: as stakeholders become less confident in the cyber transformation program's ability to deliver value, the cyber leader loses momentum, the program becomes perceived as a tick-box exercise, and visibility across the organisation fades.

By proactively avoiding these common issues associated with transformation programs and instead embracing the areas of people, change and cultural awareness that are critical for success, the cyber leader and their team can instil confidence in the cyber program and the business value that it is delivering. The key steps to ensure smooth execution include:

- Conduct a rapid assessment of the current state of your cybersecurity maturity, helping develop a solid business case for board approval.

- Secure the required budget to deliver the road map and accelerate change.

- Build a highly capable program delivery team to plan, deliver and sustain change.

- Focus your transformation program on high-value digital assets (crown jewels).

- Develop a cross-functional cyber transformation steering committee to foster accountability and accelerate critical decision-making.

## MAJOR BUSINESS PAIN POINTS

When we dig deeper into the *whys* of cyber transformation program failures, seven persistent themes emerge:

1. Deliberate and exaggerated 'bells and whistles' by cybersecurity vendors regarding the capabilities of their solutions and their involvement in the implementation and integration phases. (It is equally frustrating that some cybersecurity vendors front

their sales pitches with experienced sales engineers who are quickly replaced with less experienced and less skilled, outsourced, delivery consultants as soon as the contract is signed.)

2. Disproportionate focus on technical solutions, with the false hope that technology will be a panacea for all cybersecurity woes.

3. Ambiguous scope of digital assets to be prioritised for protection. This often leads to budget blowouts, significant delays and loss of faith in the cyber leader's ability to accelerate change.

4. Lack of a clear-cut cyber transformation road map and initiatives not aligned with the overall cyber resilience strategy and business objectives. Consequently, the cyber transformation program lacks deep meaning, and the board feels like the business is spending too much on cybersecurity, with little or unclear value delivered from the investment.

5. Lack of detailed and business-centred reporting mechanisms to constantly inform senior stakeholders and the board of the progress against stated goals.

Insufficient consideration of the complexity of the organisation, the technical landscape and other key risks that can delay or impede the rollout of key transformation activities. According to the Project Management Institute (PMI), most off-the-shelf vendors achieve economies of scale by offering generalised solutions, with each customer sharing the capital investment. Integrating these vanilla cybersecurity solutions into unique environments exposes a host of integration issues, often beyond the comprehension of these professional services firms.[79]

7. Underestimation of the ongoing operational costs or the operational capability required to maintain the ongoing effectiveness of new security solutions.

## ACTION PLAN

### Phase One: Plan to Deliver Business Value

First and foremost, the cyber leader must develop a detailed understanding of their organisation's risk landscape as well as the size and complexity of change required to address key blind spots – those areas that keep the board awake at night. To do so, the cybersecurity team must assess the current state, get agreement on the current maturity level and determine what an acceptable future level would be, considering many things: the external threat landscape, the organisation's risk appetite and the regulatory environment. It is much easier to create a compelling business case for cybersecurity capability uplift when the program is based on a solid assessment against reputable industry frameworks, such as the NIST CSF, ISO 27001, CIS Top 20 Controls, or the ACSC Essential Eight. Furthermore, it helps push areas of the highest risk to the top of the agenda.

There are five critical considerations:

1. **Obtain Board and Executive Management Buy-In for Your Cyber Transformation Program.** The cyber transformation program will flounder without unwavering support from the most senior business officers and the board. Enlisting senior stakeholder engagement from the start provides clear visibility and fosters accountability. Having senior management commit to the program helps prioritise the cyber transformation program against other changes across the business, because every dollar spent on cybersecurity represents an opportunity cost to shareholder capital. It also raises management awareness of their cyber risk position and helps diffuse cultural resistance. Once the program commences, frequently and clearly communicate progress to senior management. Masking program delays, cost overruns and other critical risks only worsens the problem and harms the cyber leader's credibility.

2. **Build a Delivery Roadmap that Is Clearly Aligned with the Cyber Resilience Strategy.** The road map must align with the organisation's cyber resilience strategy, which in turn needs to align with the overall enterprise strategy, and actively support the achievement of corporate goals. For instance, if the business hosts critical digital services and sensitive data for clients, it makes sense to prioritise the attainment of an ISO 27001 certification or SOC 2 Type 2 reporting – fast-tracking client due diligence processes and enabling business growth. Similarly, regulated enterprises must prioritise compliance activities over other nice-to-have capabilities to maintain their license to operate. Getting this right requires active collaboration with critical business stakeholders. Similarly, if the business is actively engaged in mergers and acquisitions, the cyber leader must prioritise cyber risk assurance of the target businesses as well as seamless integration of their diverse cultures and technologies.

3. **Create a Funded, Dedicated Delivery Program.** Funding and a dedicated budget for cybersecurity, governed and controlled by the program, is essential whether you are a small organisation delivering small-scale cyber change or a large organisation running a full-blown cyber transformation program. This ensures the budget is spent on the right solutions that address cybersecurity capability and control gaps, and that the program is focused on reducing cyber risk. Review and allocate the overall split of your investment budget to spend the funding in areas of highest need. In our experience, the areas that often demand substantial cybersecurity investment include identity and access management, mobile device management, security architecture, vulnerability remediation, and data protection.

That said, there is no one-size-fits-all cyber spend model; this must be informed by the maturity of your organisation and capabilities delivered to date. The budget the cyber leader requests from the board should always include a mechanism to cater for the unpredictable and accelerating cyber-threat landscape, as well as external and internal changes in the business. For instance, having a contingency budget line item under the control of the cyber risk governance steering committee can provide flexibility to allocate funds to integrate a new business-critical application with an existing MFA solution, implement tactical controls to respond to a significant newly identified threat, or extend the scope of systems reclassified as crown jewels.

4. **Hire an experienced program management team.** We have interacted with cyber leaders who have attempted to personally manage their cyber transformation programs. That is a terrible mistake – it diverts them from the other high-impact and essential aspects of their roles, such as cultivating deep relationships with key stakeholders, building high-performing teams and managing a complex web of business partners. Leading cyber leaders hire an experienced and dedicated cyber transformation program manager to manage all aspects of program delivery, including scope definition, resource planning, progress measurement, benefits realisation, cost tracking, and issue resolution – freeing up time for the cybersecurity team to focus on other value-adding and risk-reducing activities. The program manager must be empowered to make key decisions and not be relegated to administration and scheduling tasks. While the cyber leader remains accountable for the program, they must find a careful balance between keeping distance and staying deeply engaged.

5. **Define a List of Your Critical Assets and Prioritise Them.** An effective cyber transformation program is centred on the most critical digital assets (crown jewels). Even the most sophisticated enterprises recognise that attempting to apply

uniform defences across every digital asset is imprudent. Inefficient allocation of funding and resources could leave core business lines exposed to severe risk. Here are two important questions to get this essential activity going:

- Where are our crown jewels located (such as payment systems, intellectual property, core business applications)?

- Do we have a list of non-negotiable cybersecurity controls, and how have they been applied across the crown jewels?

In our experience, once a tight list of non-negotiable controls has been applied across crown jewels, the enterprise cyber risk profile substantially improves.

## Win Hearts and Minds

Most new solutions have an impact on how employees, business partners, and customers interact with technology. For example, while rolling out multi-factor authentication (MFA) across an organisation with tens of thousands of users might sound trivial because of advances in MFA technology – it is anything but. Such a complex initiative requires a dedicated change manager who can work closely with the technical teams to identify pain points the new solution will introduce, anticipate cultural resistance challenges and implement a raft of measures to smooth over the change. Communicating any cyber transformation change in advance and bringing people on the journey will be essential to the success of the program.

## Phase Two: Execution: Rapidly Deliver the Value

After securing funding, understanding key risks and developing a prioritised list of crown jewels, the cyber transformation program team must shift gears into implementation. This critical phase comprises four crucial stages.

## Define Scope, Allocate Budget, and Agree on Success Criteria for Each Project in Your Program

If left unchecked, cyber transformation programs can easily blow out in scope, as teams are tempted to do as much as they can to reduce the attack surface or eliminate every possible risk. It is vitally important to define the specific scope and prioritise the most important initiatives. There are four factors:

- Ease of implementation: Move high-impact and low-cost/low-complexity initiatives – such as rolling out MFA over cloud-based Office 365, offsite backups for critical applications or purchasing a cyber insurance retainer – to the first phase of the program. That way, the program can quickly get the proverbial flywheel turning, garner support from the business, fast-track capabilities and reduce cyber risk.

- Certain high-impact initiatives, such as mobile device management, encrypting data at rest, segmenting the network or implementing data loss prevention, must be prioritised with due care as they can prove much more complex during the execution phase than they seem on paper. For example, when employees unexpectedly push back on attempts to roll out mobile device management on their personal phones, fearing privacy concerns, the entire road map can be thrown into rough waters.

- It goes without saying that any cyber leader hired to salvage a business following a data breach, a serious cyber incident that impacted customer service delivery or a regulatory undertaking must prioritise the remediation activities that help the business regain customer trust.

- The cyber leader must anticipate future business changes and align the cyber transformation road map accordingly. For example, one CISO, through active collaboration with the business and compliance teams, realised that the business was on the verge of exceeding the number of online credit card transactions that would invoke PCI compliance requirements. Accordingly, the CISO prioritised PCI readiness in their road map.

Once the scope has been agreed with key stakeholders, the program must allocate indicative budget amounts for each project, with an appropriate percentage set aside as contingency to absorb schedule overruns, unexpected costs, and remediation activities that come to light during the delivery phase.

## Split the Projects into Short-Term Outcomes, Delivering Incremental Business Benefits with Agility

Delivering project outcomes in smaller increments through the program's life cycle ensures outcomes and benefits are delivered regularly and quickly. This demonstrates the value of the program to stakeholders on a regular basis. To help you deliver quick wins and showcase achievements regularly, adopt an agile or hybrid-agile project delivery methodology. With the latter approach, the program can use ceremonies, sprint planning, retros and showcases, while still maintaining the level of governance needed.

No cyber transformation program should be set in stone. It must be regularly revisited throughout its life cycle to ensure it is on track for delivery and adjusted to address new risks. For instance, during the Covid-19 pandemic, most cyber leaders redirected funds to minimise threats to remote work systems, protect confidential videoconference calls with MFA and beef up e-commerce security, as consumer traffic diverted from bricks-and-mortar stores to online retail.

## Establish Cross-Functional Governance and Control of the Program

A cyber transformation impacts all business areas, so it is important to obtain buy-in and support from the key stakeholders across all business units. A cross-functional cyber transformation program steering committee will provide visibility for program decisions and sends an unequivocal message that cyber resilience anchors the enterprise mission. The steering committee ratifies all key decisions, ensures the program's funds are allocated to areas of the highest risk and approves crucial changes in scope.

To be effective, the steering committee must have senior representation from all major business units impacted by the transformation, as well as key functions such as legal, risk management, technology, procurement and finance. These senior representatives can also act as ambassadors, helping warm up their business units to imminent change, promoting buy-in and overcoming resistance. In cases where most of these initiatives are outsourced, the program must establish a joint steering committee, pushing accountability to senior vendor management. A business-wide steering committee also fosters accountability and ownership, as senior executives feel they have significant skin in the game.

## Plan for the People and Process Change and Impact Assessment

Set aside some scoping and planning time to understand how the solution will fit your organisation's processes and existing technology. The solution you deliver will only be as effective as the people and processes around it that support its implementation. Too often, projects focus on planning to get the technical bits right while discounting the critical elements of impact assessment, change management, and communications, all of which should happen throughout the life cycle of the program.

## Phase Three: Operationalise – Optimise the Value Delivered

Once your cyber transformation program has delivered a new cybersecurity solution, or the cybersecurity change you are implementing has been put into action, you then need to fully operationalise the change to optimise and continuously increase the value of what has been delivered. It is important to know how well the program or project has been adopted by the receiving business units, and whether the solution or processes have been taken on. The final phase of the program focuses on maturing your program, optimising what you have implemented and measuring the success of the program.

## Embed Cybersecurity Solutions into Operations

Delivering a new cybersecurity solution is only part of the journey. There is no point in spending millions on new capabilities if no one uses them. We have seen too many situations where businesses buy next-generation firewalls that allow unobstructed access to crown jewels, data loss prevention tools left in 'passive' or 'learning' mode for years, or advanced vulnerability scanning tools that no one runs. These malpractices give a false sense of security to the board, who incorrectly assume their cyber risks have vanished because the business has invested in leading-edge cybersecurity tools surrounded by marketing hype.

Long before a program workstream is closed and victory is declared, the program team should ensure that easy-to-comprehend training guides are developed, and relevant administration teams are adequately trained. Manuals, guides and standard operating procedures (SOPs) should be written in plain language – if they resemble hard-to-read flat-pack furniture assembly manuals, system administrators and users will simply trash them and revert to their familiar routines.

Operational handover checklists should be used to sign off critical controls such as integrating new systems into the security operations centre, updating the asset inventory, server hardening and user training, prior to going live. Additionally, all new cybersecurity tools should be validated against agreed low-level design documentation to ensure they have been configured in line with good practice or vendor recommendations.

## Maintaining the Momentum of the Cyber Transformation Program

Any material change to the cyber resilience strategy necessitates rapid and concomitant change to the cyber transformation program road map. The program team must routinely revalidate the objectives of their initiatives to ensure that they are still fit for purpose, prioritised in accordance with risk appetite and aligned with business objectives. Projects deemed near obsolete, no longer aligned with enterprise goals or premised on wrong assumptions must be terminated or deferred appropriately.

Sadly, many enterprises keep throwing money into long-running cybersecurity projects despite mounting evidence that the project is doomed. This is done to save face or simply because key stakeholders have been blinded by exaggerated faith in the benefits of the project or their own capabilities. Killing cybersecurity projects initially touted as game changers or non-negotiable requires a lot of courage on the part of the cyber leader, but it creates the capacity to maintain momentum towards achievable goals.

As the transformation program matures and transitions through different phases, key stakeholders move to other roles and project teams get reshuffled. Therefore, it is important for the cyber leader to revisit the messages and reaffirm the *why* behind the strategy and overall strategic objectives – the *why* often fades with time otherwise. Leading cyber transformation program teams maintain two-way communication channels – communicating their key wins to senior management while at the same time actively soliciting invaluable feedback from key stakeholders through surveys or one-to-one meetings.

## Conclusion

The remit of the cyber leader keeps widening as boards and executives acknowledge that cyber resilience is key to surviving in the fast-paced, highly rewarding, but dangerous digital era. The struggle for cyber leaders is shifting, albeit at a slow pace, from pleading for cybersecurity funding to accelerating resilience and transforming cybersecurity practices with approved funding. It is now vitally important, more than ever, for cyber leaders to rise beyond the traditional security-operations-focused role and drive complex cyber transformation programs.

Given increasing pressure from various stakeholder groups, the expansiveness of the cybersecurity domain, and shrinking resources, delivering and demonstrating value from cyber transformation programs remains a challenge for most cyber chiefs. But this need not be the case.

In our experience, cyber leaders who have succeeded in accelerating cyber resilience did so by mastering five essential disciplines:

1. Employing strong skills of persuasion to get the most influential stakeholders on the mission from the start.

2. Resisting the urge to rush into execution and create a clear-cut road map based on a cyber resilience strategy prioritised to deliver the highest business value.

3. Anticipating major pitfalls early and implement measures to limit their likelihood and impact.

4. Regularly revisiting the transformation program and flexibly adapting it to internal and external changes.

5. Using powerful storytelling techniques to constantly reaffirm their *why* and rally the whole organisation behind the mission.

Success depends less on technical tools and more on winning hearts and minds.

# Chapter 9

# Implementing Lean and Effective Cyber Governance Frameworks

## Effective Cyber Risk Governance Is the Bedrock of Cyber Resilience

In January 2011, the Financial Crisis Inquiry Commission published its detailed report detailing the results of its examination and its conclusions as to the causes of the 2008 Global Financial Crisis. Among other findings, the report concluded that the financial crisis was avoidable. 'The crisis was the result of human action and inaction, not of Mother Nature or computer models gone haywire. The captains of finance and the public stewards of our financial system ignored warnings and failed to question, understand, and manage evolving risks within a system essential to the well-being of the American public. Theirs was a big miss, not a stumble. While the business cycle cannot be repealed, a crisis of this magnitude need not have occurred.'[80]

While this report focused on the lapses in corporate governance in relation to the GFC, the same lessons can be extrapolated to the field of cybersecurity governance. While hacked organisations are quick to describe their breaches as highly sophisticated, a list of headline cyber intrusions point to lack of executive oversight and governance as root causes. Here are some irrefutable examples:

1. The 2017 Equifax hack, that exposed personal data for 147 million, including Social Security numbers, birth dates, and addresses, primarily resulted from basic failure to patch systems and infective cyber risk reporting by the executives and the board.

2. The 2013 infamous Target data breach, which exposed 40 million credit and debit card numbers, resulted from inadequate third-party assurance and oversight.

3. The Yahoo data breach, which exposed personal information for 3 billion accounts in 2013 and 500 million accounts in 2014 and almost jeopardised the company's acquisition by Verizon, exposed some serious matters relating to disclosure of material data breaches by corporate officers. The internet giant was subsequently chastised by the United States Securities and Exchange Commission (US SEC) and the United Kingdom Information Commissioner's Office (UK ICO) for delaying material disclosures and having material and systematic gaps in its approach to safeguarding data.

4. In 2018, Facebook and Cambridge Analytica shocked the world when it was discovered that the companies had harvested data from 87 million users without consent and used it for targeted political advertising. Investigations would later point to poor data privacy policies and inadequate monitoring by key third parties.

These examples illustrate the critical role the board and senior business officers play in maintaining a resilient digital ecosystem. Without their active engagement, the cybersecurity team inevitably fail to transform culture, get strategic initiatives implemented and meet the demands of a variety of external stakeholders. Whenever a major data breach happens, it is highly likely that senior management had long ignored this important risk, relegating it as a technical matter to functional management.

This chapter proposes a series of recommendations for implementation of an effective cyber governance strategy through the following approach:

- Create tone at the top, pushing cybersecurity accountability to the most senior business executives, and keeping the board fully informed of the cyber risk profile and their fiduciary responsibilities.

- Maintain a comprehensive cyber risk profile, enabling the enterprise to direct limited resources towards areas of highest risk exposure, thus eliminating waste.

- Stay aware of the cyber threat landscape and understand the advanced persistent threats that need to be identified and managed.

- Enable good practices to ensure the business operates in a highly adaptive and responsive way in such a rapidly changing cyber environment.

- Teach organisations to become cyber resilient by embedding cyber risk governance into the bloodstream of their enterprises, making it an inevitable and inconspicuous part of strategic and operational decision-making, fostering transparency and accountability.

- Implement lean and efficient structures that can rapidly and flexibly adapt to reflect changing market needs or business circumstances.

Through these recommendations, you can expect the following benefits:

- Diffuse common tensions between security and business teams, reinforce business buy-in for important cybersecurity initiatives and promote the articulation of cybersecurity issues in business terms. Most importantly, you will be able to align the cybersecurity strategy with enterprise goals.

- Ensure senior executives are not mired in day-to-day technology operations and free up time for them to run the business and focus on the strategic aspects of cyber risk.

- Create deep and open relationships of trust, align board and management agendas.

- Give the board insight into how the board and management of similar organisations are addressing cyber risk.

- Promote business agility and efficiency as cybersecurity teams can make risk decisions faster, balancing the need to protect critical assets and speed to market.

Consider the analysis in this chapter to help frame the understanding of effective cyber governance for your enterprise. The recommendations and the nine-phase approach are supported by the analysis. Details on the nine-phase approach can be found in the Action Plan section of this chapter. Below are the top ten recommendations both organisations can benefit and gain value from:

## Top Ten Recommendations

1. **Align cyber strategy and risk management to corporate goals:** The cyber resilience strategy and risk management frameworks must be rooted in the corporate strategy and regulatory environment. Only that way can the cyber governance framework support, not impede on, corporate goals.

2. **Establish a cyber risk governance committee:** Develop a clear understanding of data privacy laws applicable to jurisdictions where your enterprise operates, as well as other external data protection obligations, such as the SWIFT Mandatory Security Controls, PCI DSS, or other contractual obligations.

3.  **Establish operational governance forums:** Used to report key matters to the cyber risk committee and support consistent implementation of security controls across the enterprise. Operational risk registers must be rigorously maintained to track detailed cyber risks, which aggregate into the corporate cyber risk register.

4.  **Encourage board level cybersecurity conversations:** The board should challenge the adequacy of risk measures against business appetite and business strategy, through the appropriate and important questions. Bring the outside in by inviting management consultants with proven ability to inform the board if they are over or underspending on cybersecurity. The cyber leader must have direct access to the board to enable candid conversations and ensure key messages are not lost in translation or needless hierarchies.

5.  **Create appropriate reporting lines:** Ideally, the cyber leader must report to the CEO, especially for companies whose survival depends on the protection of digital assets. We, however, acknowledge this is not feasible in most circumstances. The cyber leader must not report to the CIO as that creates a material conflict of interest. An alternative is for the cyber leader to report to the chief risk officer.

6.  **Ensure your cyber risk appetite is clearly articulated:** Clearly articulate the cyber risk appetite so risks are clearly understood and effectively managed, thus enabling the business to make critical decisions faster without exposing the organisation to risks beyond its capital capacity.

7.  **Simulate cyber incident response exercises:** Business leaders have a responsibility to take deliberate steps to anticipate major cyber breach scenarios and assess the adequacy of response measures through 'drills' or risk simulation exercises to identify major impacts from plausible cyber scenarios.

8.  **Purchase cybersecurity insurance:** Covering both internal and external losses resulting from a cyberattack, insulating the business from plausible, high-impact cyber breach scenarios.

9.  **Use board cyber risk metrics:** An essential tool to inform an enterprise's board of directors of the organisation's vulnerabilities and strength of its defences, two factors that an organisation can influence.

10. **Ensure you have a secure cyber governance strategy:** Implementing the recommendations in this chapter while tailoring the strategy to suit your business will guarantee your organisation is one step ahead.

## EMBED CYBER RISK GOVERNANCE INTO THE BLOODSTREAM OF YOUR BUSINESS

Throughout this chapter, you will find practical guidelines to identify and implement effective cyber governance strategies to develop a highly focused cyber resilient organisation. The role of corporate directors in cyber risk oversight has been cast into the spotlight by a succession of high-profile cyber risk events, including recent hacker incursions at Equifax, Uber, Facebook, Google and several other well-regarded corporations. Regulators are also tightening the squeeze, seeking positive affirmation from boards that their cyber risk governance structures are effective and fit for purpose.

The rising customer, investor, shareholder and regulatory expectations have merit; most data breaches have their roots in profound lapses in corporate governance, not technology, as commonly perceived. Given the stakes are so high, an increasing number of corporate directors are seeking deeper insight into cyber risk and its potential impact on their strategic priorities and regulatory compliance.

Cyber-resilient enterprises acknowledge now widely that board oversight and C-suite leadership are essential to driving any transformational change, and that cybersecurity is no exception.

Their most senior business officers and the board of directors provide unwavering support for cybersecurity programs. They role model expected behaviours and uphold the virtues of their cyber risk appetite. They embed cyber risk governance into the bloodstream of their enterprises, making it an inevitable and inconspicuous part of strategic and operational decision-making, and, as a result, foster transparency and accountability. Cyber-resilient enterprises reject needlessly complex and rigid decision-making structures that impede prompt strategy execution. Instead, they favour lean and efficient structures that can rapidly and flexibly adapt to reflect changing market needs or business circumstances.

Given the stakes are so high, the board and senior business officers should be closely involved in cybersecurity issues. This sentiment was echoed by the Committee of Sponsoring Organisations for the Treadway Commission (COSO), which stated, 'Today, more than ever, boards of directors need to demonstrate their understanding of cyber trends that could impact the organisation's ability to achieve its objectives. The board plays a fundamental role in being secure, vigilant, and resilient by understanding cyber risks and confirming preventative and detective controls are in place to manage such risks.' Simply put, totally delegating the issue of cyber risk to middle management is a risky business.

## Major Business Pain Points

Boards of directors now widely appreciate the significance of cyber risk and are seeking deeper insight into cybersecurity issues and their business implications. But despite the growing enthusiasm, most corporate directors still find cybersecurity highly cryptic and existing frameworks tedious. Predictably, a recent Deloitte study painted a grim picture regarding CEOs and directors' involvement in cybersecurity, with only 38% of polled CEOs and 23% of board members identifying themselves as 'highly engaged' in the subject.

Despite the significance of cybersecurity and growing enthusiasm from senior executives, a serious obstacle exists. Compounding this challenge, cybersecurity professionals often provide highly ambiguous cybersecurity reports, accompanied by low-level, detailed metrics, to senior business executives. Such information leaves senior business leaders frustrated or unclear about key threats targeting their businesses, the strength of their existing defences or what investment is required. Most business leaders have long perceived cybersecurity as too complex. The excessive use of security jargon – some unfathomable even to other technology professionals – further reinforces this opinion.

A wide range of cybersecurity metrics exist, including vulnerabilities, misconfigurations, and threat intelligence, but translating these into useful knowledge for business leaders remains a significant challenge. No wonder that 91% of the directors polled by NASDAQ and security firm Tanium in 2016 conceded that they don't understand cybersecurity reports.[81]

Some of the key challenges identified by enterprises are listed below:

- Limited executive buy-in into cybersecurity programs. Most business executives and boards simply don't care about cybersecurity until something goes horribly wrong, such as a major data breach, loss of a major potential deal or a regulatory undertaking.

- A growing list of poorly secured business partners without proper governance framework to oversight that risk and ensure operational effectiveness of key controls.

- Expansive cybersecurity governance frameworks often impractical for SME enterprises to implement given limited budgets.

- Heavily diluted, one-size-fits-all strategies. Attempts to implement equal governance measures over hundreds of systems and processes, each of varying business significance spells failure from the start.

- The widespread use of vain metrics that have their roots in technologies, not business risk, leaves senior management unclear of their cyber blind spots.

- The majority of cyber leaders hail from technical backgrounds and often struggle to implement risk-based governance frameworks and report up to the board in business terms. Consequently, securing buy-in is an uphill task.

How can an enterprise encourage executive leadership and improve board oversight of this vital business risk? What should enterprises do to improve their management's level of engagement with cybersecurity and cybersecurity professionals? The next steps offer solutions to these important questions.

## Close the Expectations Gap

To address this enduring challenge, cyber leaders should raise their game, move away from numbing cybersecurity vocabulary, and learn to speak the language of the businesses they work with. Boards of directors have very limited time at their disposal and are not comfortable discussing ISO 27001 reports or NIST standards. Rather, they are concerned about how cyber risk will impact new product success, business growth, the cost of capital, innovation, customer trust, profitability and other crucial business priorities.

Achieving this requires:

- Linking cyber risk to corporate objectives through developing an in-depth understanding of business operations, value chain, strategic priorities, risk appetite and regulatory environment.

- Cyber leaders to become provocative storytellers to persuade the board and executive management to act. Risk maps and detailed metrics are not enough, sustained governance requires cyber leaders to simplify cyber risk in business terms, enlisting board and executive support.

- Effective leadership includes role modelling, active participation by C-level executives in cyber drills and holding personnel accountable for maintaining robust cybersecurity controls.

- Business leaders are to embed cybersecurity into vital business processes, such as product development, digital transformation or acquisitions.

- For too long, cybersecurity professionals have advocated for greater business visibility and influence. But they also need to play their part, particularly by articulating this crucial business risk in ways non-IT business leaders find relatable and understandable.

## Establish a Cyber Risk Governance Committee

Underpinning any cyber-resilient environment is a strong governance framework. To that end, the board should establish a dedicated cyber risk committee comprised of senior business, technology and risk executives tasked with ensuring the business maintains strong defences against current and emerging cybersecurity threats. They should also ensure that the business is not exposed to risks outside its determined risk tolerances.

The cyber risk committee should be chaired by the cyber leader. Acceptance of this responsibility by the cyber leader naturally elevates this critical role within the business. Senior business officers, such as the chief executive officer, chief information officer, general counsel, public relations officer, chief customer officer, chief operations officer and the chief financial officer should all be part of the cyber risk committee. *Figure 8.1* shows an illustrative example.

*Figure 8.1*

BOARD OF DIRECTORS

CYBER-RISK GOVERNANCE COMMITTEE (CHAIRED BY THE CISO)

| Monthly cyber security governance forums (Chaired by CISO) | Monthly third party cyber security governance forums (Chaired by CISO) | Business unit level operational risk forums (Chaired by BU CRO) |
|---|---|---|
| Chief Information Officer Chief Information Security Officer Cyber Security Managers Business operations Legal Technology Risk Managers | Chief Information Security Officer Commercial vendor management Business operations Legal | BU Chief risk officer BU aligned security managers BU enterprise risk managers Senior BU business and technology management |

Above: Suggested structure for cybersecurity operational governance forums

Source: The Five Anchors of Cyber Resilience

The committee should be responsible for:

1. Ensuring the enterprise has a strong grasp on its most valuable digital assets, revalidates this grasp frequently and implements a mandatory set of non-negotiable controls around each asset.

2. Keeping an eye on emerging threats, regulatory changes, key stakeholder expectations (of customers, business partners, shareholders and investors) and adjusting management priorities as required.

3. Ensuring that the business maintains a fine balance between customer digital trust and convenience, and that cybersecurity acts as a key business enabler, not an inhibitor of innovation or agility.

4. Reviewing and communicating the enterprise's cyber risk appetite and ensuring its intent is clearly understood and institutionalised into critical decision-making processes.

5. Keeping the board of directors fully informed about the enterprise's cybersecurity posture (challenges, capabilities and key initiatives to improve the risk profile).

6. Maintaining a pragmatic, business-aligned cyber risk scorecard to measure the operating effectiveness of critical controls.

7. Ensuring the business maintains a highly engaging program to promote positive risk-aware behaviours across employees, customers and business partners.

8. Engaging external consultants to benchmark the maturity of the enterprise's cyber risk profile against similar enterprises to identify key improvement opportunities.

9. Ensuring the enterprise maintains a suitably qualified, motivated and well-funded cybersecurity team with appropriate reporting structures.

10. Reviewing and challenging the enterprise's cyber assurance program to ensure areas of high risk are subject to independent reviews and all findings rated 'high' are promptly addressed.

11. Actively participating in cyber risk drills, ensuring all plausible scenarios are regularly tested and the enterprise maintains enough capital reserves to absorb cyber incident management activities.

12. Ensuring critical responsibilities are clearly understood. This includes authorising disconnection of transactional systems

from the internet in the event of a breach or contacting key customer segments and the media when required.

The advantages of establishing a cross-functional cyber risk committee are clear – it helps diffuse common tensions between security and business teams, reinforces business buy-in for important cybersecurity initiatives and promotes the articulation of cybersecurity issues in business terms. Most importantly, it aligns the cybersecurity strategy with enterprise goals. The cyberthreat landscape and technology landscape are changing at breathtaking speeds. Accordingly, the cyber risk committee should provide detailed cybersecurity updates to the board on a regular basis.

To maximise the value of the cyber risk committee, enterprises should establish operational cyber risk governance forums to support consistent implementation of cybersecurity controls across the enterprise and report key matters to the cyber risk committee. This approach ensures senior executives are not mired in day-to-day technology operations and frees up time for them to run the business and focus on the strategic aspects of cyber risk. Operational governance forums may include, but are not limited to:

1. Monthly cybersecurity governance forums to track progress against key strategic initiatives, operational scorecards, material incidents and assurance programs.

2. Monthly third-party governance forums to track cybersecurity service level agreements (SLAs), operational scorecards and assurance processes over high-risk service providers and partners.

3. Business-unit-level cyber-governance forums comprised of senior business unit (BU) business and technology management. The forums should include cybersecurity managers, be chaired by the BU chief risk officer (CRO) and oversee the effectiveness of security controls and improvement initiatives.

## Encourage deeper board-level cybersecurity conversations

Despite the importance of technology to corporate strategies, most board members still lack technology experience. It's no longer enough for the board to 'note' cybersecurity reports on a quarterly basis. Effective cyber risk management requires the board to challenge the adequacy of risk measures against business appetite and business strategy.

To have a good grasp of the enterprise cyber risk posture, the board needs to ask several important questions:

1. What are our high-risk information assets, and do they have appropriate cybersecurity defences? (For example, are they running on vendor-supported infrastructure updated with the latest security patches?)

2. How do our cybersecurity capabilities, resourcing and spending compare with industry peers?

3. What are our current cybersecurity strategic initiatives and how do they support the overall mission? Are they aligned with enterprise goals to account for current and future needs?

4. How effective are our cyber breach response capabilities and have they been tested?

5. How effective are our cybersecurity assurance procedures for key business partners (especially those charged with handling sensitive information or connecting to the corporate network)?

6. How does the residual enterprise-level cyber risk rating compare with our board-approved risk appetite, and what activities are in place to reduce our business risk exposure?

7. What were the top data breaches and other cyberattacks in our industry and how has the business applied lessons learnt from those incidents?

The board should also consider inviting management consultants with proven ability who work across multiple customers to join the board in order to 'bring the outside in'. These external advisors can offer insight into how similar enterprises are tackling rising cyberthreats and anticipated regulation changes or could inform the board if they are over or underspending on cybersecurity.

These interactions must be handled with care for three key reasons:

1. External consultants without a nuanced understanding of the enterprise's technology landscape and constraints can fuel board-management mistrust.

2. Several consultants promise 'no obligations' advisory. But obligation-free consultancy is a fallacy – the reality is these consultants hope to sell a broad range of technologies or advisory services to fix the discussed cybersecurity concerns. Sidestepping the cyber leader, therefore, increases the odds that external consultants may exaggerate the enterprise's cyber risk exposure, persuading the board to invest in valueless initiatives.

3. There is also a slight possibility that management consultants themselves may be interested in the cyber leader role. This significantly affects their objectivity and can result in needless restructures, derailing key cybersecurity programs.

External advisors should, therefore, complement, rather than replace, internal governance and reporting structures. The key to navigating this challenge is having external advisors present their insights to the board in the presence of the cyber leader. This approach has two benefits: it creates open relationships of trust, where the board and management have mutual agendas, and doubly informs the board and management of how similar organisations are addressing cyber risk.

The board should develop a positive but sceptical attitude when interacting with management, as management may be inherently biased to overstate the effectiveness of controls and downplay the organisation's vulnerabilities, especially when management incentives are tied to cyber risk metrics.

## Simulate Your Cyber Crisis Responsiveness

No matter how good a cyber resilience framework is, it's bound to get better if it is regularly tested and refined. The board has a responsibility to ensure that a comprehensive cyber crisis management plan is in place and response capabilities are regularly tested against high-impact scenarios. Stress testing cyber response capabilities in controlled environments validates key assumptions, uncovers defective procedures and clarifies key responsibilities – reinforcing muscle memory and instilling business confidence.

Furthermore, cyber scenario drills answer some important questions:

- Who makes critical decisions during a cyber crisis event, such as paying ransom if vital business files are rendered inaccessible without up-to-date backups?

- Does the organisation have up-to-date, offline backups to recover essential business processes if production systems are rendered inoperable or corrupted?

- Does the enterprise have cyber incident response retainer to ensure prompt access to incident response and forensics experts in the event of a data breach?

- Who is authorised to speak to the media, regulators, key customers or shareholders in the event of a major data breach?

- Which business functions are a priority if IT resources are significantly constrained by a cyberattack?

- Does the enterprise have pre-canned messages for call centre staff to provide consistent messages to customers in the event of a data breach?

- What has been the extent of incident response tests, e.g. has the organisation conducted full-blown red teaming exercises to validate the capabilities of the blue team?

Attempting to make these critical decisions during a cyber emergency can lead to significant missteps, conflicted messages or internal squabbles, aggravating an already dire situation.

## Clearly Articulate Your Cyber Risk Appetite

Enterprises thrive by taking measured business risk, but stumble if these risks are not clearly understood and effectively managed. Business leaders are constantly making intelligent trade-offs between how much risk they are willing to take in pursuit of enterprise goals. A clearly articulated cyber risk appetite statement – a formal articulation of the organisation's willingness to accept cyber risk – is a vital tool to enable an enterprise to make critical decisions faster without exposing the organisation to risks beyond its capital capacity. The cyber risk governance committee should formulate the cyber risk appetite and the board should ratify it, at a minimum, annually.

An effective cyber risk appetite is one that's clearly understood by all employees, is actionable, measurable and supported by clear roles and responsibilities. The board of directors have ultimate responsibility to ratify the cyber risk appetite, ensuring it supports the enterprise's objective and doesn't constrain innovation. This necessity was emphasised by a report by the Senior Supervisors Group, which stated, 'The board of directors should ensure that senior management establishes strong accountability structures to translate the RAF [risk appetite statement] into clear incentives and constraints for business lines.'

Most cyber risk appetite statements, however, are vague and don't provide any meaningful guidance to operational teams. For instance, a cyber risk appetite that states that the enterprise has a low-risk appetite for the loss of its business and customer data only stimulates boredom.

When formulating the enterprise's cyber risk appetite, business leaders should be guided by two factors: the enterprise's capacity to absorb the accepted risks should they materialise and its enterprise mission. An effective cyber risk appetite is also tightly linked to an organisation's high-value digital assets, and takes into consideration external obligations to customers, investors, shareholders and regulators.

Below are some practical examples that illustrate a variety of risk appetites.

## Has Appetite

- Connecting employee-owned devices to a corporate network if they undergo required security procedures.

- Partnering with third-party business or technology providers that have been assessed as having medium or low cyber risk exposure to pursue unique capabilities, provided enough governance and monitoring processes are implemented to ensure the firm is not exposed to risks outside its tolerance.

## Has Limited Appetite

- Partnering with third parties whose cyber risk exposure has been assessed as 'medium', provided there is a solid commitment to address associated issues within a specific time frame.

- Acquiring new digital solutions with known vulnerabilities provided the vendor has reasonable, contractually enforceable commitments to address them.

## Has No Appetite

- Partnering with third-party suppliers whose cybersecurity risk exposure has been assessed as 'high'.

- Using public cloud environments to host high-risk information assets, such as intellectual property that underpins the enterprise's mission.

- Deliberate breach of security policies and associated procedures by employees.

- Taking the organisation's digital assets to high cyber risk countries that have not been certified by the cybersecurity team.

- Putting new digital offerings with known high-rated vulnerabilities into production.

- Allowing line managers to neglect validating access rights for their direct reports within a stipulated time frame.

- Exempting any non-negotiable cybersecurity control on high-risk systems, e.g. storing sensitive customer records in unencrypted form.

- Unjustified delay in applying critical vendor patches on high-risk applications.

Technology, cyber risk and the business environment are all evolving at breathtaking speed. An enterprise cyber risk appetite statement should therefore be constantly tightened or relaxed in line with evolving circumstances.

## Implement Third-Party Security Governance

Cyber-resilient enterprises know that in today's fast-paced business environment, they need to partner with external suppliers to access innovative solutions, lower costs or to enable them to refocus on their core areas of differentiation. But cyber resilience businesses don't enter these alliances blindly – most debilitating cyberattacks emanate from poorly secured third-party environments. Cyber-resilient enterprises manage this complexity by implementing risk-based cyber assurance programs over their suppliers, enabling the enterprise to adapt quickly to changing market opportunities, stimulate innovation, and access unique capabilities, all while minimising exposure to cyber threats. The following section summarises some of our key recommendations for managing this risk.

### Top Seven Recommendations

1. **Clarify third-party assurance roles and responsibilities** The role that governs cyber assurance over critical suppliers should be clearly defined. Designate someone with enough organisational clout to make important decisions. This individual liaises with procurement teams, the CIO, CISO, general counsel and relationship managers, to ensure these risks are considered from the outset and managed throughout the lifetime of the relationship.

2. **Create an inventory of third-party suppliers** You cannot govern what you don't know. Once roles and responsibilities are assigned, you must develop and actively maintain an inventory of all suppliers with remote access to your network, as well as those that process, store and transmit sensitive corporate or customer data.

3. **Write legally enforceable contractual clauses** Formally documented and legally enforceable contractual clauses underpin any robust security assurance program for third-party suppliers. During the contract negotiation phase, business leaders must have a clear understanding of the cyber risks associated with each relationship, and ensure appropriate clauses are agreed on from the outset and baked into contracts.

4. **Conduct third-party cyber assurance reviews** The board should challenge the adequacy of risk measures against business appetite and business strategy through appropriate and important questions. Bring the outside in by inviting management consultants with proven ability to inform the board if they are over or underspending on cybersecurity. The CISO must have direct access to the board to enable candid conversations and ensure key messages are not lost in translation or needless hierarchies.

5. **Create a third-party cyber assurance framework** Every potential supplier must undergo rigorous cyber assurance reviews prior to being onboarded. Senior management, in line with the corporate cyber risk appetite statement, must approve or veto suppliers whose cyber risk profile has been designated as high or critical. For smaller companies, rely on the vendor's assurance framework (penetration test reports, SOC 2 Type 2 assurance reviews, internal audits, etc.) to place reliance on the operating effectiveness of controls, rather than being bogged down in endless reviews.

6. **Segment suppliers according to risk** Segment your suppliers into different categories based on the criticality of the outsourced business function and third-party risk exposure. The result of this exercise is a clearly segmented supplier risk profile in three risk categories: high, medium and low. Nailing this provides a strong foundation on which to build a risk-based assurance model.

7. **Deploy technical controls over vendors with remote access to enterprise network** Adopt the least privilege principle, only giving remote access when there is no other cost-effective way for the vendor to deliver their services. Such access must be restricted to specifically segmented zones, channelled via secure virtual private networks and protected via multi-factor authentication.

## Embed Legally Enforceable Clauses into Supplier Contracts

Contracts must expressly require the suppliers to comply with a minimum set of security and privacy requirements. Without clearly stipulated clauses, it is very difficult for the enterprise to implement any reasonable governance or assurance over third-party suppliers. Managing security and reporting back to business partners requires ongoing financial commitment, and suppliers often push back when required to provide reports or perform activities not stated in the contract. This also leads to business partnerships punctuated by disputes or legal proceedings.

Procurement teams must engage security and legal teams from the start to ensure these requirements are considered early in the negotiation stage, and security sign-off is only provided once enforceable security and privacy requirements are agreed on. This also provides a basis for service level agreement monitoring and ongoing security reporting. There are several baseline requirements to consider here, and these are discussed next.

## The supplier must:

a. Provide independent assurance reports to attest to the operating effectiveness of key controls, such as the SOC 2 Type 2 report, ISO 27 001 certification, or Payment Card Industry Data Security Standard (PCI DSS). These should be provided at least annually.

b. Provide the right to audit the design and operating effectiveness of key security controls (those relevant to the enterprise or its regulators) in the event of a systemic control breakdown or legal investigation.

c. Comply demonstrably with applicable data protection and privacy laws, not engage subcontractors without express approval from the enterprise, and only host data within approved jurisdictions.

d. Adhere to applicable data breach notification laws, including notifying the enterprise, without unreasonable delay, of any data or privacy breach, as well as results of subsequent investigations.

e. Engage an independent, suitably qualified firm to regularly conduct penetration tests on critical applications and fix material vulnerabilities within agreed SLAs.

f. Maintain formal, up-to-date policies and procedures for the administration of information security.

g. Implement robust user access management controls, including tight control of privileged access.

h. Not engage subcontractors to handle, process or transmit the enterprise's data without express written permission.

i. Maintain a robust security awareness program covering all staff and contractors with access to the enterprise's systems and data.

j.  Notify the enterprise, without unreasonable delay, of any data or privacy breach.

k.  Share the results of post-security-incident reviews and forensic investigations, including measures to deter recurrence.

l.  Maintain up-to-date network security defences, including intrusion prevention systems, network access controls, anti-malware, advanced threat protection, and real-time security monitoring.

m. Protect access to high-risk applications using multi-factor authentication.

n.  Protect sensitive data, at rest or in transit, using industry-standard encryption, and implement robust encryption key management processes.

o.  Maintain effective patch management and vulnerability assessment processes, including a vendor-supported digital fleet.

p.  Engage an independent, suitably qualified firm to regularly conduct penetration tests on critical applications.

q.  Share the outcomes of audits and penetration tests within agreed time frames, including actions to address key matters.

r.  Implement data loss prevention controls to detect and prevent leakage of sensitive data.

s.  Maintain highly resilient digital architecture, including frequent offsite data backups.

t.  Conduct regular disaster recovery and business continuity tests and share results within stated time frames.

u. Not host data in foreign jurisdictions without the explicit written permission of the enterprise.

The supplier security requirements above are for illustrative purposes only. Requirements for each supplier relationship should be driven by the level of risk associated with the arrangements, relevant laws and regulations, and should reflect each enterprise's risk appetite.

The significance of getting this right from the outset is hard to overstate. Requesting security assurance reports later in a relationship is complex; and without legally enforceable clauses, suppliers will likely push back, leaving an enterprise with no recourse in the event of disputes or systemic control breakdowns. This too, however, has its challenges. For instance, large cloud service providers will unlikely agree to a 'right to audit clause' with a medium-sized corporate customer. This comes down to leverage. Hence, it's important to set realistic expectations upfront, as well as ensure that security-related contractual requirements are reviewed and signed off by the legal team and business owners.

## Conduct Supplier Due Diligence

Next we provide 20 essential questions an enterprise should ask potential suppliers during the due diligence phase. This list is not exhaustive, of course. There are several other questions enterprises can ask, depending on the level of risk, nature of the relationship, as well as external obligations. There are also several industry practice frameworks enterprises can leverage when managing security within supply chains, such as:

**NIST Special Publication 800-161** – Supply Chain Risk Management Practices for Federal Information Systems and Organizations.

**PCI Data Security Standard (PCI DSS)** – Information Supplement: Third-Party Security Assurance.

**Shared Assessments Third-Party Risk Management Toolkit** – A suite of best practice third-party risk management tools including the SIG Questionnaire Tools, SCA Procedure Tools, VRMMM Benchmark Tools, and the GDPR Privacy Tools.

| Domain | Key Questions to Third Party |
|---|---|
| 1. Cybersecurity Governance | Who is responsible for cybersecurity governance within your enterprise? Please explain cybersecurity governance forums in place, their composition and cadence.<br><br>Note: Companies where the board and C-level executives have limited visibility and engagement in cyber risk are a red flag. |
| 2. Cybersecurity Function Structure | To whom does your cybersecurity team report? Companies with a dedicated CISO, who has direct reporting line into the CEO, demonstrate stronger commitment to cybersecurity and their teams feel more prepared to deal with cyber risk than those that report into IT, according to the ISACA 2019 Global Security Survey. |
| 3. Data Privacy and Security Obligations | What external data protection/ cybersecurity obligations do you have to abide by (PCI DSS, mandatory data breach reporting requirements, global data protection requirements [GDPR], etc.). Are there any material compliance gaps? |

| Domain | Key Questions to Third Party |
|---|---|
| 4. **Compliance with Industry Frameworks** | Have you aligned your cybersecurity with industry best practices, such as National Institute of Standards & Technology (NIST), SANS TOP 20, ISO 27001, PCI DSS, or similar? What mechanisms have you implemented to confirm compliance? |
| 5. **Disaster Recovery Planning** | Do you have a comprehensive disaster recovery plan that's been approved by senior management? Does the disaster recovery plan cover all critical systems and supporting infrastructure? How often is the disaster recovery plan tested, and what were the results of the previous test? |
| 6. **Security Assurance** | What independent security assurance frameworks do you comply with? Examples include PCI DSS, ISO 27001, SOC 2 Type 11 audits, FEDRAMP. How often do you engage a suitably qualified party to validate the operating effectiveness of your key controls?<br><br>Note: Organisations that don't have their own independent assurance processes demonstrate significant immaturity in managing cyber risk and should be handled with caution. |

| Domain | Key Questions to Third Party |
|---|---|
| 7. Penetration Testing | Do you regularly engage a suitably qualified third party to conduct security testing against industry practice (web application testing, network security review, infrastructure security testing, application code review, remote access security and wireless security review)? Can you share the latest reports as well as advise how material findings were addressed? |
| 8. Cybersecurity Incident Management Policy | Do you have a comprehensive process to promptly detect, contain, respond to and eradicate cyber threats from your environment? Do you have a 24/7 security operations centre (SOC)? Is your SOC in-house or do you outsource to a managed security services provider? If outsourced, please provide details. |
| 9. Data Protection | Can you describe mechanisms in place to protect sensitive/confidential data at rest and in transit? Please provide details regarding data encryption standards, user authentication, access controls, etc. |
| 10. User Access Governance | Do you use industry-standard tools to protect privileged user accounts within your environments? Please specify the privileged access management tools used and related governance processes. How often is user access to critical systems validated by management? Describe the process to remediate identified exceptions? |

| Domain | Key Questions to Third Party |
|---|---|
| 11. Personnel Security | Do you conduct background checks on staff and contractors with access to critical systems prior to employment? |
| 12. Supplier Security Governance | Do you outsource any key IT or data security functions to third parties? If so, what are the outsourced services and related service providers? What assurance mechanisms are in place to ensure these providers maintain effective cybersecurity governance processes? |
| 13. Supplier Remote Access | Do you have suppliers/business partners with remote access to your network? If so, what controls are in place to tightly control such access? |
| 14. Secure Systems Development Policy | Describe key controls in place so security requirements are baked into the application during design stage, and appropriate assurance mechanisms are employed to ensure that no applications are deployed into production environments with exploitable vulnerabilities. This preserves the integrity, confidentiality and availability of corporate and client data. |
| 15. Developer Education | How often are developers trained in secure coding practices, and what procedures are in place to ensure compliance? |

| Domain | Key Questions to Third Party |
|---|---|
| 16. Security Awareness | What strategies are in place to educate staff and contractors on key security threats, and any practical tips to detect and prevent cyber risks? What processes have been implemented to measure the effectiveness of security awareness culture? |
| 17. Data Loss Prevention | What processes do you have in place to detect and block the exfiltration of sensitive or confidential data? Describe data loss prevention technologies and processes to prevent data breaches from insiders, intentionally or by human error. |
| 18. Threat Intelligence | What reliable sources do you subscribe to stay abreast of latest and potential threats and attacks impacting your industry? How is this data used to adapt defences? |
| 19. Patch Management | Detail controls in place to ensure critical patches are adequately tested and rapidly deployed to reduce exposure to exploitable vulnerabilities. Do you have any critical systems running on obsolete infrastructure? |
| 20. Data Jurisdiction | Where is your data processing and storage centre hosted? What procedures are in place to notify clients should confidential/ sensitive data be moved to certain jurisdictions? |

## Limit Vendor Remote Access to the Network

As we learned from the Target breach, suppliers with remote access to the enterprise network can present soft avenues for threat actors to exploit and gain access to the enterprise network, escalate privileges and cause substantial harm. To manage this risk, the enterprise must adopt the least privilege principle, only giving remote access when there is no other cost-effective way for the vendor to deliver their services. Such access must be restricted to specifically segmented zones, channelled via secure virtual private networks and protected via multi-factor authentication. Furthermore, an up-to-date list of all vendors with access to the network, including their respective access rights, must be maintained and validated frequently, at least quarterly.

## Conclusion

Despite the billions of dollars invested in cybersecurity solutions every year, not much has changed. The bad guys keep outsmarting enterprises – pilfering billions of sensitive records, manipulating stock markets, stealing trade secrets and committing several other egregious acts. It's become clear that change driven solely by technology will not suffice; real transformation needs to start up higher, with the board holding management accountable for maintaining strong cyber defence and response measures.

## CYBER LEADERS ON THE MOVE STORY 3

**Vandana Verma – Security Relations Leader, Snyk. OWASP Global Chair, Cybersecurity Women of the Year winner, CLP scholarship recipient.**

When we sat down with Vandana Verma, one of CLI's distinguished alumni, he enquired about the genesis of her incredible journey to understand how those formative years shaped her into the global change-maker she is today.

'I was born and raised in Delhi, India. I'm still in India. I travel a lot, but India is home,' Vandana warmly opened the conversation. 'My family are all in Delhi, including my two siblings, a brother and a sister, each going well in their careers.'

One of Vandana's primary school teachers left a lasting impression, as the best teachers do, and instilled in Vandana the virtue of only competing against herself. 'My teacher told me to always compete with myself; that will take you a long way,' Vandana recalls. 'That has stuck with me. My field needs a lot of enthusiasm and competition, but a healthy one.'

In high school, Vandana had a choice between medical or engineering subjects. Not one to follow the grain, Vandana pursued mathematics and biology. Recalling that time fondly, Vandana describes, 'It's like being in two boats at the same time, and you don't know which one is going to sail and even if it sails, whether it will capsize.'

While in college, Vandana dabbled in networking computers and routers. In addition to her scientific pursuits, Vandana earned an MBA, solidifying her understanding of the business world, leadership, and management. She loves stepping out of her comfort zone and trying new things.

'You grow from the things around you. Even if you don't have anything if you have things to learn, it will take you places,' Vandana remarked.

Vandana kickstarted her career at Wipro, one of the largest technology consulting companies globally. 'You realise it's an ocean, and there's so much to do!' she exclaimed. At Wipro, Vandana was assigned a task in cybersecurity, birthing her career in this booming industry. Staying with Wipro for five years, Vandana accumulated hands-on experience in core cybersecurity domains such as network security, vulnerability assessments and security operations. During this intense tenure, often characterised by numerous night shifts, she configured firewalls, routers, switches, SIEMs and various other solutions, further deepening her technical knowledge.

She left the Indian multinational conglomerate to join IBM, further cementing her network security credentials. From here, Vandana joined Accenture as a security and information administrator. She put her hand up when roles opened up on Application Security. With minimal experience, Vandana was given three months to upskill herself in application security. Being thrown into the deep end was undoubtedly nerve-wracking, but it turned out to be one of Vandana's best career choices.

At this time, around 2012-2013, DevSecOps and DevOps emerged as hot topics. 'I was introduced to OWASP in 2012, which I only knew as a testing guide. I thought the foundation only produced web code,' Vandana laughed, 'Within a year, I realised it was so much more.'

OWASP, or the Open Web Application Security Project, is a free knowledge-sharing platform and global non-profit online community. OWASP produces freely available articles, methodologies, documentation, tools, and technologies in web application security. With regional chapters, each with hundreds of members and multiple projects, OWASP is one of the leading global cybersecurity professional associations.

The OWASP Bangalore chapter lead encouraged Vandana to immerse herself in the OWASP community. She took heed, marking a critical turning point in her career. 'I got to meet people from OWASP and the prominent application security players.'

Vandana's involvement in OWASP grew. In 2017, she was asked to lead the Bangalore chapter, a decision that took a few months to make. As Vandana aptly puts it, this was serendipitous and worked for good. OWASP launched Women in AppSec the following year, and Vandana was appointed the Asia lead.

High on the list of impressive moments in an awe-inspiring career was

2019 when Vandana was asked to keynote at an OWASP conference in Washington, DC. There, she talked about diversity with incredible passion in front of thousands. 'It was not just gender diversity; it was about colour, age, different fields, ethnicity,' Vandana reveals. 'There is something to learn from everyone, and that is what cybersecurity is all about,' Vandana expands, 'It is like a buffet with different dishes.'

I was curious to understand how she felt before such a momentous keynote. 'Being a vice-chair for women in App Sec is one thing. Speaking in front of over a thousand people is a different feeling. There was a lot of pressure to get it right,' Vandana narrated. Redirecting the adrenaline from fear and nerves into preparation, Vandana went through multiple iterations of her slides and had her presentation peer-reviewed to ensure the message landed correctly.

Vandana's speech also addressed research into the cybersecurity skills gap. This gap, Vandana suggests, could be partly due to job seekers' hesitancy in applying for jobs where they meet 99% of the criteria. Vandana believes talking about diverse topics and making them comfortable could give people the confidence they need to start applying. 'If you have the right attitude, you will learn the skills on the job,' she states.

The keynote would prove pivotal, catapulting Vandana onto the global stage as an authority on diversity in cybersecurity. That same year, Vandana applied to join the global board of OWASP. The board consists of just seven people: the Chair, Vice-Chair, Secretary, Treasurer, and three members at large. She decided to ignore the critics and take a leap of faith. Surrounding herself with supportive colleagues remains one of her secret weapons. 'It is important to have friends that support your crazy ideas,' Vandana grinned.

'I received the highest number of votes for the Treasurer position,' Vandana recalled. The following year, she was appointed vice chair of the OWASP global board. After two years, she was voted chair of the OWASP global board position.

Not only does Vandana Chair OWASP, which is volunteer work, but she is also a member of the Black Hat Asia Review Board and multiple other conferences, including Grace Hopper India and OWASP AppSec USA, to name a few.

Vandana loves to pay it forward. She founded InfoSec Kids in 2020 to educate kids about the vital subject of cyber security. The idea was born out of conversations with police, which revealed a clear need to educate kids and their parents about cyber risks and safe cyber practices. 'When we were growing up, we didn't have smartphones. Nowadays, kids have access to smartphones, and it's important that we take care of them,' Vandana explained with incredible passion.

With a lot of dedication to volunteering, I was curious to learn what Vandana's bread and butter is. 'I work for Snyk and am their first employee in India,' Vandana explained, 'I am their security relations leader in the APJ and ANZ regions. I connect with CISOs and organisations to help them address their application security challenges.'

I am always curious to understand regrets or big challenges, so I asked Vandana to reflect on her stellar career and any things she might want to change. Vandana simply notes that her biggest challenge was her shyness. Describing herself as an introvert, Vandana explained her journey to overcome fear and intentionally nurture confidence, weapons she continues to deploy with success.

Last year, Vandana won a Cybersecurity Woman of the Year award, which gained her a scholarship into our Cyber Leadership Program. 'Winning an award is not what matters,' Vandana humbly emphasises, 'But if it connects you to people or teaches you something, that is what matters.' Vandana remains in touch with most of her CLP classmates, embodying the spirit of togetherness upon which we founded the CLI. Vandana believes her success lies in curiosity and willingness to reach out for help. 'Never shy away from connecting with anyone or asking a question. It is always good to ask and to learn from others. It doesn't make you any less of a person,' she underscored.

It is clear Vandana has a lot of wisdom to share. I asked for some closing remarks for anyone trying to break into security but doubting themselves due to gender, ethnicity, experience, or other self-imposed limitations. 'Be you!' Vandana remarked. 'Never doubt yourself. Many times, other people don't judge us; we judge ourselves,' Vandana states. 'People are so wrapped up in themselves that no one cares whether you succeed or fail!' she emphasises. To overcome doubts, Vandana reiterates the importance of discussing your problems with friends and mentors. 'When you start discussing your doubts, you realise either you pass or fail,' Vandana explains. 'And even if you fail, you still get experience,' she concluded.

# Chapter 10

# Writing Board Reports with Clarity, Persuasion and Impact

### The Rising Imperative for Effective Cyber Risk Reporting

Cyber risk has skyrocketed to the top of most corporate profiles after decades of being relegated to the edges of the technology enterprise. The push has been from by a variety of factors, but chiefly: seemingly unstoppable high-impact cyberattacks, increased personal liability on personal directors, and persistent lobbying by investors, shareholders, customers and business partners.

Consequently, CISOs are rising on a strong and favourable tide – globally, more and more corporate directors are now aware of the strategic implications of cyber risk and are willing exercise their cyber risk oversight responsibilities.

But a serious obstacle stands in the way despite this growing enthusiasm. Most cybersecurity reports are still rooted in technology not business. They are littered with valueless and low-level metrics, leaving boards unclear about their key risks or the investment required to boost their defences. Predictably, a 2023 Heidrick & Struggles report in the US exposed that just 14% of seats on boards had cybersecurity expertise of any kind.[84] This was corroborated in Australia by the Australian Prudential Regulation Authority (APRA), which found that management reporting on information security to the board is not fit for purpose and unlikely to enable meaningful discussion.[83]

If there is one thing we have learnt through our work as cyber leaders across several industries, as well as through assessing hundreds of board packs presented by cyber leaders as part of our flagship Cyber Leadership Program, it is this: there is no one-size-fits-all cyber risk reporting. The effectiveness of your reports boils down to these things that we teach in the course: clearly understanding your unique business context, your business value chain and what information matters most to your board. By mastering these timeless fundamentals, you can boost your credibility and advance your cyber transformation agenda – regardless of industry vertical or geography.

But let's pause a little and explain why effective cyber risk reporting is one of the most important predictors of your success as a cyber leader. There are three strategic benefits:

1. Your ability to clearly tie cybersecurity transformation to the strategic business goals and mission of the enterprise will create a strong shared sense of purpose, and get the board and key decision makers to throw their full weight behind the execution of your strategy. You will also drive deeper and meaningful conversations with corporate directors, and allay their fears as well as accelerate the approval of your cybersecurity budget.

2. Whether in business, politics or civil life, all transformational leaders have one thing in common – they are exceptional communicators. Delivering sharp executive reports will boost your brand as a business-centred cybersecurity executive. Mediocre cyber risk reports, on the other side, position you as a functional leader who hasn't earned a seat in the C-suite. You can have the highest performing team or the best cybersecurity strategy, but if you can't effectively communicate at an executive level, your impact will be greatly diminished.

As we say in our trademark Cyber Leadership Program (CLP), the role of the CISO is quite straightforward – you tell the board what you are going to do, you execute on that promise and then come back and tell the board what you have done. Your cyber risk report is the critical window through which the board gets an unfiltered view into the progress of the cyber transformation program: the material risks your enterprise faces as well as emerging issues. Providing sharp insights helps the board exercise its cyber risk oversight responsibilities more effectively.

Effective cyber risk reporting is no longer a nice-to-have soft skill for you as a cyber leader. It is a necessity that can define your success or failure in the C-suite. We can say confidently that getting this right will fuel your cyber leadership journey. Presenting to boards of directors has been one of our highest honours, but, it has also been one of our greatest tests. Done right, effective communication can open up tremendous opportunities and turbocharge your career trajectory.

We have produced this comprehensive chapter to help CISOs close the strategic disconnect between the board and the cybersecurity function. Left unaddressed, cyber resilience will remain a pipedream for most enterprises. We back these strategies for two reasons:

- These are not academic theories but proven techniques we use to successfully enlist the support of corporate executives and boards within enterprises we work for as virtual CISOs.

- We have corroborated each of these strategies with hundreds of cyber leaders/CISOs across multiple verticals who have gone through our intensive Cyber Leadership Program (CLP).

Cyber leaders will significantly up their game if they embrace the following recommendations:

## Top 11 Recommendations

1. Develop an in-depth understanding of your board. By knowing their cybersecurity skills levels and expectations, you will be able to steer away from cookie-cutter cyber risk reports and provide business-contextualised and insightful information to the board.

2. Using a combination of clear-cut explanations and cyber risk maps, educate the board on your most critical risks, and give them assurance that you have established a robust strategy to bring risk to within appetite.

3. Avoid numbing the board with cyber industry clichés, information they already know, or valueless metrics. Rather, cut straight to the chase by highlighting key risk, changes to the risk profile, updates on strategic projects, emerging risks, as well as whatever specific information the board has requested.

4. Write a succinct and compelling executive summary that hooks board members from the first line and leaves them wanting to learn more. The quality of your executive summary determines if the board members will bother reading the rest of the report, so make it count.

5. Create a healthy balance by educating the board about active risks but also giving them clear insight into emerging risks and opportunities.

6. Write your drafts freely and swiftly before pruning every sentence to its cleanest form, a writing concept referred to as killing your darlings. Once done, ask the CRO, CFO or another C-suite executive to peer review your drafts – we are too close to our creations to identify their flaws. It's very difficult to recover from bad first impressions, so make sure your final report is succinct and accurate.

7. Resist the temptation to filter the bad news and inform the board of critical blind spots. If your company's capabilities are lagging behind its industry peers, the budget is too tight or key initiatives are at risk, then say it. Courage and transparency are the hallmarks of leading cyber leaders.

8. This is a balancing act – emphasising urgency to the board without creating a belief that the sky is falling. Avoid exaggerated terms like best-in-class, bleeding-edge, world-class or fireproof. These commonplace terms will harm rather than advance your integrity.

9. To maximise effectiveness, you must centre the board's attention on crown jewels.

10. Shun technical jargon. Rather, emphasise the *why* by rigorously tying the cybersecurity initiatives and risks to broader business goals and corporate values. To achieve that level of clarity, you must understand the business value chain, replace fluffy ideas with concrete details and express them in the business language: money.

11. Develop business-centred cyber resilience metrics. These are an effective way to track, measure and analyse the cyber health of the organisation. Key risk indicators (KRIs) should inform the board, via brief and clear commentary, of current management initiatives to address measures that are outside of tolerance, including specific target dates.

## Current Board Cyber Reporting Challenges (The Old Ways of Doing Things)

There are several challenges with existing cyber risk reporting frameworks and strategies. Here are the top 12 most pervasive problems in our experience:

1. Most cyber leaders hail from technical backgrounds. The technical lingo (CVEs, zero-trust, zero-days, next-generation

firewalls) that made them superstars in functional roles means very little to the board and senior executives. Furthermore, the skills required to gain access to the board and leave a lasting impression – skills such as storytelling, persuasion, influencing and executive presence – are hardly taught in the dozens of certifications cybersecurity professionals acquire over the years. Their leadership gaps loom large when new cyber leaders are suddenly thrust in front of executive committees and boards.

According to the NACD, company directors usually get huge volumes of material to review, often in excess of 500 pages.[84] Some of these reports are crowded with metrics on organisational performance but offer limited clear information to guide quality decision-making and provide insights into the organisation's future. This view was supported by an article in *Harvard Business Review*, which stated that directors complained, 'PowerPoint decks were way too long, too granular, or simply uninformative.'[85]

There is limited interaction between boards and the cyber leader, even now cyber has become one of the most critical risks for many organisations. According to a study published by *Harvard Business Review*, fewer than half (47%) of boards interact with their cyber leaders regularly, and almost a third of them only see their cyber leaders at board presentations.[86] This means that directors and security leaders do not spend enough time together to have a meaningful dialogue about cybersecurity priorities and strategies. This also creates another material problem – in some cases, as information is relayed through non-technical business executives, there is increased likelihood that key facts will be distorted, bad news filtered or important cyber risk information simply delayed.

A growing number of corporate directors now appreciate the significance of cybersecurity and are willing to play their part. But despite this growing enthusiasm, a serious obstacle stands in the way. Most cybersecurity reports are too technical and complex. Predictably, a staggering 90% of corporate directors still complain that they do not understand cybersecurity reports.[87] This same issue was emphasised by a *Harvard Business Review* article, which stated that the disconnect between the cyber leader and board lies with the former's difficulty in translating technical jargon into business language (such as risk, reputation, and business resilience).[88]

Most board papers are way too long, backward-looking, internally focused, downplay bad news and are hard to comprehend – as noted in research conducted by the Chartered Governance Institute UK & Ireland.[89]

A large proportion of boards still don't have deep cybersecurity expertise. A recent study painted a grim picture of cybersecurity governance with only about half of Fortune 100 companies having a director on their boards with relevant cybersecurity experience.[90] Fortune 200 and 500 companies fare even worse with only 9% having cyber-savvy directors. This creates a serious challenge – boards become passive recipients of cybersecurity reports with the inability to ask penetrating questions or influence the strategic cybersecurity direction. This leaves a significant gap for some silver-tongued cyber leaders to sell the utopian view of the world and sweep bad news under the carpet. The board has to then deal with the real-life scenario during a major crisis.

1. Cyber risk is bundled into enterprise-wide risk reports and is often denoted as a single dot on an enterprise risk profile with no granularity to give directors and top business officers clear visibility into the cyber risks they face, and their business implications.

2. These helicopter-type cyber views often lack the clear management strategies required to bring cyber risks within appetite: that is, who is responsible, and how will high-rated risks be turned green.

3. No credible methodologies to demonstrate progress towards target state (mitigating risks to within appetite). There are five root causes: cyber risks not quantified, lack of business-centred key risk indicators (reports are solely qualitative), reports are littered with too many irrelevant details, overreliance on audits to provide a view of cyber risk profile, and fearmongering with far-fetched threat scenarios.

4. Template-based rolling status updates on cyber risk with zero context into the key changes since the previous board update, status of previously agreed actions, current cyber risk profile, and how planned initiatives will change the cyber risk profile.

5. Use of 'industry-standard capability maturity' as the main driver of cybersecurity initiatives rather than risks and controls that are contextualised to business circumstances.

6. Cyber risks are measured using different scales as compared to other enterprise risks, making it harder for directors to prioritise cyber risk remediation against a myriad of other initiatives.

This confusion dents the cyber leader's credibility, reinforcing the long-held stereotypes that cybersecurity teams are cost centres and lack business acumen. This loss of business confidence has cascading effects, stifling additional budget requests and blocking the cyber leader's continued access to the board.

## COMMUNICATE CYBER RISK WITH CLARITY, BREVITY AND PERSUASION

Most organisations will never achieve cyber resilience unless they get their corporate directors actively engaged in cyber risk oversight. It is well documented that the success of any major transformation program hinges on the unwavering support of the most senior business officers, and cyber resilience is no different.

But the tide is turning. Given the high stakes, an increasing number of corporate directors are seeking deeper insight into cyber risk and its potential impact on their strategic priorities and regulatory compliance. There are a number of factors at play, chiefly, tightening regulatory screws, insistent lobbying by a variety of external stakeholders and increased personal liability of corporate directors. For instance, most board members got a wake-up call in the first month of 2019, when the former officers and directors of Yahoo agreed to pay $29 million to settle charges that they breached their fiduciary duties in their handling of customer data during a series of cyberattacks from 2013 until 2016.[91] Up until then, shareholders had not been successful in holding companies accountable for data breaches.

But despite the growing enthusiasm, most corporate directors still find cybersecurity highly cryptic and existing frameworks tedious. To remediate this, cyber leaders must up their game and learn to communicate this important subject with clarity, brevity and persuasion. In the following section, we provide 12 practical recommendations to help cyber leaders create insightful and polished board reports, boosting their credibility, and improving cyber resilience.

## ACTION PLAN

1.  **Know Your Board Members and Pre-Empt Their Expectations** The board's perception of cyber risk is likely to be influenced by information they receive from other boards they sit on. For example, a board member who presides over companies in highly regulated industries is likely to be concerned about key aspects of relevant prudential standards, while a director who sits on a board of a high-tech company is likely interested in the protection of intellectual property and trade secrets. Developing an intimate knowledge of your board and their competencies will sharpen your insights rather

than bore the board with information they don't care about or already know.

To get this right, the cyber leader must engage the chief executive officer, chief risk officer, company secretary or any board member they have access to and ask these questions, as a minimum: Who is on the board? What are their competencies or professional backgrounds? Do board members preside over companies that have been hacked before, and what was the root cause of such data breaches? What specific information has the board asked for?

Cyber leaders must also acquaint themselves with any cyber risk oversight courses their board members are pursuing, as these will also influence the board's cybersecurity concerns and questions. For instance, a director who is a member of the National Association of Corporate Directors (NACD) is likely to be conversant with the association's five principles of cyber risk oversight[92]: namely, cybersecurity as a strategic risk, legal and disclosure implications, board oversight structure and access to expertise, an enterprise framework for managing cyber risk, and cybersecurity measurement and reporting.

One virtual CISO client of ours had a reputable lawyer on the board. The same director also sat on multiple boards for companies whose long-term survival hinged on their ability to protect high-value intellectual property from clandestine competitors and rogue nation states. Armed with this knowledge, they proactively explained initiatives in flight to comply with mandatory data breach regulations and prevent leakage of intellectual property – key concerns for this director. Pre-empting these matters will help allay board fears and boost the cyber leader's credibility.

## 2. Give the Board Insight into Major Risks and Vulnerabilities

The role of the board is to ensure the organisation's cyber risk management framework is fit for purpose and that management has established a robust strategy to mitigate major gaps. The board cyber risk report must therefore focus on key risks and respective management responses. Using a combination of clear-cut explanations and cyber risk maps, the cyber leader must address the following key risk matters, as a minimum: key cyber risks that sit outside the board-approved cyber risk appetite, updates on strategic initiatives to close key risks, how cyber transformation aligns with strategic goals, compliance with external obligations, and management responses to emerging risks. As Michelle Daisley and Lucy Nottingham wrote, 'Effective risk oversight is only possible when the board has comprehensive, clear visibility on risks the organisation is facing and taking, as well as its steps to mitigate and manage them.'[93]

3. **Don't Bore the Board with Information They Already Know or Don't Need** Avoid numbing the board with cyber industry clichés, information they already know or valueless metrics. Avoid long-winded generic introductions explaining threat actors and their motivations, generic industry statistics or telling the board, 'It's no longer a matter of if, but when your organisation will be hacked.' This cyber lingo has been in circulation for a while and has long lost its punch. Most of your board members likely know who the bad nation states are and their motivations. Obviously, a cyber leader responsible for protecting critical infrastructure may need to talk about nation state-related threats, but a better way is to cut straight to the chase and talk about the critical risks you face and what you are doing about them.

4.  **Write a Compelling Executive Summary** Remember that your cyber risk report is competing for attention against several business-critical matters. Write a succinct and compelling executive summary that hooks board members from the first line and leaves them wanting to learn more. The quality of your executive summary determines if the board members will bother reading the rest of the report. So, make it count – articulate the purpose of the report, discuss key changes to the risk profile, share updates on your transformation program and convey the specific outcome you require from the board. Identify the key messages you want to express to the board and articulate them as briefly and clearly as humanly possible.

A wise editor once observed that the easiest decision a reader can make is to stop reading. The same applies to your board reports – you must make every word count and hook corporate directors from the start. Writing something that's intriguing and maintaining the formality of board reports, however, is a careful balancing act. The idea is to get straight to the point and emphasise why the board should care deeply about what you are about to say.

Board members are some of the toughest groups you will ever face as a cyber leader. They're incredibly impatient because their schedules are tight – within a few hours they must make difficult trade-offs, high-stakes decisions on capital allocation, oversee regulatory compliance, mergers and other pressing matters. Boards have limited patience for long and meandering presentations with no clear-cut big reveal. Without a strong start, you risk being cut off before halfway through your presentation, or your monotonous five-page paper will simply lie there like dead fish.

The executive summary elevates your most critical points and recommends specific action for the board to address. That's why you should make it count. No matter how long you have been allocated on the agenda, pretend your entire slot will be cut to five to ten minutes. This will force you start with the information the board really cares about – update on strategic projects, risks sitting outside of appetite, material incidents, key recommendations and a clear call to action. Express those points as clearly and briefly as possible from the start, then move on to flesh out key topics as required by your board. But if the board has expressly requested you to present on a specific matter, such as a material incident or imminent regulation, then you must focus on that before delving on any other matters.

The first step is to ask yourself, what is the critically important power point that you want board members to take away from the meeting? Then make sure every part of your report is furthering that supreme goal. This could be a refreshed cybersecurity strategy, a revamped cyber risk profile, a summary of the annual red teaming exercise or a near miss.

Here are some examples. You may want the board to approve a cyber transformation strategy, or to inform them of critical security issues at a company they are targeting for acquisition. If you are seeking budget approval, have you built a compelling story that ties cybersecurity spend to business goals, and elevates it above other competing priorities? If the board can't fully fund the strategy, have you given an alternative plan B with clear articulation of the risks associated with the trade-offs? You could want the board to note key risks sitting outside of appetite, how you responded to a major vulnerability that threat actors exploited to cripple one of your competitors, or the result of a major assurance project. Sometimes you want to appraise the board of an imminent regulation and your level of preparedness. The reality is your paper will include a few key matters, but you must get to what the board cares about right away and use the rest of your presentation or paper to advance that important goal.

Cato, a Roman statesman once said, 'Grasp the subject, the words will follow.' This is as true in in cyber leadership as in politics. Nailing that power point requires a great deal of consultation. If you are new to the cyber leader role, read a few prior board reports and associated meeting minutes. If you have access to the board, ask them what they want to hear about and prioritise that above your own views. Ask the board administrator or company secretary if there are actions carried from the previous meeting, or information requested. If you don't have access to the board, ask the CEO to share their views on the board's information needs.

It's best to write the executive summary after finishing your board report, because if you go the other way, you risk leaving out key information. Remember to keep the executive summary short and sweet, but make sure that it's a standalone document from which directors can take specific action without the need to go through the entire report as that's often the case.

This also helps during the presentation time. When you know what your key message is, you will leave a lasting impact even if your slot is cut down from thirty minutes to ten, even five minutes.

5. **Talk About Emerging Risks** The cyber risk report will naturally cover key risks, vulnerabilities and major incidents. But solely discussing historical events is akin to a driver who exclusively focuses on the rear-view mirror. Leading cyber leaders create a healthy balance, giving the board clear insight into the risk profile and also anticipating future risks and opportunities. If the industry is experiencing a spike in specific high-impact attacks, then explain how you have adapted your strategy to address those concerns. If a peer organisation was breached due to supply chain vulnerability, then discuss how you have tightened your third-party assurance program. Equally important, explain how you are adapting your strategy to support business goals and the digital transformation agenda.

## 6. Prune Your Drafts to Their Cleanest Form

a. Good writing is rewriting. If any of your peers struggle to understand a section, then rewrite it because it's likely that the board will struggle too. Get someone to proofread your report and fix any formatting, grammatical, spelling and punctuation issues.

b. Make sure you can articulate the key messages in ten minutes, even if you are allocated more time on the agenda. As part of the Cyber Leadership Program, we require cyber leaders to present their strategies within ten minutes. Why? Because, in our experience, most board meetings often run behind schedule, and cyber leaders often struggle to convey important messages within squeezed time frames. Be clear with key decisions you want from the board, key risks directors should be aware of, major achievements, and how you are adapting your strategy as new risks emerge. Presenting this important subject in ten minutes feels impossible, but there are no two ways about it. Getting this right requires the cyber leader to rehearse the presentation until it feels like second nature.

c. Limit the use of passive sentences because they project a passive mind and reluctance to take responsibility. For example, a phrase like 'The delivery of the mobile device management solution was missed' only raises questions: Who was responsible for missing the deadline? What are the regulatory or business ramifications? What is required to bring this critical initiative on track? Does the business have any mitigating controls? Occasional passive sentences are OK, especially when the subject receiving the action is the important part of the sentence. Equally important, replace useless adverbs (like extremely, definitely, truly, very and really) with strong verbs. For example, 'Multi-factor authentication is an extremely effective control' can be 'Multi-factor authentication is a robust control'.

d.  You must therefore keep your writing formal and avoid sensationalising issues. Always back your assertions with concrete data or independent control verification. You are more believable when you say, 'Our cybersecurity was rated 4 out of 5 against average industry maturity of 3.5 by a recent audit against the NIST framework conducted by a big consulting firm,' than baselessly telling the board that you consider your cyber risk as low, moderate or high.

e.  Replace tame or cautious language with definite assertions, which inspire confidence in your leadership and drive important points home. Don't tell the board what you believe, tell them what you know. Words and phrases like 'I believe', 'highly likely', 'probably', 'it's my understanding', or 'industry practice' do not inspire confidence and leave the board unclear about key gaps, and what they need to do. Replace these hesitant statements with declarative sentences. If you don't know – just say it and come back with facts as soon as you gather them. Avoid hedging verbs, such as *seem, tend, look like, appear to be, think, and believe,* as they portray uncertainty and doubt.

f.  It's important to back up your report with concrete details, but overuse of statistics and benchmarks can also confound the board, especially in the body of the report. Studies show that the impact of the first statistic diminishes quickly once you throw in the second one and is further dampened by throwing multiple numbers.

7. **Be Bold and Discuss the Bad Stuff** American General George S. Patton famously started a Second World War speech by saying to his soldiers, 'You are not all going to die. Only 2% of you right here today will be killed in a major battle.'[94] By pre-empting the bad news first, he then focused on the good, as well as what his soldiers needed to do to defeat the enemy.

You certainly don't have to start with the ugly side like General Patton, but his message serves as an important reminder that life is not all smooth sailing – the seas *are* rough out there and bad situations do happen. Unfortunately, some cyber leaders actually increase those risks by avoiding talking about them, and how to mitigate them.

You must resist the ever-lingering temptation to filter the bad news, and inform the board of directors of your critical blind spots. If your capabilities are lagging behind your industry peers, your budget is too tight or key initiatives are at risk, then say it. Courage and transparency are the hallmarks of leading cyber leaders. If you succumb to pressure and downgrade a material risk, then things go wrong (which they will), you will lose your credibility and likely your job as well. But if you stick to your guns and call out the bad stuff, your credibility will go up when the risk inevitably materialises.

One consistent theme we have noted is that many cyber leaders already knew of the key issues the business ignored way before a major breach occurred. But they either didn't feel empowered to speak up or their message was carefully massaged as it moved up corporate hierarchies.

Let's illustrate this with a practical example. Once, a new CISO that we collaborated with joined a healthcare organisation. They noted that the business was allowing staff to connect their personal devices to Office 365 and download email. This information, unfortunately, contained spreadsheets with thousands of personally identifiable and sensitive health records. When the CISO proposed rolling out an opt-in mobile device management solution to the executive committee, the proposal was met with fierce resistance. Some senior leaders accused the CISO of a 'big-brother mentality', attempting to monitor their online activities.

When the CISO documented the risk acceptance in the next report, a few executives were further infuriated – no one wanted mobile device management (MDM) on their phones, or had the courage to accept the risk. Several months later, a healthcare administrative officer travelled back to their home country in Europe, where they lost their iPhone. Because the organisation had no ability to remotely wipe the device, or ascertain the security controls on the personal device, this triggered a potential reportable data breach in accordance with Australian privacy law. The board was incensed. The CISO's job was saved by one factor – they refused to be intimidated and downgrade what they clearly knew was a major risk.

Let's discuss some of the bad news you must fearlessly report upward:

a. Toxic cybersecurity culture whereby the business defaults to risk acceptance, including some material issues that can be cost-effectively mitigated. An example is the procurement team that engages high-risk third parties without proper security due diligence, always citing project timeline or costs.

b. Reluctance by the IT team to address high-rated audit findings or aged vulnerabilities, citing resource constraints or other lame excuses.

c. Poor cybersecurity training uptake or low user access management reviews because line managers don't care much about their cybersecurity responsibilities.

d. The cybersecurity function is way behind the industry average in security funding, delaying the implementation of critical controls.

e. Unknown security risks – it's impossible for the CISO and their team to know everything. Be open with what you don't know, as well as what you are doing to expose and manage key risks. An example is the unverified supply chain cyber risk posture.

f. Major incidents at peer organisations the like of which you are still exposed to (the same vulnerabilities).

g. Key risks outside of appetite such as crown jewels that don't have offline backups or are exposed to the internet without MFA.

Wherever possible, tell the board what the organisation is doing to address a negative situation and who is doing it. For example, you could say, 'The modernisation project to decommission obsolete infrastructure and fix critical vulnerabilities has been delayed due to unforeseen technical challenges. The vulnerable systems have been migrated to a separate network segment to reduce their exposure to threats.'

You must also avoid exaggerated statements or high-flown language that masks major issues or paints an idealistic view of the world. Instead of gold standard cybersecurity assurance just say 'industry standard'. In the same vein, a devastating cyberattack could be stated as a high-impact cyberattack more objectively.

Lastly, don't use stretched benchmarks for the sake of it. For instance, saying you are spending less than your peers because your security spend is 16% of the IT budget against a financial services industry of 20% can be quite misleading if your business is in the wealth management industry. Most of the FSI security spend benchmarks reflect the situation at large global banks. These large banks have a much different cyber risk profile, tighter regulations, and deeper pockets when compared to wealth management companies. Leave exaggerations to politicians. Replace generalisations with clear arguments backed by detailed evidence. At the Cyber Leadership

Institute we recommend an 80:20 rule – 80% factual information, 20% the cyber leader's analysis or interpretation of that information.

8. **Use Visuals to Grab the Board's Attention** Visuals can grab people's attention and engage them in ways that words cannot. This makes it critically important for CISOs to balance their communication to the board with impactful words and compelling imagery.

The overriding goal for writing to the board is clarity – empowering them with solid insights to effectively exercise their cyber risk oversight responsibilities, prompt two-way dialogue and actively engage in cyber transformation.

Most of your content will naturally be text or as dictated by your board reporting rules. Most companies have clear-cut board reporting templates that leave little room for imagery, and those dictates must be respected.

There are three reasons to inject key graphics where feasible – to break monotony, emphasise the underlying point and engage the board. Your overall aim should always be clear communication and a logical flow of ideas. Without visualisation, isolating the most critical risks or key initiatives at risk would be a very difficult task.

Let's illustrate this with a simple yet highly effective graphic as shown in *Figure 10.1.*

## Figure 10.1

| | Identify | Protect | Detect | Respond | Recover |
|---|---|---|---|---|---|
| Group Level Maturity | | | | | |
| Australia | | | | | |
| New Zealand | | | | | |
| Singapore | | | | | |
| Japan | | | | | |

| Maturity Levels | Level 0: Incomplete | Level 1: Initial | Level 2: Managed | Level 3: Defined | Level 4: Quantitatively Managed | Level 5: Optimizing | |
|---|---|---|---|---|---|---|---|

*Figure 10.1* is a depiction of cybersecurity maturity across four business subsidiaries after conducting an initial capability maturity assessment. The graph depicts overall cybersecurity maturity across the five NIST domains – Identify, Protect, Detect, Respond, Recover – assessed using the capability maturity model integration (CMMI).

It's important for the cyber leader to share insights with the board regarding how serious the gaps are and how management plans to improve matters. You could, for example, say that while the detective abilities in Japan are red (or lowest rated), your program will prioritise implementing a 24/7 SOC in Australia because that subsidiary generates 60% of the group's operating income, or is disproportionately targeted by advanced threat actors. The bottom line is that imagery should always be accompanied by solid commentary, especially when it comes to high-rated matters.

It's also important to minimise subjectivity and ensure that each conclusion is backed by rigorous evaluation and credible data (ideally conducted by an independent party). Casually changing colour codes without solid arguments will reduce the credibility of your reports. If the imagery contradicts your text in any way, beware – the board will likely take away the message communicated by the visual.

What visuals matter most will vary from one organisation to the next. In principle, a great visual should help the cyber leader depict the health of their cyber environment in the simplest and most defendable form. You must go beyond the *what* and articulate why things got to an undesirable state and what's being done about it. Take the time to identify the key message or emotion you want to convey and choose graphics that reinforce and advance the core message. Imagery is a powerful tool. It can evoke emotions, convey complex ideas and engage an audience on a deeper level than mere words.

9. **Don't Fearmonger or Play the Victim** The purpose of your cyber risk report is to inform the board of your material risks and assure them that you have established a high-impact program to accelerate change. Complaining projects a tone of weakness and harms your credibility. Remain professional and use data-based metrics to back your assertions, rather than resorting to exaggerated promises like, 'A game-changing 24/7, AI-driven security operations centre that will give the organisation complete visibility into all threats.'

10. **Centre Your Reporting on Crown Jewels** Remember that not all cyber risks are created equal. To maximise effectiveness, you must centre the board's attention on your crown jewels – the most important digital assets that underpin your intellectual property, trade secrets, competitive advantage or products that your clients value the most.[95] A simple yet effective tool is the cyber risk indices (available in **Appendix C**), which informs the coverage of critical controls, e.g. MFA and data encryption across your crown jewels.[96] You're better off informing the board that your online retail application does not have MFA enforced than saying you have six to seven common vulnerabilities and exposures (CVEs) without providing business context.

11. **Communicate with Clarity** Shun cyber jargon (zero-trust, zero-day, APTs, CVEs). These pompous phrases can make you feel sophisticated, but they say nothing of value to the board. As William Zinsser said, 'Jargon is the lingo of people in specialised fields who have infected each other with their private terminology and don't think there is any other way to say what they mean.'[97]

    Here is an example to illustrate how you can convey key messages with clarity: We have embarked on a program to attain a SOC 2 Type II certification by DD/MM/YYYY. Widely considered the globally accepted cybersecurity assurance report, SOC 2 Type II certification will save $100,000 per year by eliminating duplicate third-party audits, accelerating the onboarding of new institutional clients, creating competitive advantage and freeing up time for security staff to drive transformational projects.

12. **Define Business-Centred and Insightful Cyber Risk Indicators** A good set of cyber resilience metrics or key performance indicators is an effective way to track, measure and analyse the cyber health of the organisation. They establish a consistent mechanism to gauge management's commitment to cyber resilience, reinforcing discipline and accountability. For them to be valuable to the board, cyber risk metrics should refrain from reporting on vain measures whose aim is to arouse emotions without driving real change.

    For example, telling the board that the cybersecurity team stopped 7 million spam emails last month does not provide any value. Advising the board, however, that the organisation

277

is running outdated email threat prevention technologies will prompt them to fund the modernisation of cybersecurity capabilities.

Cyber leaders, working collaboratively with senior business stakeholders, should define a set of cyber KRIs to achieve the following five objectives, as a minimum:

- Provide timely cyber risk information to senior executives and the board, helping them redirect resources towards areas of highest concern.
- Act as an early warning sign, informing key decision makers of what is likely to go wrong.
- Prompt management action to dig root causes and take corrective action before the negative consequences materialise.
- Provide feedback by demonstrating the operating effectiveness of critical controls.
- Enable benchmarking of capabilities and transfer lessons learnt from one business unit to the other.

There are several guiding principles to help cyber leaders develop insightful cyber risk metrics:

- KRIs must be identifiable pieces of information that are indicators or proxies of the current or potential level of a key risk. More often, they relate to current active risk but that may not have negatively impacted the enterprise yet.

- A good set of KRIs should maintain the right balance between negative events that may happen (leading KRIS) or risks whose impacts have materialised (lagging KRIS). Leading KRIs are generally more valuable as indicators of potential risks than lagging KRIs, especially at senior levels. So, at board level you would typically focus on leading KRIs.

- By focusing on key risks (not the entire risk universe), the cyber leader will drive deeper and quality board conversation towards risks the most critical risks. Your KRIs should therefore largely align to your active cyber risk profile.

- The KRI must tie strongly to the risk being tracked. Said, differently, a change in the KRI should correspond to a shift in risk profile.

- KRIs should be actionable. Any KRI outside tolerance must drive concrete management actions with C-level accountability.

- KRIs should ideally be objectively measurable and fact-based. Randomly assigning traffic light colours wastes the board's precious time.

- KRIs should be able to be collected from current management processes, i.e. you should report the metrics that management is using already to manage a process, not blindly dump a set of main metrics evangelised as best practice.

Now that we have established a solid foundation to build cyber risk indicators, how do you bring them to life? There are four key steps:

- Identify your top cyber risks, ideally starting from your active cyber risk profile. For each key risk, identify a set of potential KRIs. Note that some KRIs will relate to multiple risks and vice versa.

- Map the KRIs to your selected controls framework (e.g. NIST) to assess whether you have balance in your selection of KRIs and coverage across the key domains (e.g. Protect, Detect, Respond, Recover).

- KRIs are dynamic, so start with metrics with existing data and beef them up as reliable data becomes available.

- Agree on the frequency of reporting with key stakeholders and align that with key risk management reporting dates.

Effective cyber KRIs give the board deep insight into the efficiency of key controls. The cyber leader must, therefore, inform the board via brief and clear commentary of current management initiatives to address measures that are outside of tolerance, including specific target dates. Metrics identified as red should be accompanied by a brief commentary articulating the plausible business impacts, the likelihood of the risk materialising and existing compensating controls if any. To demonstrate these essentials, we have provided an illustrative (industry agnostic) cyber risk report in **Appendix C**.

## In conclusion

There is certainly no one-size-fits-all approach to cyber risk reporting – there are still more strategies enterprises can implement – but we believe the above recommendations will materially uplift cyber board reports, give directors deeper insight into the material risks and capabilities, and lay stronger foundations for cyber resilience.

## SAMPLE CYBER RISK BOARD REPORT

### Cyber Resilience Strategy Update

<name>, Chief Information Security Officer (CISO)

### Issue / Purpose Statement

To update the board on the progress of changes in <company xyz>'s cyber risk profile and update on progress made against the strategic road map since the last brief on DD/MM/YYYY.

### Recommendation and Action from the Board

1. **Note** the cyber transformation program update and actions to bring at-risk initiatives back on track.
2. **Discuss** the status of <company xyz>'s key cyber risk metrics and related management actions to address controls outside risk appetite.
3. **Note** key changes to the cybersecurity budget resulting from changes in strategic initiatives.

## Background and Summary

Effective cyber resilience sits at the heart of <company xyz>'s strategy. Embedding security into the DNA of everything we do helps <company xyz> securely accelerate digital transformation, sustain operational stability and maintain a licence to operate – all of which are core elements of maintaining public trust. Although we cannot eliminate cyber risk completely, we are constantly adapting our strategy to internal and external changes.

In May 20XX, management commissioned a Big Four consulting firm to independently benchmark our cybersecurity capabilities against peer organisations. The review assessed <company xyz>'s capabilities as stronger across seven of ten domains, when compared against our peers. The assessment results, combined with management's own risk assessment, recommended multiple initiatives to further boost business cyber resilience. Here are the top five recommendations:

1. **Crown Jewel Protection** – Refocus and accelerate our efforts to ensure 100% coverage of our non-negotiable controls across <company xyz>'s most valuable digital assets (crown jewels). By prioritising the protection of crown jewels, we will doubly reduce the cyberattack surface and lower the cost of security.

2. **Adopt the Domains of NIST (National Institute of Standards and Technology) Cybersecurity Framework** – By leveraging this reputable framework, we will promote common cyber language, meet external obligations, simplify board cyber risk reporting, as well as improve cyber stress testing.

3. **Deliver Sustainable Enterprise Cyber Resilience and Privacy Risk Management** – Broaden the enterprise cyber resilience risk assessment to include privacy requirements. Eliminate duplicate effort and simplify data protection capabilities.

4. **Enhance Cyber Aware Culture** – Build a culture where cybersecurity is entrenched in our operations and implement additional training to high-risk communities.

5. **Refine Cyber Risk Governance** – Include departmental heads from product development and acquisitions departments in the company-wide cyber risk governance committee to support <company xyz>'s accelerated regional expansion and secure-by-design strategic priorities.

## Background and Analysis

Following the cyber resilience review, the Group CISO facilitated multiple workshops with senior business and technology stakeholders to agree on key priorities. Here is a summary update on the status of the five agreed priorities:

## 1. Accelerate Cyber Transformation

*Figure 10.2* provides a snapshot of the progress made against the board-approved three-year cyber resilience road map. Eighty per cent of Phase 1 Cyber Transformation Program initiatives (designed to mitigate all extreme cyber risks) are on track for delivery by DD/MM/YYYY. The rollout of an enterprise mobile device management solution, to protect corporate data stored on personal devices, is now at risk due to unanticipated pushback from staff. A senior change manager has been appointed to enlist staff buy-in and ensure seamless change. In the meanwhile, we have minimised the amount of corporate data staff can download to personal devices.

*Figure 10.2*

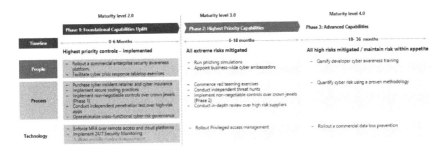

## 2. Adopt the NIST Cybersecurity Framework

- <Company xyz> has adopted the NIST cybersecurity framework (NIST CSF) as its reference framework. A capability maturity assessment against the five NIST domains, as well as updating security policies and standards in line with this framework is in progress.

- Management has established a detailed cyber assurance calendar to continuously stress test our key controls and determine our ability to rapidly respond to high-impact cyberattack scenarios. A tabletop exercise conducted during the last quarter against a ransomware attack on our online retail platform concluded that while our capabilities are on par with industry practice, management lacks complete visibility into critical data backup and restore capabilities. An independent review of these critical controls has started.

## 3. Deliver Sustainable Enterprise Cyber Resilience and Privacy Risk Management

- After Phase 1, management will refocus cybersecurity spending on areas of the highest risk and systems that support <company xyz>'s competitive strategic goals. By shifting beyond minimum key controls and regulatory obligations, we will position cybersecurity as a strategic business enabler and competitive differentiator.

- In addition, the scope of the enterprise cyber resilience risk assessment has been broadened to include privacy considerations in light of stricter data protection laws and the importance of safeguarding confidential customer data to our long-term brand value. This unified approach will eliminate duplicate effort and simplify data protection capabilities.

## 4. Develop a Cyber-Resilient Culture Change Program Strategy

From the outset, we placed people's hearts and minds at the centre of our cyber resilience strategy, given 95% of successful security attacks are the result of human error. Our cyber aware cultural transformation program is multifaceted, including short and sharp monthly security training videos, a cyber awareness ambassador program, ongoing phishing simulations, secure-by-design gamified developer training, and role-modelling by senior business leaders (tone at the top).

Following a recent near miss, in which threat actors attempted to divert X million supplier payment through advanced phishing tactics, we boosted payments-out-related controls by introducing specialised training to payment teams, activating system-enforced dual payments authorisations, as well as mandating out-of-band verifications for any payments over $100,000.

## 5. Revamped Cyber Risk Governance Structure

- In 20XX management established a cross-functional cyber risk committee to challenge the adequacy of the cyber resilience strategy, set the tone at the top, and embed cyber risk governance into major operational decision-making. The committee has recently been reconstituted to include product development and acquisitions executives to support new strategic priorities (developing products that are secure-by-design and expanding market share through accelerated M&A activities).

- We have operationalised an initial set of 12 cyber key risk indicators (KRIs) to give the board sufficient visibility into <company xyz>'s material cyber risks and resilience capabilities (refer to **Appendix D** for detail).

## 20XX Cyber Resilience Investment Plan

The FYYY investment plan has been revised to XXM from the previous XXM to reflect <DESCRIBE CHANGED CIRCUMSTANCES> and is still on track to deliver the CRI target score / capability maturity score of XX by the end FYYY.

This investment is an addition to the business-as-usual (BAU) budget of $XXX, making a total of approximately $XXX. This takes our cybersecurity spend to 10% of our IT budget, at par with our peers.

## Conclusion

While our cyber resilience transformation is designed to mitigate all high-rated risks, management will constantly revise the strategy to strike the right balance between opportunity and risk. Getting this right requires everyone to play their part, from senior executives to frontline staff. We will provide the next update to the board, outlining progress made against the board-approved strategy, in MM/YYYY.

## Cyber Key Risk Indicators

There aren't any straightforward responses to the rapidly evolving cyber-threat landscape, but multiple credible studies agree that the majority (80%–90%) of high-impact cyber intrusions result from a lack of basic cybersecurity defences. This assertion is backed by the United States Computer Emergency Readiness Team (US-CERT), which attributes 85% of security incidents to failure of the same five defensive actions. The following metrics, designed in collaboration with business stakeholders, are aimed to give the board insight into key controls around our crown jewels, key risks and top essential / fundamental controls.

| Domain | Measure | Management Commentary | Responsibility |
|---|---|---|---|
| 1. Strategic Initiatives | 80% | Eighty per cent of Phase 1 Cyber Transformation Program initiatives (designed to mitigate all extreme cyber risks) are on track for delivery by DD/MM/YYYY. The rollout of an enterprise mobile device management solution, to protect corporate data stored on personal devices, is now at risk due to unanticipated pushback from users. A program change manager has now been assigned to minimise impacts and enlist staff buy-in. In the meanwhile, we have minimised the amount of corporate data staff can download to personal devices. | Chief Information Officer – DD/MM/YYY |
| 2. Third-Party Security Assurance | 80% | We have conducted standard third-party security assessments across 100% of our suppliers, as well as detailed assessments across 80% of our high-risk suppliers. We are on track to complete the residual 20% by end of year. | Chief Information Security Officer – DD/MM/YYY |

| Domain | Measure | Management Commentary | Responsibility |
|---|---|---|---|
| **3. Crown Jewels Key Controls Coverage** | 80% | Eighty per cent of our most valuable digital assets (crown jewels) have a complete set of non-negotiable cybersecurity controls implemented and operating effectively. A crown jewels protection program (focusing on privileged access management and multi-factor authentication rollout) is targeted for completion within the next 12 months. | Chief Information Security Officer – DD/MM/YYY |
| **4. Security Culture** | | Over the last quarter, 95% of our employees and contractors completed their security awareness training. One hundred per cent of developers completed specialised secure coding training, which helps us bolt security into the DNA of our product development. One hundred per cent of executives and directors completed their cyber risk oversight training. | Chief Human Resources Officer – DD/MM/YYY |

| Domain | Measure | Management Commentary | Responsibility |
|---|---|---|---|
| **5. Remote Access Security** | | We have enforced multi-factor authentication (MFA) across all remote access to the enterprise network, including third-party access and cloud platforms. One hundred per cent MFA coverage has significantly reduced the risk of unauthorised access to our network through stolen credentials. | Chief Information Officer – DD/MM/YYYY |
| **6. Mergers and Acquisitions** | | Conducted comprehensive security reviews across all 5 newly acquired businesses and kickstarted remediation projects to ensure acquired entities do not introduce excessive cyber risks. No recent acquisition materially changed our cyber risk profile. | Chief Information Security Officer – DD/MM/YYYY |
| **7. Vulnerability Management** | 50% | Twenty per cent of our high-value digital assets are running on aged software, no longer supported by vendors. These systems support 50% of our revenue lines ($4.2 billion). These vulnerable systems expose the business to a heightened risk of business disruption through ransomware attacks or unplanned outages. As the platform modernisation project is underway (targeted for DD/MM/YYYY) these systems have been migrated to a separate network segment with tight network restrictions. | Chief Information Officer – DD/MM/YYYY |

| Domain | Measure | Management Commentary | Responsibility |
|--------|---------|----------------------|----------------|
| 8. Cyber Crisis Preparedness | | Conducted 4 comprehensive tabletop exercises attended by business and technology executives to assess response capabilities against 3 high-impact scenarios:<br><br>• Ransomware attack against core business platform<br><br>• Confidential / sensitive customer data exfiltration<br><br>• Distributed denial of service attack on our online retail platform.<br><br>Our response measures were assessed as robust, and cyber crisis response measures have been updated to address gaps. | Chief Information Security Officer – DD/MM/YYY |
| 9. System Access Reviews | 80% | Eighty per cent of all staff and contractor access to the network and high-value business applications were reviewed by line managers during the last quarter. These ongoing reviews ensure that user access is granted sparingly, terminated staff accounts are revoked, and segregation of duties is maintained. Outstanding reviews have been escalated to relevant general managers (GMs). | Chief Information Security Officer – DD/MM/YYY |

| Domain | Measure | Management Commentary | Responsibility |
|---|---|---|---|
| 10. Security Monitoring | 80% | Ninety per cent of crown jewels are configured to send security logs to the security operations centre, monitored 24/7 by a global team of experts. All 50 critical security events detected during the last quarter were actioned within business agreed SLAs, and neutralised with no downstream business or customer impacts. A program onboard the remaining 10% of high-value digital assets is planned to complete by DD/M/YYYY. | Chief Information Officer – DD/MM/YYY |

# Chapter 11

# Leading with Courage
# During a Crisis

This chapter was a collaboration between Cyber Leadership Institute and Chris Gray, Managing Director of Twenty6forty4 Communications. Chris is an experienced public relations, executive communications and crisis management professional. He is reachable via email: chris@twenty6forty4.com.au

## Leading with Empathy and Integrity During a Crisis - Leadership Lessons from Johnson & Johnson (J&J)

In 1982, an unknown criminal contaminated J&J Extra-Strength Tylenol capsules with cyanide. The criminal resealed the packages and deposited them in approximately six pharmacies and food stores in the Chicago area of the US. A high-stakes crisis ensued; the evil act claimed seven unsuspecting victims.[98]

J&J provided a lasting crisis management model by taking strong and decisive leadership, taking ultimate accountability and prioritising its moral responsibility for profits. This famed and oft-quoted response has come to represent exemplary leadership in crisis management.

There are some critical lessons cyber leaders and business executives can draw from J&J's crisis management.

J&J's leadership sent a clear message from the outset: public safety was their primary priority. They quickly established toll-free numbers for the concerned public; and sent 450,000 telex messages to doctors, hospitals and trade groups. Even more critical, J&J stopped any Tylenol advertising.

a.   J&J took immediate selfless action by ordering all 31 million bottles of Tylenol capsules to be removed from US store shelves. Furthermore, J&J ordered more than 8 million tablets to be tested for poison, and 75 were found to contain cyanide. As a result of this recall, J&J lost more than US$100 million immediately, and its share price declined by 7%.[99]

b.   J&J demonstrated that strong leadership is the bedrock of strong crisis management. James E. Burke, J&J's chairman, pushed himself to the front lines, and personally managed a dedicated committee to produce tamper-proof packaging. Similarly, the cyber incident response must be led by highest-level business executives, ideally the CEO.

c.   Johnson & Johnson employed a forgiveness and sympathy strategy: seeking to win forgiveness from the public and create acceptance for the crisis. The company provided the victims' families with counselling and financial assistance even though they were not responsible for the product tampering.[100] Likewise, hacked enterprises can maintain customer trust by offering customers complimentary identity protection, darknet monitoring or credit monitoring services.

Thanks to its response, Johnson & Johnson was able to re-establish the Tylenol brand name as one to the most trusted over-the-counter consumer products in America. We can apply the same principles.

This chapter aims to serve as a complete set of end-to-end strategic considerations (beyond technology considerations) during major cyber crisis response.

## Being ready for the inevitable

This chapter proposes a series of recommendations for the implementation of a cyber incident response strategy through the following approach:

- Sending an unequivocal message to the board and most senior business officers that it's not a matter of *if* but *when* the organisation will experience a damaging data breach

- Transforming fortress mentality culture into one that underscores business resilience and maintaining customer trust in the event of the inevitable

- Developing a comprehensive set of complementary activities to stress test the organisation's cyber resilience, and continuously identify improvement opportunities

- Striking the right balance between cyber defence and response when allocating scarce financial resources

- Enlisting the buy-in and active engagement of the board and most senior business officers through rigorous tabletop exercises

Through these recommendations, you will be able to:

- Keep up with the rapidly changing cyber-threat landscape and adapt defences accordingly.

- Create a culture that acknowledges that while the cyber leader is an integral member of the cyber response team, a holistic approach is required to manage the media, communicate to customers, regulators, business partners, staff and the board.

- Expose critical blind spots and clarifying key roles and responsibilities, thus ensuring rapid response during a cyberattack.

- Prioritise what matters and focus on cyber breach scenarios that could materially harm the organisation, instead of spreading scarce resources thinly across all potential risks.

## DESIGNING A HIGH IMPACT CYBER RESPONSE STRATEGY

No matter how big or small, every enterprise faces the daunting task of defending itself against increasingly brazen, well-funded and capable cyber-threat actors. There is no underestimating the difficult situation most enterprises find themselves in. Enterprises cannot afford to delude themselves about the current state of affairs. Protection against the soaring threat of cybercrime has never been more critical. Discounting cybercrime is not just negligent: it's dangerous.[101]

A Ponemon Institute study analysed the cost of reported data breaches from 507 organisations across the globe and found the average cost of an incident was $3.9 million. Businesses that respond poorly in a crisis lose an average 20% market value, while those that respond effectively gain an average 10% market value. That's a 30% differential.[102]

As this cyber menace continues to unfold, so too are jurisdictions tightening privacy laws. For instance, the EU's General Data Protection Regulation (GDPR) will impose fines up to 20 million euros or up to 4% of the annual worldwide turnover, whichever is greater. In the case of a personal data breach, GDPR mandates that the 'controller shall without undue delay and, where feasible, not later than 72 hours after having become aware of it, notify the personal data breach to the supervisory authority competent per Article 55 unless the personal data breach is unlikely to result in a risk to the rights and freedoms of natural persons'.[103]

Leading cyber leaders acknowledge that the fortress mentality is outdated and recognise the significant role played by preventative controls. At the same time, they invest proportionately in response measures, ensuring the organisation can promptly bounce back from high impact data breaches, retain customer trust and turn crises into opportunities.

This chapter aims to provide an end-to-end view of cyber incident response, including:

- Minimising the impacts of a cyber incident and helping the organisation to rapidly return to its business-as-usual state

- Conducting a cyber risk assessment based on business risk

- Containing the incident to minimise further damage to the business

- Responding to a cyber incident through a multifaceted cyber incident response team

- Establishing an incident response and a crisis management assurance program

- Leading through a crisis

## Top Ten Recommendations

Design a high impact and cost-effective cyber response strategy with the help of our top ten recommendations.

1. **Establish a cyber incident response team (CIRT) and lead from the top.** An essential aspect of cyber incident response preparation is establishing a multidisciplinary cyber incident response team (CIRT) with sufficient authority to invoke appropriate mitigations in the event of material cybersecurity incident without delay. The CIRT assesses, contains and responds to cyber incident breaches above a specific threshold. Also, the CIRT is tasked with evaluating the severity of the incident, business impacts, legal ramifications, reporting obligations as well as taking drastic action, such as approving disconnecting critical systems from the network.

   While the cyber leader remains an integral part of a cyber crisis response team, high-stakes cyber crises must be led by very senior business officers. Ideally, the CEO should assume this vital role. However, it can be any other senior business officer with authority to make big decisions, such as the CEO's chief of staff, an experienced PR hand, or an assistant general counsel.[104]

2. **Establish a relationship with law enforcement and threat intelligence communities.** Law enforcement agents discover a high proportion of damaging cyber incidents. For example, the FBI informed Target of its 2013 (now infamous) payment card breach that exposed millions of payment card details. An effective cyber incident response program requires active collaboration with law enforcement agents.

   Equally important, the organisation must actively subscribe to reputable threat intelligence bodies, such as the US-Computer Emergency Readiness Team ('US-CERT'), the US Department of Homeland Security's Automated Indicator Sharing, SANS's Internet Storm Center, Virus Total, Cisco's Talos Intelligence, Virus Share's Malware Repository, Google's Safe Browsing, National Council of ISACs' Member ISACs and The Spamhaus Project.[105]

3. **Purchase cyber insurance and provision for unknown costs.** The board of directors, in exercising their fiduciary responsibilities, should ensure that the organisation maintains a comprehensive cyber insurance plan covering both internal and external losses resulting from a cyberattack. Cyber insurance protects an enterprise against internal and external losses from cyber-related breaches, such as business disruption costs, replacement of impaired digital assets, legal expenses and regulatory fines, forensics and incident remediation, third-party damages, customer fraud protection and customer communications.

   Furthermore, the CISO must engage the CFO to ensure that the organisation has sufficient financial provision to absorb unplanned expenses in the event of a material cyberattack.

4. **Maintain a robust cybersecurity assurance program.** No matter how robust a cyber resilience framework is, it's bound to get better if regularly tested and refined. To that end, the CISO must establish a robust cyber incident response assurance program comprising executive tabletop exercises, red teaming reviews, dark web monitoring, threat hunting exercises, etc. These reviews must inform management of the organisation's preparedness and opportunities to bolster existing defences. Equally important, ensure that all contracts with third parties, business partners and suppliers contain legally enforceable incident response and data breach notification clauses.

5. **Prioritise incidents that matter.** Managing cyber incident response is not dissimilar from managing other aspects of business risk. The cyber incident response plan must prioritise rapid response to critical and high-rated threats. In the absence of a risk-based approach, the CIRT will be drawn into unessential matters. Examples of a significant cyber incident include confirmed leakage of market-sensitive information, board deliberations, sensitive executive communications or other information that underlie competitive advantage (such as inventions, trade secrets, proprietary formulas and processes, prototypes and blueprints, technical designs, advanced research, manufacturing plans, software code, corporate and pricing strategies).

6. **Create a culture where staff openly admit mistakes and promptly report security incidents.** Create a culture that encourages employees to own up and report cybersecurity breaches or near misses, rather than punishing perceived wrongdoers. When employees promptly report cybersecurity breaches or mishandling of sensitive information, the organisation can quickly invoke a cyber response plan, preventing downstream harm to its customers or business partners. Consider this example. A payments staff falls victim to a well-crafted business email compromise scam and transfers millions of dollars to cyber crooks. If the employee owns up to that mistake and reports the incident, the organisation can contact its bank and attempt to stop or reverse that transaction. Conversely, if the employee thinks they will be punished, they will sweep the mistake under the carpet, leading to irreversible, substantial losses.

7. **Invest in a cybersecurity incident response retainer.** The reality is most cyber incident response missions are complex and beyond the capability of most internal cybersecurity teams. To address this risk, the CISO must purchase a cybersecurity response retainer that gives the organisation accelerated access to top-tier cybersecurity incident responders, forensics analysts and other experts, in the event of a breach, thus reducing downstream incident impacts.

   But before you subscribe to a security incident response retainer, check the provisions of your insurance policy to determine if your cover provides a similar service. That way, you can avoid procuring redundant services. Alternatively, if you purchase an incident retainer before buying insurance cover, ask your insurance provider to provide a discount to factor in your proactive security measures. Cyber leaders, however, must not gain exaggerated comfort from incident retainers. Incident retainers guarantee a maximum number of hours; you will still need to purchase additional expertise in the event of a complex breach.

## 8. Maintain a highly tuned, actively monitored security operations centre.

One consistent message from us at the Cyber Leadership Institute is that cyber resilience is about making radical business choices and sticking with them. Cyber incident monitoring is no different: to be effective, the cybersecurity team must prioritise the monitoring of alerts from high-risk applications, such as domain name servers, data loss prevention (DLP) systems, Active Directory, cloud monitoring consoles, DHCP servers, firewalls, internet proxies, authentication systems, radius servers, business-critical applications, and VPN servers. Equally important, unusual events (such as logins from jurisdictions the organisation doesn't have a presence in) must be prioritised. Furthermore, the cyber leader must ensure that sufficient security logs are adequately retained as these will be required for in-depth forensic reviews or criminal investigations.

## 9. Back up, back up, back up.

A fundamental control to minimise impacts from inevitable cyberattacks is to consistently back up all high-value data and ship it offsite to an environment not exposed to the same threats. Codespaces, a once-thriving cloud-based source code repository firm, was wiped out of existence when an attacker breached its cloud console and deleted production files and backup files that were accessible from the same console.[106] Codespaces's demise highlighted a fundamental point: it's not enough to replicate data across two interconnected sites; a skilled attacker can hop across one environment to another and wipe both environments. Storing critical backups offsite is essential to guaranteeing an enterprise's survival.

Backing up data sounds easy and straightforward, but most enterprises don't consistently back up their files. According to *Storage* magazine, over 34% of companies do not test their backups, and 77% found that their tape backups failed to restore.[107]

### 10. Know your crown jewels.

We have covered this in detail in previous chapters, but it's worth underscoring again. Maintain a detailed inventory of your crown jewels, the essential digital assets that underpin the organisation's life. Capture essential details (servers, applications, databases, interfaces, etc.) as this information will help expedite incident assessment, containment, and eradication processes. Attempting to gather this pertinent information during a disaster can lead to terrible missteps or prolonged network intrusions.

## MAJOR BUSINESS PAIN POINTS

Our experience and interviews with peer cyber leaders, business executives and corporate directors have revealed numerous challenges relating to cyber incident response. Four stand out for their persistence and implications.

1. Cyber-threat actors are increasingly agile and inventive, developing stealthy programs that can easily evade traditional security defences, thanks to a growing base of resources and absence of regulation, which often stifles innovation for legitimate enterprises. Consequently, the majority of threat actors burrow themselves deeply within enterprise networks, silently exfiltrate data and remain undetected for a long time.

2. Similar to challenges cyber leaders face across several domains, limited executive involvement in cyber incident response preparation remains the gravest challenge. Executive tabletop exercises rarely happen, and in the limited circumstances when they do, senior business leaders delegate middle managers to participate. Predictably, when a cyber incident unfolds, chaos ensues. Organisations fail to own up, and media responses are botched, messages inconsistent and key stakeholders are overlooked. Lack of strong and decisive leadership during a cyber crisis spells disaster for any enterprise. It leads to damaged customer trust, significant regulatory fines, cancelled business contracts and even bankruptcy. Attempting

to make critical decisions under pressure leads to finger pointing, hesitation or hastily taking wrong public stances that lead to substantial brand damage.

3. Another consistent mistake we see is smaller organisations, whose budgets are squeezed and staff fatigued, attempting to build cybersecurity monitoring and response capabilities in-house. Leading cyber leaders, on the other hand, outsource these advanced capabilities to organisations that can deliver advanced monitoring capabilities at scale. That way, they can focus their resources on driving value-adding transformational activities, while not straining their teams with an endless barrage of worthless security alerts. Keeping up with a rapidly changing threat landscape is a complex task whose scope exceeds the capacity of most organisations.

4. Even cyber leaders who have successfully built world-class security monitoring programs seem to make a common mistake. In our experience, organisations often don't have sufficient visibility into their digital ecosystem. Logs from critical systems, such as authentication systems or software-as-a-service (SAAS) platforms, are often overlooked. Leading cyber leaders acknowledge that building a security monitoring program is a journey with no finish line. They also embed security monitoring into the systems development life cycle and only commission new systems once security monitoring has been configured.

## ACTION PLAN

### 1. Cyber Incident Prevention

Before rushing into detection and response, the cyber leader must conduct a detailed assessment of the environment to ensure adequate controls are in place to prevent high-impact incidents from occurring at all. As the adage goes, prevention is better than cure. A proper preventative controls regime not only reduces the probability of threat actors getting into your environment but also minimises business impacts when the inevitable happens. Here are eight examples of critical preventative controls:

- **Tighten Control Over Privileged Access:** Use a commercial password vault solution to protect passwords for privileged accounts to all your high-value applications and critical IT infrastructure. A password vault will encrypt, securely store, and automatically change and manage passwords for administrative and service accounts, significantly reducing the likelihood of their compromise.

- **Encrypt Sensitive Data at Rest:** High-value data, such as health records, passwords, and board papers, must be encrypted at rest, and in transit, using industry-grade encryption tools.

- **Segment Your Network:** Design a network infrastructure to isolate digital assets into different segments based on risk. A segmented network makes it significantly harder for an attacker to compromise one system and hop on to others, a concept called 'lateral movement'.

- **Enforce Multi-Factor Authentication:** Mandate multi-factor authentication (MFA) for access to high-value applications, transactions, or users accessing your network from remote locations.

- **Create a Cyber-Savvy Workforce:** Deliver a risk-based security awareness program to empower staff with the knowledge to detect advanced phishing threats, as well as promptly report missteps.

- **Tighten Your Email and Internet Security Gateways:** Deploy robust DNS filtering, spam control, URL isolation, sandboxing, blocklisting, SSL decryption and inspection, etc. to lessen the number of cyber threats that reach end users.

- **Deploy Application Safelisting:** Deploy commercial tools to prevent unverified or unauthorised applications from executing on all high-value systems. When properly configured, application safelisting can significantly boost system security and stability and mitigate software licensing issues.

- **Harden Your Environment:** Configure firewalls to block access to known malicious IP addresses, disable all unrequired services and ports and ensure devices and systems are up to date with patches and antivirus updates.

## 2. Incident Identification

Once the preventative measures are in place, the next phase involves implementing relevant measures to detect and report security incidents promptly. Often a cybersecurity incident is reported by an employee, a business partner, or identified by SOC analysts, but there are several other cyber incident identification avenues, including:

- Alerts generated by technical monitoring systems, such as data loss prevention tools and security monitoring centres

- Suspicious activities reported by users to a centralised security mailbox

- System intrusions reported by business partners or managed technology services providers

- Anomalies identified by advanced assurance activities, such as threat hunting or darknet monitoring reviews

- Suspicious activities or confirmed data breaches reported by law enforcement agents or customers

- Targeted threats from known cyber-threat actor groups

- Active campaigns targeting the industry reported by the threat intelligence community

## 3. Incident Assessment

Once a material incident has been identified, the cyber incident response manager must conduct the initial assessment, using the cyber risk rating guidelines provided in *Table 11.1* for example. To do this effectively, the cyber incident manager must ask the following questions:

- What critical business systems have been compromised by the threat actor?

- Is the identity of the threat actor known (is this an internal or external threat actor?)

- When did the attack start? Is it still unfolding, or has it now been contained?

- How did the attacker gain access to the environment? Examples include exploiting a known vulnerability, stolen credentials, poorly secured third-party access, targeted phishing attack, or other back doors.

- Has any sensitive/confidential information been stolen? Was that information encrypted with encryption keys appropriately segregated?

- Is the organisation the primary target, or is it just a victim of an industry-wide, opportunistic attack?

- What are the known impacts of the data breach?

Proper incident analysis is a vital step for two reasons. First, without a rigorous evaluation of incidents, the CIRT members will be distracted from their day-to-day strategic roles by unessential noise. Second, in the absence of clear-cut guidance, material incidents may fall into the cracks, leading to severe customer backlash or regulatory fines.

**Table 11.1: Cyber Incident Rating Guidelines**

| Domain | Business impacts | Examples |
|---|---|---|
| High / Critical rated events | • Severely degrades mission-critical systems and services.<br><br>• Exposes staff or civilians to the risk of physical harm.<br><br>• Inhibits the organisation's ability to deliver essential services to a substantial segment of its customers or critical business partners. | • Theft of market-sensitive information, board deliberations, sensitive executive communications, inventions, trade secrets, proprietary formulas and processes, prototypes and blueprints, technical designs, advanced research, manufacturing plans, software code, or pricing strategies.<br><br>• Extensive corruption or deletion of core production systems and data.<br><br>• Leakage of a large set of customers' personally identifiable or sensitive data, such as dates of birth, social security numbers, tax file numbers, payment card details, addresses, or medical records.<br><br>• Distributed denial of service attacks on core business applications, leading to sustained loss of essential services.<br><br>• Access to critical records blocked by ransomware, with no immediate access to up-to-date backups, impacting essential business operations. |

| Domain | Business impacts | Examples |
| --- | --- | --- |
| | • Results in material breach of privacy laws or contractual obligations.<br><br>• Exposes the business to sustained negative media scrutiny. | • Several business applications or end users incapacitated by destructive malware.<br><br>• Public-facing organisational website defaced by threat actors.<br><br>• Domain name service (DNS) compromised and threat actors harvesting customer credentials.<br><br>• Staff fallen victim to business email compromise scam and substantial amounts of money extorted. |
| Moderate-rated events | • Less severe events are likely to impact a smaller group of users, disrupt non-essential services and breaches of network security policy. | • Unauthorised provision of administrative users by IT or outsourced providers.<br><br>• Reconnaissance activity that attempts to gather information for future attacks.<br><br>• Malware affecting a limited number of end users' devices.<br><br>• Unauthorised changes to security configurations.<br><br>• Connecting unauthorised devices to the corporate network. |

## 5. Incident Containment

Once the cyber incident response manager rates the cyber incident as high or critical, the CIRT is notified, which in turn challenges or confirms that assessment. If the CIRT confirms the materiality of the incident, it authorises incident containment activities to control the impacts of the confirmed intrusion, stop the adversary from spreading to other segments of the network, and accelerate the return to business as usual.

An effective containment strategy also provides a vital window for developing a tailored remediation strategy. The CIRT should be involved in the cyber containment phase as it requires some critical decisions, such as shutting down a system or an entire network segment. Some essential cyber incident containment activities include:

Disconnect infected computers from the network, shutting them down entirely or disabling specific services. However, the cyber response team should attempt to isolate affected systems without simply powering them off, as doing so may make the investigation more difficult and result in lost evidence or data.[108]

Shut down routers, switches and other relevant network appliances to isolate an infected segment of the network from the more extensive network.

Deploy missing critical patches to remove exploited vulnerabilities and confirmed back doors.

Reset passwords for all potentially compromised accounts or disabling administrator accounts.

Block suspected IP addresses or access from specific geographic locations through firewall filtering or relevant security gateways.

Enforce multi-factor authentication (MFA) on all remote access.

Block confirmed malware sources (e.g. email addresses and websites) on email gateway, internet proxies or firewalls.

Inspect security logs and blocking threat actors back doors or command-and-control channels. The absence of these, however, doesn't mean the attacker has left your environment.

Block all administrator access from remote locations.

Effective cyber incident containment requires prompt and decisive action. Containment must, however, be executed with care as the following common missteps can jeopardise cyber incident response:

- Prematurely disconnecting customer transactional systems without proper communications in place.

- Falsely believing that a threat actor has been eradicated from the environment and unintentionally alerting the attacker of an activated response.

- Inadvertently tampering with or destroying forensic evidence.

Once the containment measures have been undertaken, SANS recommends response teams back up essential files before wiping and reimaging any system, and retaining the forensic image of the affected system(s) using industry-standard tools such as Forensic Tool Kit (FTK) and EnCase.[109]

## 6. Critical Incident Response

Once the incident has been provisionally confirmed as critical, the CIRT will assemble and take the following key actions:

- Confirm the criticality of the incident based on the information provided and the organisation's incident assessment guidelines.

- Authorise critical cybersecurity containment activities, such as shutting down entire network segments.

Authorise the activation of the cyber incident retainer based on the assessment of the internal team's capability to respond. The CISO must understand the regulatory environment before the team engages in forensic exercises. For instance, the PCI DSS standard mandates certified entities only engage with a vetted and independent Payment Card Industry Forensic Investigator (PFI) listed on its website.

Engage the general counsel to assess the legal implications of the breach and activate regulatory notification procedures, based on applicable data protection laws and contractual obligations. To do so, the legal team has to answer many questions: What data protection laws apply in jurisdictions we do business in? What are our data breach notification contractual obligations with our business partners? What nature of the information was compromised? How long has the information been stolen? What mitigating controls were in place to deter an unauthorised party from exploiting that information and harming customers? What is the legal opinion of external parties?

Approve the appointment of external lawyers as soon as possible to collaborate with internal attorneys to manage the incident response.

As part of enlisting forensics experts, obtain legal counsel to ensure reports requiring legal privilege will be protected from public disclosure. A **case in point is the 2023 Optus case**. Optus is one of the largest telecommunications companies in Australia and it suffered a major data breach in 2022. The Australian Federal Court rejected Optus's claim of legal professional privilege in 2023 over an expert forensic investigation report prepared by consulting giant Deloitte. Optus sought to withhold the report from being disclosed, arguing that it was subject to legal privilege. However, the Australian Federal Court ruled against Optus finding that the report did not meet the necessary 'dominant purpose' criteria for such protection.[110]

In line with the business continuity plan, prioritise teams that have access to constrained resources based on the severity of the incident and impacted processes.

Agree on the protocol to advise staff (e.g. IT teams, call centre staff, executive management or board members of the confirmed data breach) and next steps.

- Authorise external communications to key stakeholders, such as business partners, vendors, cyber insurance underwriters, data breach coaches and public relations firms. A list of potential stakeholders is included in *Table 11.2*.

- Confirm public relations protocols (who is authorised to contact the media, and does the organisation have access to public relations experts or a data breach coach as part of its cyber insurance provisions?)

- Determine and authorise immediate steps to minimise customer harm from the confirmed data breach, such as offering opt-in credit protection, darknet monitoring or identity monitoring.

*Table 11.2*

| Internal stakeholders | • Board of directors and executive management team<br><br>• IT staff, legal team, call centre personnel, public relations, relationship managers |
|---|---|
| External stakeholders | • Customers, insurance providers, public relations consultants, incident response experts, data breach coaches, identity protection providers<br><br>• Key business partners, supplier or vendors<br><br>• Data privacy commissioners, e.g. who, when and how?<br><br>• Taxation offices<br><br>• Securities exchange commissions<br><br>• Federal police<br><br>• Key suppliers/business partners and engagement protocols<br><br>• Employee unions |

There are several technical measures the organisation can take at the same time to eradicate the threat actors and revert to business as usual. These include:

- Rebuilding infected systems (often from known 'clean' sources).

- Replacing compromised files with clean versions.

- Installing patches, changing passwords, and tightening network perimeter security, such as firewall rulesets.

- Testing systems thoroughly including security controls.

- Confirming the integrity of business systems and controls.

According to Microsoft, organisations make a huge mistake of purchasing an assortment of expensive security tools in a sheer panic during a disaster. In the end, none of these tools are ever deployed or used and they did not need to be purchased in the first place. It's important for the cyber leader to defer its acquisition until after the team has conducted a detailed root cause analysis and determined the tool is essential to prevent future incidents.[111]

## 7. Maintain a Robust Assurance Program

As Theodor Reik wrote in his essay 'The Unreachables', 'It has been said that history repeats itself. This is perhaps not quite correct; it merely rhymes.'[112] Like many banks during the Global Financial Crisis, the majority of enterprises are ill-prepared to deal with unanticipated, highly targeted and debilitating cyberattacks. These attacks can be much deeper and more prolonged than imagined, leading to major financial shocks, which result from significant operational losses, share price declines or customer litigations. It can even threaten the existence of an enterprise in extreme circumstances.

Stress testing cyber-response capabilities in controlled environments validates key assumptions, uncovers defective procedures and clarifies key responsibilities reinforcing muscle memory and instilling business confidence.

Business leaders have a crucial responsibility to play here. They need to take deliberate steps to anticipate major cyber breach scenarios, assess the adequacy of response measures and set aside sufficient capital to absorb the shocks should each scenario eventuate.

To achieve this, business leaders can engage external consultants to facilitate desktop cyber risk simulation exercises or 'drills'. These drills must be attended by senior business, technology, and risk stakeholders, as well as cybersecurity experts. During these drills, business leaders identify business impacts from extremely plausible cyber scenarios. For example: a sustained distributed denial-of-service (DDoS) attack rendering essential digital services inaccessible: a wide-scale sensitive data breach or extensive contamination of production data.

Narrowing down critical cyberattack scenarios is necessary because attempting to anticipate every possible attack scenario is not feasible. Once the stakeholders have agreed on plausible scenarios, the next step involves quantifying associated impacts and determining how much capital should be set aside. Quantifying financial impacts from cyber breaches is still in its infancy, and this is where external consultancy can provide insight using their wider industry exposure.

Cybersecurity response simulations should achieve five key objectives:

- Assess the ability of different departments – cybersecurity, IT, public relations, finance, legal counsel, the senior leadership team – to come together and respond to a hostile cybersecurity incident. When effectively executed, these drills can clarify previously ambiguous responsibilities, dysfunctional relationships and cross-departmental tensions. Resolving identified gaps early enhances the organisation's response capabilities.

- Inform business leaders of their most critical digital assets, the strength of their existing defences, and what alternative business controls can be put in place in the event of a sustained breach. In this context, cyber drills reveal the difference between perceived versus actual cybersecurity.

- Challenge the priority of teams and business functions. For example, does the enterprise know which team has the highest priority to the business continuity site in the event of an internet outage resulting from a sustained DDoS attack?

- Inform business leaders of malfunctioning business controls, such as obsolete crisis management plans or out-of-date business documents. For instance, in the event of a cyberattack or breach, an enterprise may resort to manual payments but realise only too late that authorised cheque signatories have long left the enterprise.

- Clarify crisis response roles and responsibilities, as well as escalation procedures, specifically when addressing the following questions:

   Who is responsible for authorising customer communications in the event of a significant sensitive data breach? Who liaises with regulators, investors, suppliers and critical business partners? Who is allowed to respond to media enquiries in the event of data breach fallout? Who notifies the board? Does the enterprise have pre-canned messages for call centre staff to provide customers with consistent messages once a breach has been publicly announced? Who authorises ransom payment in the event of a debilitating ransomware attack?

Although the last question may sound absurd, business realities are much more complicated than people think. When critical files are rendered inaccessible, senior leaders may need to make a tough call.

Given the current environment of heightened cybersecurity awareness, it is tempting for stakeholders to overstate potential impacts from cyberattacks. Exaggerating potential implications of cyberattacks unnecessarily locks in capital that could be invested in defensive controls or other value-adding initiatives. External consultants or internal audits can play an integral part by independently challenging the model used to quantify cyber risk likelihood and impacts, and ensuring that agreed-on capital levels are ratified at the right level.

## Cyber Crisis Management

Our world is full of disruption, volatility and unpredictability. In the case of a cyberattack, how you communicate with stakeholders can have a significant impact on your company's bottom line and brand reputation. It may even determine whether you remain in your job.

Brand reputations are built over the years but can be compromised or even ruined in minutes – your brand is as important as your organisation's financial health. Providing accurate and quick communication to the senior leadership team (SLT) or cyber incident response team (CIRT) is critical for the containment and eradication of, and recovery from, the incident. Yet, communication is often the weak or forgotten link. Here are some recommendations to close those gaps.

## PROVIDE STRONG AND DECISIVE LEADERSHIP

## Being Cyber Crisis Ready

For cyber preparedness to be operating at an optimum level, all planning elements and responses must work in unison. Crisis communications must be embedded in your cyber risk plan and be included in ongoing reviews, monitoring and testing to ensure success.

The communication principles and approaches in dealing with cyber incidents are similar to how other crises are managed. The key is to be prepared, rehearsed and ready to respond at any time. Agility, nimbleness and speed are essential. The C-suite or SLT must be heavily involved, and the cyber leader must convene regular crisis meetings.

In most cases, the SLT will have a spokesperson that will deal with the media and handle interviews. For this reason, the cyber leader role is vital as you will need to deliver information about the incident via clear, concise messaging that is free of technical jargon. You will effectively need to understand and convey details around what is happening right across the organisation, covering 'the server room to the boardroom' so to speak.

The following are three steps that should be considered in your crisis communication planning.

## Step 1. Identify and Assess the Risks

Take time in the planning stage to review and think about all the possible stakeholders the organisation deals with who could be affected by a cyber incident. List those key stakeholders that should be notified. Consider how much information they need to know. For instance, the CIRT may require a more detailed analysis compared to your suppliers. As well as including employees, partners and customers in this planning, don't forget that government authorities may also need to be notified, depending on the scale of the cyberattack, and in line with the current legislation concerning where your business resides and where your customers are located.

After listing the stakeholders, consider the various potential scenarios, and detail the risks. When considering the situations, understand the nuances between an 'issue' versus a 'crisis'. An issue is a low-level incident, while a crisis is a more catastrophic incident that can have a financial, legal and reputational impact. Many threats can be minimised via early detection, but a simmering issue unaddressed can quickly turn into a crisis.

## Step 2. Understand How to Respond

Most large enterprises will already have crisis plans at the ready, which includes a crisis communications component. Your scenarios for cyber threats and attacks must be included in these plans. For small-to-medium-sized enterprises, this may require more work and collaboration, as depending on the industry sector, your risk management plan may not be as robust as a large enterprise's, or might not consider the implications of a cyber crisis. This is more important now than ever as many businesses have rushed to move online quickly during the Covid-19 pandemic and have staff working remotely from home. While security may not have been a top priority for some organisations, this has now changed.

Make sure to consider all the various departments within your organisation that should be included in your plan. For instance, does HR have training in place for employees who have become victims of a phishing attack? Does the communications team understand the various types of cyberattacks that could occur, such as domain name system (DNS), phishing and ransomware?

Once you have mapped your stakeholders and your risks, you need to pressure test the plan through crisis exercises. During the testing, you must contribute to the messaging and get to know the CIRT and their specific roles.

## Step 3. What the Business Can Do and Say

In the heat of the battle, there are seven things the SLT must do when implementing the crisis plan and preparing to communicate. As a cyber professional, providing guidance and information around these seven points will significantly aid the team and help contain the incident more quickly:

- Focus on actions, not outcomes. Early in an incident, focus communications on the actions your company is taking to investigate and remediate the security incident. This often includes steps like notifying law enforcement, hiring forensics experts to help in the investigation and any general steps being taken to remediate the issue. Avoid disclosing numbers or otherwise scoping the incident until there is forensic certainty around these facts.

- Keep customers as your North Star. In all messages, focus on how you are helping to protect customers versus going into detail about how the incident happened, or who was behind it. Often the media will want to know more about the attack itself or other facts that would help produce a more exciting or sensational story. However, these details often do little to help address customers' concerns or needs. Focusing on providing actionable guidance is likely to be more helpful to your customers, and regulators, who are often most interested in how the company is protecting its constituents.

- Determine facts of the incident ASAP (what DO you know).

- Assess gaps (what DON'T you know ... but should).

- Think of the questions and answers your CEO or SLT might be asked (think of the worst-case questions).

- Provide 1–2 key messages (what do you want the business to say).

- Think of proof points if possible (detailed evidence of the business's history and good work).

*Table 10.3* outlines seven things your business should always say in a cyber crisis and seven things it shouldn't.

*Table 10.3*

| Do | Don't |
| --- | --- |
| Post information regularly in a highly visible location. This can be a physical location or virtual – email, the company intranet, or a Slack or Facebook channel. | Rush to announce the scope of the breach before in-depth forensic investigations. Revising the numbers multiple times erodes confidence. Most of the initial estimations are wildly off the mark. Tell customers what you know, what you are doing, and when you will update them next. |
| Take complete ownership and be transparent. | Play the blame game or avoid responsibility. |
| Be on the front foot and keep your employees, customers, shareholders and relevant stakeholders informed of the incident. Provide facts, and how the business has responded so far. | Delay informing employees, customers, shareholders and stakeholders. In 2017, Equifax took 6 weeks to tell customers. It seems several senior business executives were unaware of the breach, shorting, and selling stocks. Yahoo was breached in 2013 and 2014 but disclosed in 2016 and 2017. |
| Explain how the business is cooperating with authorities (where relevant). | Pre-empt findings or actions by authorities or discuss possible litigation that might result. |
| Describe the efforts being made to deal with the immediate situation. | Predict potential implications for the business. |

| Do | Don't |
|---|---|
| List what you'll do next and how you'll maintain communication. | Lie or try to hide the truth. |
| Be clear in your communication, express compassion and sympathy to those affected. | Be unclear. A case in point is Equifax's 2017 data breach, whose press release was too heavy on corporate jargon, impersonal and full of unclear phrases. Equifax was also widely condemned for including a binding arbitration clause that precluded data breach victims from suing Equifax. |

## How the Media Operate in a Crisis

Understanding how media works in a crisis will help prepare you further. In a crisis, speed to market, especially acting to get on the front foot with the media, is essential. The journalists want information quickly and may even be ahead of you (or think they are) by talking to outside parties, such as those affected by the breach, your partners and suppliers.

As tempting as it will be to say nothing, the designated spokesperson (and there should only be one) must say something. Ignoring the media will only push them to other sources to fill the void, which can lead to inaccurate or incorrect information and cause further damage. Initially, the spokesperson may not need to say a lot when the breach is first discovered.

Still, if ignored, control of the message and story can be lost, resulting in additional financial and reputational costs. Regular and brief statements and updates are better than infrequent, lengthy ones.

You can assist the SLT team and spokesperson in remaining factual and on-point.

Make sure you continue to update the SLT and relevant stakeholders as more information is discovered about the nature of the breach. That way, the media is informed as the situation evolves. This shows the business is taking action, concerned and working towards a solution.

## The Role of Social Media in a Crisis

Social media can be a friend or a foe in a crisis but plays a vital role, nevertheless. Consider Equifax, which one day after disclosure, tweeted, 'Happy Friday! You've got Stevie ready and willing to help with your customer service needs today!' That heartless tweet prompted several negative replies. For instance, one irritated Twitter user responded, 'Stevie, can you help repair my life your company just ruined?'[113]

In your cyber plan, direct the communications team to monitor social media and alert you if there is chatter on these channels that could be about a data breach or a cyberattack. Social media can provide an early warning system, as many issues pop out there first and can lead to a crisis if left ignored.

In conclusion, planning, preparing and testing are the keys to managing a cyberattack when it occurs. Communication is an essential component of your cyber crisis plan. It's important to remember that while you might not face the media or manage the communication directly yourself, your knowledge means you are best placed to advise and explain to the SLT when a breach occurs.

# Chapter 12

# Managing Cybersecurity Risks in Mergers and Acquisitions – The Essentials

## Mergers and Acquisitions a Preferred Target for Threat Actors

A decade ago, a leading cybersecurity firm, FireEye, sounded alarm bells when it discovered that cybercriminals had been hacking more than 100 companies, investment advisers and law firms, in search of market-moving information about deals.[114] Since then, high-profile, M&A-related cyber incidents continue to surface with increased frequency and impacts. Consider this – after the hotel giant Marriott acquired Starwood Hotels in 2016, the media publicly announced in 2018 that a major data breach had occurred at the acquired company, exposing personal information of approximately 500 million guests. The breach started in 2014, prior to the acquisition, but remained undetected for almost four years.

Cybersecurity concerns discovered after a deal is closed often present costly risks that had they been factored into the deal negotiations may have led to its dissolution. **Sixty-five per cent experienced buyer's remorse**, regretting the deal due to previously uncovered cybersecurity concerns.[115]

Merger and acquisition deals always involve a balance of speed and risk: speed to get the deal closed before valuations increase and to leverage new business opportunity (unlock value), versus the risk of not doing adequate due diligence. *Table 12.1* illustrates cyber risk and value opportunities.

Cybercriminals have historically exploited the hysteria that characterise M&A activities to target key staff with sophisticated phishing attacks. This risk was highlighted by the Australian Cyber Security Centre (ACSC), which cautioned, 'During major organisational change, staff may find they are under pressure to accept the validity of requests for data, payment or access from people they don't know, and cannot easily verify the identity and authority of. Malicious actors use this pressure to increase the likelihood of successfully using techniques such as business email compromise.'[116]

As the Verizon-Yahoo deal brought to light, target organisations may be tempted to conceal material cybersecurity issues in their environment, fearing such information may undermine their deal prospects or significantly lower valuations.[117] Provisions in M&A often focus on the IT operations and legal ramifications, not on the changes to corporate security governance and changing threat profile of both entities. Information and cybersecurity need to take equal account of people, processes and technology.

## MAJOR BUSINESS PAIN POINTS

Companies continue to pursue mergers and acquisitions to eliminate competition, diversify product offerings, achieve economies of scale, access unique capabilities and penetrate new customer segments. Each stage of the M&A presents unique challenges. Here are three examples:

1. Integrating dissimilar systems and technologies increases digital complexity. Many enterprises are still saddled by legacy applications difficult to protect with modern security solutions. Complex digital environments are inherently harder

to protect as additional technologies may require unique skill sets as well as additional patch windows, hardening guidelines, and vulnerability scanning.

2. M&A negotiation strategies, pricing and associated sensitive information – such as the target company's growth strategies or financial projections, taxation issues, contracts, customers, intellectual property and key employees – are a high-value target for criminals who use them to gain from illegal market manipulation. Also, if this sensitive information falls into the wrong hands, it may dent deal prospects or result in serious regulatory issues.

3. Employees of the target company may become anxious about the fate of their jobs and be tempted to export high-value information such as product development plans, proprietary algorithms, and client-confidential documents to external drives or public cloud environments. This risk is higher for businesses whose prospects depend on the diligent protection of intellectual property, such as high-tech firms. M&A transactions, therefore, heighten insider cybersecurity threats.

M&A risks should be managed just like other business risks, despite the myriad challenges that threaten the viability of deals and participating firms. Here are ten actionable strategies to reduce business risk.

## Top Ten Recommendations

1. Engage early and bring together the cyber leaders of both companies. Uncover previous security incidents and their root causes. Conduct in-depth due diligence looking into cybersecurity capabilities, key risks, compliance obligations, governance, assurance reports (e.g. SOC 2 Type 2 reports), threat landscape, prior data breaches, etc.

2. Embed cybersecurity into new corporate governance obligations, i.e. charters for new board, risk and audit committee constructs.

3. Secure the immediate – communicate clear guidance to those handling highly confidential information (M&A-related transactions), secure dealing rooms, clean desk policy, special handing, etc. Step up security monitoring during the highly confidential stages.

4. Consider the people and culture risk. Step up security awareness for all employees and extend to senior executives/board (cyber threats to personnel, M&A data leakage as a result of human error, theft from both organisations intellectual property by disgruntled employees, etc.). Empower with knowledge to slow down and be vigilant about sophisticated spear phishing attacks.

5. Recognise the business security opportunity and value early – embed business-focused enterprise security architecture expertise within the integration team to exploit security capabilities and cost savings that support key integration objectives (e.g. identify opportunities to unify technical solutions, reduce run costs and reduce architectural complexity).

6. Review the combined regulatory landscape and scope of applicability and identify any toxic combinations (e.g. areas of the business that must be kept separate). Prepare now and take account of incoming directives and legislation that will impact cybersecurity, privacy, and broader data protection.

7. Before day one review cyber resilience and breach response practices. Build new playbooks for the merged entity and communicate with executive and operational team members so all are clear on how to deal with a major security incident or cyber crisis.

8. Know your crown jewels and new threat profile – reinstate what's mission-critical in terms of assets (information, products, business applications, cloud applications, etc.) on both sides.

9. Rationalise current security programs and consider where there are likely to be areas of duplication. Hold off any major technology investments until both cyber leaders have met.

10. And finally, build a plan for day one, and subsequent stages, including a target operating model for security risk governance and commercial competitive advantage.

## ACTION PLAN

The following three-phase approach to assessing an M&A target's cybersecurity, information risk management and compliance programs will help prevent unwelcome surprises and unforeseen liabilities. It will also drive greater efficiency and unveil areas that could unlock new value. Ensuring M&A cybersecurity before, during, and after the deal increases business value in areas of revenue and customer satisfaction, as well as lower costs.

### Phase 1: Pre-Announcement and Initial Due Diligence

Begin by asking some key questions that will help you prioritise and understand the fundamental capabilities of the two organisations. A Strength, Weakness, Opportunities and Threats (SWOT) analysis will provide a view of how an enlarged organisation will look from a security perspective.

Key questions include:

- Do both companies have a chief information security officer (CISO) who is responsible and accountable to the CEO and board of directors?

- Who are the key people dealing with sensitive information, are they fully aware of the protocols they should be following? (It's possible they're restricting information flow through misinformed precautions. Good security could enable this process.)

- Do these teams have the right tools to protect sensitive information, such as encryption of data in transit and at rest?

- What are the existing security compliance certificates?

- Is there a code of conduct that provides expected workforce behaviour and responsibilities related to data security? If so, does it describe sanctions for non-compliance?

- Does the target organisation have a compliance and security governance committee? If so, have the charter, membership, cybersecurity key performance indicators, and information risk management processes been reviewed to ascertain their comprehensiveness?

- What are the existing security compliance certificates worldwide (e.g. PCI DSS, ISO 27001)? A lapse in compliance state will cause customer contractual issues and heavy fines.

- Is there a formal program for managing third-party service providers? If so, have recent revisions been made to accommodate any new regulations and supply chain risk?

- Can the impact of insider threats and data leaks be minimised by identifying key insider-related risks and increased monitoring pre- and post-merger?

- Have recent assessments or audits been conducted on compliance, data security programs, or both? If so, are remediation activities underway to close any gap?

- Have copies of cyber insurance policies been obtained and reviewed? Are there appropriate levels of cyber insurance coverage?

- Are there potential cybersecurity centres of excellence that can be exploited?

- How can changes in threat profiles and known vulnerabilities (those that will affect the merged organisation's reputation) be mitigated? Could external benchmarking such as Bitsight provide quick insight into cyber risk posture?

- Are there existing initiatives or projects that should be put on hold due to the merged organisation's combined capabilities?

- How will the new executives, board members and operations personnel respond to a major cybersecurity breach?

- And finally, what could be included from a cybersecurity perspective in a customer and partner outreach program to build confidence and maintain trust? For example, roundtables with client CISOs.

## Phase 2: Prior to Definitive Agreement

The intention is to ratify the initial target model and understand what may impact the M&A from all sides. We recommend the following actions:

- Articulate information and cyber risk in a formal company register, notify the board of directors, and provide risk treatment planning advice.

- Review governance/oversight committee meeting minutes and attachments to verify adherence to charter, agendas and documented risk management processes.

- Review corporate governance charters and ensure cybersecurity is included in the revised audit and/or risk charter.

- Cross-check policies and procedures against regulations to ensure complete compliance and make it easier to integrate the companies (e.g. ITIL, PCI DSS, ISO 27001).

- Ensure that only those jobs that require access to sensitive information will have permission.

- Engage in discovery conversations about the location of crown jewels on both sides.

- Review specific policies and procedures related to reporting complaints, major cybersecurity incidents or privacy violations, and major breach assessments/notifications.

- Review cyber resilience, business continuity and disaster recovery plan – which are the critical systems, who are the decision makers and what is the communication plan hierarchy for crisis management?

- Request an inventory of service providers with information about the services they provide, minimum information shared, due diligence conducted in hiring their services, security incident notification requirements, and replacement vendors for critical services.

## Phase 3: After Signing Definitive Agreement and Integration

This stage involves detailed work aligned with the first stage of the plan (day one), ensuring a high-level integration plan is in place and active as soon as possible. The detailed plan will be split between governance, cyber strategy, risk management, audit and others.

Recommended actions include:

- Review all documented activities to test business continuity, disaster recovery and emergency cyber resilience plans. Build a cyber crisis management playbook (a subset of crisis management) and agree on table-top exercises with operations and executive teams across the merged companies.

- Review information risk management processes in detail, including prior risk assessment decisions to assess the compatibility of risk tolerance.

- Review logs and other documentation regarding major security incidents, privacy violations, complaints, breach risk assessments and conclusions, notification plans and previous activities (if any).

- Begin running enterprise-wide information and cyber risk assessments covering crown jewels, primary physical locations, security standard scores or benchmarks, and risk profiles of executives and key support staff.

- Request details of any reported breaches, regulatory investigations and external audits.

- Request copies of compliance and security attestations, assessments or audits from high-risk service providers.

- Audit the adherence to procedures that establish, modify or terminate access to sensitive information.

- Review remediation activities from recent compliance and data security audits or assessments and completion timelines for ongoing audits.

## KEY CONSIDERATIONS

Once you have completed key activities across the three stages above, the next step includes diving deeper into specific risk management domains.

## 1. Corporate Governance

Information governance, cybersecurity and risk management are increasingly key topics for discussion in the boardroom. This interest should peak when a merger and acquisition (M&A) is announced.

There are three key cybersecurity and information risk considerations:

1. When a company has begun an M&A transaction,
1. The role of directors who serve on multiple boards, and
1. Taking a top-down approach.

Companies face increased risk during the time of acquisition, such as:

- Common financial investor and shareholder-themed social engineering lures to gain information likely intended for use in insider trading.

- Breach notification laws will affect the entire brand, no matter which business is compromised. It is important to rationalise cyber crises management plans in both organisations early to support a harmonised approach when rapid response is required.

- One of the companies may not take security as seriously as the other so it's important that there's a common understanding and executive cyber awareness to the changing risk profile.

- Data shows an average of 200+ days for companies to detect advanced persistent threats, so the impact of a cyber deficiency in an acquired company may not be visible immediately.[118]

- The acquirer may not be engaged sufficiently in cyber due diligence to uncover weaknesses and allocate resources quickly enough.

## Directors who serve on multiple boards face special issues:

- Cybersecurity is a corporate-wide and boardroom issue that must be evaluated to meet fiduciary duty standards.

- Boards cannot simply rely on management, and they should be aware of comparative cybersecurity practices with other companies on whose boards they serve.

## Taking a top-down approach:

A business's ability to identify, prevent, detect and respond to a major cyberattack is challenging. The complexity of M&A activities can further reduce the board's visibility into the company's cyber risk posture.

The three-layer defence model provides a framework for reviewing cyber crisis practices and communication protocols with the board ahead of the formal merger date.

Revised corporate governance charters (board, audit, risk committees) should explicitly include cybersecurity terms. Furthermore, clear-cut executive level KPIs will help reinforce the mandate.

*Figure 12.1*

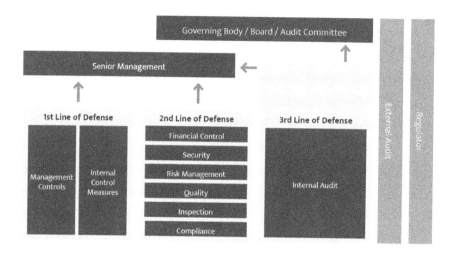

## 2. People and Risk Aware Culture

The clear lesson from the significant rise of security incidents around the world is that people matter as much as, if not more than, technology. Ninety-five per cent of all security incidents involve human error – technology, in fact, can create a false sense of security.[119] Therefore, it's important to build an exceptional culture of high performance that consistently minimises risk. Like Admiral Mike Rogers, who oversaw the US Cyber Command, said: 'We have got to get beyond focusing on just the tech piece here. It's about ethos. It's about culture ... how you man, train, and equip your organisation, how you structure it, the operational concepts that you employ.'[120]

Due to the urgency that often surrounds M&A transactions, companies rarely have time to assess culture with respect to security during due diligence. And since culture issues seldom stop proposed transactions, it becomes the responsibility of security (the cyber leader) and business leaders, including CEOs, to raise the importance of maintaining and developing a risk aware culture.

Instituting a rigorous program to address a risk-aware cultural integration – with clearly stated objectives and a link to measurable business results – can help reduce security-related incidents that may undermine the value of a deal and the brand of the merged company longer term.

Here are two of the considerations:

• **Maintain cybersecurity ambassadors/champion programs** – Security awareness program owners from both companies should maintain existing activities and look to extend specific training to high-risk areas such as M&A deal making, executives and HR departments. Include the issue on the agenda of regularly scheduled steering committee meetings to drive home the importance of a risk-aware culture.

• **Consider the strengths of existing cultures and their compatibility** – When two companies merge, the combined security leadership often assumes they should retain the leading cultural attributes of each. Cultural strengths, however, are sometimes incompatible; therefore, it will be important to create a shared vision and apply this consistently from the top down. Building and nurturing a culture of high reliability will require the personal attention of the CEO and the board, as well as substantial investments in training and oversight.

## 3. Unlock Value with Enterprise Security Architecture

It is strategically advantageous to build enabling security objectives into the fabric of a merged organisation rather than playing perpetual recovery. Each company and associated business units have worked very hard to build trust and goodwill. The cyber leader can consider taking an enterprise security architecture approach and delivering it as a strategic business toolset, enabling the merged organisation to create competitive value-creating opportunities.

Client identity and access management (IAM) is a key capability to make this work. Client IAM should be seen as a key integration activity, leveraging the capabilities we have today (EDM, SSSO, Federation, etc), as an initial transitional stage.

An appropriately aligned framework has distinct advantages, including:

- Having a business-aligned security strategy and architecture to help articulate the bigger picture and set a common language of understanding for the merged organisation. This will embolden the business to leverage security capabilities to manage strategic risks and create a competitive advantage in the industry and market.

- Developing and deploying new business solutions ensures that the business environment remains safe and secure and maintains integrity through change.

- Enabling the identification and remediation of current risks and issues, allowing the business to operate within acceptable tolerance limits of its risk appetite.

Other security business opportunity examples worthy of further discussion include:

- De-duplicating and leveraging security centres of excellence between the two organisations.

- Exploiting security architecture segmentation by considering how upfront costs can be reduced significantly, while also reducing the risk of serious data breach – focusing on the crown jewels.

- Leveraging security assets, expertise, resources and best practices across the enlarged organisation.

- Leveraging cyber capabilities such as threat intelligence, threat prevention, detection, and incident response capabilities.

- Reprioritising current security programs to focus and prepare for the merger, optimise effort and identify cost savings enables reduced delivery time and cost.

- Exploiting service products that have a cyber element to them and potentially cybersecurity-specific services such as consulting services across the wider industry segments.

## 4. Evolving Security and Privacy Legislation

Businesses that span across geopolitical boundaries defy traditional security governance, adding a layer of complexity that makes it confusing to know who has the authority, what is the applicable law, and how it is enforceable by people, processes and technology. The convergence and overlap in scope of applicability, as well as regional applicability in legal and industry security frameworks, needs to be fully understood and documented. This will require board and C-level involvement as the impact of not following the rules can have far-reaching consequences.

Data breach notification laws are a global patchwork, often conflicting with new legislation that is being introduced all the time. Understanding what's just around the corner and the potential consequences of non-compliance is challenging. The EU's GDPR for example, has global impact, and requires breach notification within 72 hours, with fines imposed of up to 4% of annual turnover.[121]

Staying on top of legislation requires:

- Preparing ahead and taking a risk-based approach within each mandate. It is not a tick-box exercise.

- Increased focus on developing and maintaining a security awareness program (board level and to all employees).

- Understanding existing security compliance certificates worldwide. Furthermore, determining organisational compliance with relevant security compliance frameworks, such as the National Institute of Standards and Technology, PCI DSS, ISO 27001, Payment Card Industry Data Security Standard, International Organization for Standardization's 27001 certification. A lapse in compliance state may result in customer contractual issues and heavy fines.

- Stronger collaboration between legal and security teams.

- Identifying and mapping regional, national and sub-national cyber legal rules, wherever you do business.

- Developing, updating and maintaining written policies and procedures, including on governance by the board of directors.

- Extending the same level of rigour to your third-party suppliers, to reduce supply chain cyber risk.

- Regularly testing and updating all assessments, safeguards and protocols, before and after new mandates come into force.

## Conclusion

We have provided a comprehensive list of considerations when considering cybersecurity risk and business opportunity during mergers and acquisitions. We recommend you use our three-phase approach action plan as a guide during M&A processes.

# Chapter 13

# Sustaining Resilience Through Crises and Constant Change

## Case study – 2017 Maersk Cyberattack

In June 2017, Maersk was hit by the NotPetya ransomware attack, one of the most devastating cyberattacks in history.[122] NotPetya was initially believed to be a ransomware attack, but it quickly became apparent that its primary function was to disrupt and destroy. The malware spread rapidly throughout Maersk's global network, encrypting files and rendering systems inoperable. This attack disrupted operations across 600 container vessels, port and terminal operations, and the company's internal networks.

Maersk's response to the NotPetya attack was widely praised for its effectiveness and transparency. Here are the five key aspects of their incident response and recovery strategy:

1. **Rapid Response and Communication**: Maersk immediately assembled an incident response team comprising internal IT staff, cybersecurity experts and external consultants. The company prioritised transparent communication with its customers, stakeholders and the public, acknowledging the extent of the impact and their steps to address the situation. The shipping giant didn't try to sweep the incident under the carpet, play the blame game or attribute the outages to some inexplicable network or power supply issue. They were brutally honest throughout the entire ordeal.

2. **System Recovery and Data Restoration**: With critical systems encrypted and operational data locked, Maersk undertook an enormous recovery effort. The company reinstalled over 4,000 servers, 45,000 PCs and 2,500 applications in a span of ten days – a process that typically would take six months. Critical to their recovery was the existence of an offline backup in Ghana, which had escaped the NotPetya encryption due to a power outage, allowing Maersk to restore much of its global operations. The response went beyond technical measures to minimise operational impacts to its customers. The shipping company reimbursed many of its customers for the expense of rerouting or storing their marooned cargo. One Maersk customer described receiving a seven-figure cheque from the company to cover the cost of sending his cargo via last-minute chartered jet.

3. **Learning and Improvements**: Post-recovery, Maersk focused on learning from the incident to improve its cybersecurity posture. The shipping giant invested in advanced cybersecurity infrastructure, enhanced incident response protocols and fostered a culture of cybersecurity awareness across the organisation. Maersk also emphasised the importance of collaboration and information sharing within the industry to bolster collective defences against future cyber threats.

4. **Focused on Facts**: Maersk focused on facts, publicly announcing that the cyberattack had come from 'a previously unseen type of malware'. They avoided the sensationalist language that most companies resort to, for example, labelling an attack 'unprecedented and highly sophisticated' when in most cases the threat actor has exploited a vulnerability whose patch had been released several months prior. Maersk stuck to the facts and avoided speculation on matters they had not yet zeroed in on. Their external communications were absent of emotional language.

**Outcome and Lessons Learnt**: The NotPetya attack on Maersk served as a wake-up call for the global shipping industry and beyond, highlighting the importance of cybersecurity resilience and the need for robust incident response capability. Maersk's ability to rapidly recover operations and transparently communicate with all stakeholders set a benchmark for handling such crises. Furthermore, the incident underscored the critical need for regular data backups, continuous improvement of security practices, and the benefits of a transparent and cooperative approach to cybersecurity within the global business community. This case study exemplifies how even the most well-prepared organisations can be vulnerable to sophisticated cyberattacks, but also how an adaptive response and recovery strategy can mitigate the impact and strengthen future resilience. The Maersk chairman went one step further, sharing lessons learnt to the global community at the World Economic Forum where he stressed that Maersk had worked not only to improve its cybersecurity but also to make it a 'competitive advantage'.

## The Need for Sustained Cyber Resilience

Cyber resilience is no longer just about defending against attacks and securing assets; it's about developing an adaptive capability that enables an organisation to withstand and recover from inevitable disruptions. It's about anticipating external and internal changes and preparing to seamlessly pivot strategies. Whereas operational excellence ensures that the cybersecurity program's day-to-day functions are maintained and optimised, it delivers sustainable risk reduction and drives value and efficiency across the organisation through a tightly controlled function.

This chapter provides sharp insights into strategies you can wield to sustain resilience and embed operational excellence during times of constant change. It explores the strategies, challenges and triumphs of cybersecurity programs that have managed to sustain momentum, adapt to evolving threats and align with rapidly changing organisational structures and business models.

## Top seven recommendations:

1. **Understanding Resilience in Cybersecurity** – Resilience in cybersecurity is multifaceted and goes beyond traditional defence mechanisms. It encompasses the ability to anticipate, withstand and recover from disruptions while maintaining essential functions and services. A resilient cybersecurity program is agile, adaptable and robust in the face of adversity. Done right, a well-balanced cyber resilience program has the potential to maintain (and in some cases improve) the organisation's reputation after a high-impact attack.

2. **Anticipating and Mitigating Threats** – One of the cornerstones of resilience is the ability to anticipate and mitigate threats before they materialise. This involves continuous monitoring of the threat landscape, proactively identifying exploitable vulnerabilities and implementing pre-emptive mitigations. By staying ahead of emerging threats, organisations can significantly enhance their resilience posture and minimise downstream impacts.

3. **Adapting Response and Recovery** – Cyber resilience also requires an adaptive response and recovery strategy. Organisations must have robust incident response plans that enable them to react swiftly and effectively to security incidents. This includes procedures for containing high-impact incidents, rapidly restoring high-value digital assets and conducting post-incident analysis to prevent recurrence.

4. **Building a Culture of Resilience** – Cultivating a culture that values and prioritises security at every level of the organisation is central to resilience in cybersecurity. This involves fostering awareness and accountability among employees and empowering them to play an active role in safeguarding sensitive information and assets. Resilient organisations create a mindset that not only reduces the likelihood of damaging attacks but also one that improves collective response measures.

5. **Embedding Operational Excellence** – Security programs operate efficiently and effectively where there is operational excellence. This encompasses a range of practices to optimise cybersecurity operations, enhance visibility and control and drive continuous improvement across the organisation. Three of the key components of operational excellence are streamlining security operations by automating routine tasks, implementing standardised processes and workflows, and leveraging technology to augment human capabilities. Doing so reduces manual effort, minimises errors and ensures rapid response.

6. **Enhancing Visibility and Control** – Operational excellence includes implementing robust monitoring and detection capabilities to identify and respond to threats in real time. You can minimise the downstream impacts on your staff or customers by enhancing visibility across all high-value digital assets and closing all the material blind spots.

7. **Driving Continuous Improvement** – Operational excellence is not a static goal but a continuous journey with no finish line. To sustain it, you must regularly assess your security posture, identify areas for enhancement and close identified gaps. This is a multifaceted discipline that includes regular security assessments and audits, analysis of incident data to identify trends and patterns, and investment in training and development programs to keep security teams abreast of the latest threats and technologies.

While not flashy, operational excellence and resilience are the bedrock of sustained cyber transformation. By sustaining them, you can streamline key processes, boost efficiency through automation, augment human effectiveness, lower operational costs, and most importantly, keep the business rock solid in the face of rapid change.

## Adapting to the Ever-Changing Threat Landscape

Cybersecurity leaders must remain ever vigilant and agile in an era marked by swift technological advancements and the escalating sophistication of cyber threats. To effectively adapt, cyber leaders must implement processes and embed cultures that drive learning and evolution. This agility is underpinned by a comprehensive system to gather and distil threat intelligence into actionable insights for technology teams to neutralise material threats pre-emptively.

Such a system for adapting to evolving cyber threats is predicated on a multilayered understanding of strategic, tactical, and operational threat intelligence. Strategic threat intelligence offers a macro view of the cyber threat landscape, focusing on long-term trends, the evolution of cyber-threat actors and their underlying motivations.

Tactical intelligence, by contrast, zeroes in on the specific tactics, techniques and procedures (TTPs) utilised by cyber adversaries. This intelligence helps cybersecurity teams develop actionable tactical responses. It enables cybersecurity teams to refine their defence strategies, ensuring they are tailored to counter the latest offensive tactics by threat actors. This layer of insight helps teams stay ahead of attackers and adapt defensive postures in real time to neutralise threats as they emerge.

Operational threat intelligence provides the most immediate and detailed insights into an organisation's threats and vulnerabilities. It offers a granular view into specific cyber threats, their vectors and potential impacts. This intelligence layer enables cybersecurity teams to rapidly implement specific countermeasures and respond to active threats.

Moreover, collaboration and information sharing with external entities such as industry peers, cybersecurity alliances and governmental agencies, arms cybersecurity teams with more comprehensive threat intelligence insights to rapidly close loopholes and adapt defences.

## Adaptive incident response and recovery

Organisations must have robust incident response plans that enable them to react swiftly and neutralise security incidents. These include procedures for containing and mitigating the impact of breaches, restoring affected systems and data and conducting post-incident analysis to identify lessons learnt and areas for improvement.

There are three critical components that form the backbone of a robust cybersecurity strategy:

- **Comprehensive Incident Management and Response Framework**: This should not only prioritise the rapid detection and containment of threats but also ensure a systematic approach to eradicating the threat actors from the network. This includes clear communication plans for internal and external stakeholders, defined roles and responsibilities for the incident response team and the use of forensic tools to analyse and learn from the breach. The framework must be regularly updated and tested through drills and simulations to ensure its effectiveness under highly plausible cyberattack scenarios.

- **Resilience Through Redundancy and Flexibility**: Beyond the immediate incident response, building resilience into the IT infrastructure itself is the next critical. This involves the implementation of redundancy in key systems and data backups to ensure business continuity even in the face of disruptive cyberattacks. Organisations should also adopt agile methodologies to quickly adapt their security measures in response to evolving threats. This includes the ability to dynamically adjust security protocols, deploy patches and update defences as new threat intelligence becomes available.

- **Post-Incident Evolution and Continuous Improvement**: The cycle of resilience is incomplete without a rigorous post-incident analysis phase. Following a security breach, organisations should engage in a thorough review of the incident to identify not just the root causes but also the effectiveness of their response as executed. This analysis should extend beyond technical aspects to include organisational, procedural and human factors. Learning from these incidents enables the continuous improvement of security practices and incident response strategies. It's also crucial to share these insights, when appropriate, with the broader cybersecurity community to contribute to the collective resilience against cyber threats.

By focusing on these expanded areas, organisations can develop a more robust and adaptive incident response and recovery capability.

## Fostering a Cyber Resilience Culture

Building a resilient cybersecurity culture goes beyond the implementation of robust technologies and processes. It fundamentally revolves around people at every level of the organisation. This people-centric approach to cybersecurity resilience acknowledges that while technology plays a crucial role in defence mechanisms, the behaviours, attitudes and awareness of every employee are equally critical in safeguarding an organisation against cyber threats. Emphasising the human element in cybersecurity strategies involves nurturing an environment where security is everyone's responsibility, promoting continuous learning and fostering open communication about cyber risks and best practices.

Comprehensive Incident Management and Response with a People Focus: The development of a comprehensive incident management and response framework that places a strong emphasis on the human elements is at the core of fostering a resilient culture. This includes empowering employees with the knowledge and tools to identify and report potential threats, ensuring that there is a clear understanding of roles and responsibilities in the event of an incident, and fostering a blame-free environment where the focus is on learning from incidents rather than finding fault. Training and simulation exercises are vital as they not only prepare teams for potential cyber incidents but also reinforce the culture of vigilance and collective responsibility.

Cultivating Resilience Through Redundancy, Flexibility and Empowerment: The cyber leader should focus on cultivating a flexible and adaptive mindset among employees. This involves encouraging innovation and creative thinking in problem-solving, providing continuous education on the evolving threat landscape and empowering employees to take initiative in improving security practices. A resilient culture values and rewards flexibility and adaptability, recognising that the cybersecurity landscape is constantly changing and that staying ahead requires an agile and informed workforce.

Post-Incident Evolution Focused on People and Continuous Learning: A resilient culture thrives on continuous improvement and learning, especially in the aftermath of security incidents. This means engaging all levels of the organisation in post-incident reviews, fostering an environment where lessons learnt are shared openly and ensuring that improvements are implemented in a way that enhances both technological defences and employee awareness and behaviours. It's about shifting the mindset from a reactive stance to a proactive one, where every employee feels responsible for contributing to the organisation's cybersecurity resilience.

Engaging with the Broader Cybersecurity Community for Collective Resilience: Building a resilient cybersecurity culture also extends beyond the organisation's boundaries. It involves actively participating in the broader cybersecurity community, sharing insights and best practices, and collaborating on threat intelligence. This not only enhances the organisation's own resilience but also contributes to the collective security of the digital ecosystem. Encouraging employees to engage with external cybersecurity communities, attend conferences and participate in forums can bring new ideas and perspectives that enrich the organisation's culture of resilience.

Emphasising the People Aspect in Every Initiative: At every level, from onboarding new employees to executive decision-making, the emphasis on the human aspect of cybersecurity must be evident. This means integrating cybersecurity awareness into the core values of the organisation, making it a part of everyday conversations, and ensuring that everyone, from the newest recruit to the CEO, understands their role in maintaining and enhancing cybersecurity resilience. By doing so, organisations can create a culture where cybersecurity is seen not just as a technical requirement but as a shared responsibility that is integral to the organisation's success and integrity.

## Navigating Organisational Change

Understanding and addressing the substantial challenges as they arise is largely about being prepared, for example, during strategic shifts, mergers and acquisitions (M&A), or when restructuring an organisation. These pivotal periods can unsettle established cybersecurity practices and introduce new vulnerabilities, making the role of cybersecurity leaders crucial in steering the organisation safely through these transitions. Maintaining cybersecurity resilience during such periods is not just about defence but about strategic foresight and adaptability.

To sustain cyber resilience during complex change, cyber leaders must collaborate closely with executive management, HR and other departments. They must understand how organisational changes impact cybersecurity.

For example, the M&A process demands rigorous due diligence to uncover and mitigate potential cyber risks. The expertise of cybersecurity leaders is indispensable here. They are tasked with evaluating the cybersecurity posture of the target entity, pinpointing risks and liabilities, and formulating an integration plan that not only secures the digital assets of the merged entity but also aligns with their overarching cybersecurity strategy.

Cybersecurity leaders can ensure that their organisations not only withstand the challenges of transition but also emerge stronger and more secure. They do this by engaging stakeholders effectively, reassessing risks in light of organisational changes, conducting thorough due diligence during M&As and cultivating a culture of continuous improvement. The way forward demands strategic insight, collaborative effort and a relentless pursuit of cybersecurity excellence, ensuring the organisation remains resilient and adaptive in an ever-changing digital landscape.

## Embedding Operational Excellence in Cybersecurity

Operational excellence is about creating an environment where cybersecurity practices are not only optimised for utmost efficiency, control and visibility, but are also deeply ingrained in the organisation's culture. Operational excellence is about promoting an ethos of relentless improvement.

We offer the following ten recommendations to build operational excellence into the DNA of the cybersecurity function.

1. **Have deep environmental awareness**: Identify all assets, assess their vulnerabilities and prioritise them according to their level of risk. This forms a strong foundation for a differentiated security model that not only optimises security resources but also reduces the crown jewels' exposure.

2. **Automate security deployments**: Legacy security tasks are often time-consuming, tedious and error-prone. To mitigate this, cybersecurity teams must prioritise automated standard builds, tests and deployments, thus creating repeatable patterns and significantly cutting down human error.

3. **Ensure complete visibility**: Set up 24/7 monitoring across your network and leverage automation to discover new assets,

eliminate false positives, and ensure logs from high-value digital assets are collected and analysed, and that bona fide incidents are promptly mitigated.

4. **Create a culture of automation**: Automate ruthlessly to reduce manual effort on repetitive work with no enduring value, improve release velocity and minimise human-induced errors.

5. **De-identify personally identifiable information**: Do this when exporting to non-production environments, external parties with no business need to keep the entire record, and host systems in geographical data centres that align with your data protection laws.

6. **Adopt a zero-trust philosophy**: Minimise your blast radius by making sure resources are only accessible to authorised users with a specific intent through automated policies and guardrail controls.

7. **Minimise the attack surface**: Reduce the attack surface by disabling any services needlessly exposed to the internet and enforcing MFA on all remote access and SaaS applications.

8. **Prioritise high-impact security controls**: Focus your limited resources on high-impact controls like automated privileged access management, MFA, application safelisting, and network segmentation.

9. **Standardise builds, tests and deployments**: By eliminating human-induced errors for repeated processes.

10. **Incorporate 'secure-by-design' principles**: Embedding security considerations into the design phase of all projects and processes ensures that security is an integral part from the outset. This 'secure-by-design' approach minimises

vulnerabilities and reinforces the organisation's security posture. This concept aims to enhance security while reducing the cost and effort associated with addressing vulnerabilities at later stages.

## The Science and Art of Tracking Progress

Defining and measuring success within the cybersecurity domain is challenging but it's key to building trust in your program. Tools that effectively track progress provide a structured way to assess the impact of cybersecurity initiatives and are a guide to understanding how well an organisation is protecting their digital assets.

Key performance indicators (KPIs) and metrics, when thoughtfully selected and aligned with the specific objectives of the cybersecurity program, serve as invaluable instruments for this purpose. These include a variety of quantitative measures, such as the number of incidents detected and resolved, the speed of response and recovery from incidents, and the overall reduction in the organisation's exposure to cyber risks. Such metrics offer tangible data points that reflect the program's effectiveness in maintaining the integrity and availability of information systems.

However, the story of a cybersecurity program's success extends beyond these quantitative assessments. Qualitative evaluations are equally vital in painting a full picture of a program's effectiveness. Feedback from stakeholders across the organisation can reveal insights into the perceived strengths and weaknesses of the cybersecurity posture. This feedback, coupled with compliance assessments with relevant industry standards and best practices, adds depth to the understanding of the program's success.

The integration of cybersecurity metrics into the organisation's broader business analytics and reporting mechanisms further elevates their importance. By illustrating how cybersecurity initiatives support business objectives, such as protecting brand reputation, ensuring customer trust and safeguarding proprietary information, cybersecurity leaders can demonstrate the intrinsic value of their programs to executive leadership and board members.

## Cultivating a Culture of Continuous Improvement and Sustainability

The cybersecurity arena is dynamic. New threats emerge daily, exploiting new vulnerabilities. It's a constantly changing environment as new technologies are introduced, and new processes and policies are implemented. Complacency is an ever-present risk as resting on your past successes can lead to vulnerabilities and misconfigurations. Organisations must integrate continuous testing and learning into their cybersecurity strategies. This approach prepares the organisation to defend against known threats and equips it with the agility to respond to new challenges as they arise.

Top-tier cybersecurity leaders are increasingly integrating continuous testing, assurance and learning to deliver a more sustainable risk posture. This involves assessing existing security measures through methodologies such as penetration testing, red team exercises, purple teaming, controls assurance testing and tabletop exercises.

These assurance activities provide insights into potential vulnerabilities and incident response capabilities, but more importantly, the effectiveness of key controls. Continuous assurance practices, including security audits/thematic reviews, vulnerability scanning, security monitoring, incident response, and compliance assessments, also play a crucial role in maintaining operational resilience and robustness. By embracing a culture of continuous learning and improvement informed by assurance activities, executives, business leaders, board members and regulators can feel confident that a rigorous approach to maintenance is being applied.

Learning involves using the insights gained from testing to refine and improve cultural practices. It requires an organisational culture that values learning from failures and successes alike. This culture encourages transparency and open communication about cybersecurity incidents and near misses; this culture fosters an environment where every member of the organisation is engaged in improving cybersecurity resilience.

## Examples of Testing, Assurance and Learning Methodologies

Several testing methodologies have proven effective in refining and maturing the robustness of cybersecurity defences. Among these, the following stand out for their ability to provide actionable insights to the cyber leader:

**Penetration Testing** – Penetration testing is a proactive security assessment to identify vulnerabilities in an organisation's systems, networks and applications. It involves simulating cyberattacks to uncover weaknesses that malicious actors could exploit. This typically includes the following five steps:

1. **Scope Definition**: Define the scope of the penetration test, including target systems, applications, and testing methods, ideally prioritising internet-facing workloads.

2. **Threat Modelling**: Identify potential attack vectors and prioritise targets based on their criticality and exposure.

3. **Vulnerability Identification**: Conduct reconnaissance and vulnerability scanning to identify potential entry points.

4. **Exploitation**: Attempt to exploit identified vulnerabilities to gain unauthorised access or escalate privileges.

5. **Documentation**: Document findings, including exploited vulnerabilities, potential impact and recommended remediation actions.

**Example**: A financial institution engages a team of certified ethical hackers to perform penetration testing on its online banking platform. The testers identify vulnerabilities such as SQL injection and weak authentication mechanisms, demonstrating the risk of unauthorised access to sensitive financial data. The organisation uses these findings to implement patches, strengthen access controls and improve its overall systems development life cycle.

**Red Team Exercises** – Red team exercises simulate offensive cyberattacks against an organisation's infrastructure, applications and personnel, to assess its resilience and response capabilities. Unlike penetration testing, which focuses on identifying vulnerabilities, red team exercises evaluate the organisation's ability to detect, respond and recover from sophisticated threats. This typically includes the following five steps:

1. **Scenario Development**: Create realistic attack scenarios tailored to the organisation's industry, threat landscape and risk profile.

2. **Execution**: Launch coordinated cyberattacks using advanced TTPs commonly employed by real threat actors.

3. **Detection Assessment**: Evaluate the organisation's ability to detect and respond to simulated attacks in real time.

4. **Response Evaluation**: Assess the effectiveness of the organisation's incident response procedures and mitigation strategies.

5. **Debriefing**: Conduct a post-exercise debriefing session to analyse findings, identify areas for improvement and develop action plans.

**Example**: During a red team exercise, a team of experienced cybersecurity professionals covertly simulates a ransomware attack on a manufacturing company's industrial control systems (ICS). The exercise assesses the organisation's ability to detect the attack, contain its spread and recover normal operations. Observing how the organisation's security operations centre (SOC), and incident response team, handle the simulated attack identifies and addresses weaknesses in detection and response capabilities.

**Purple Teaming** – Purple teaming does the same as the red team but does so in close collaboration with the defensive team (blue team) to enhance an organisation's security posture as they go. In these engagements, the purple team simulates attacks openly, while blue teamers defend against them. The focus is on knowledge sharing and skill development as they go. This typically includes the following five steps:

1. **Objective Alignment**: Align with blue team objectives to ensure a collaborative approach to cybersecurity attack and testing.

2. **Scenario Development**: Design realistic attack scenarios that challenge the organisation's defences and detection capabilities.

3. **Execution**: Conduct the exercises and simulate attacks, and blue teamers defend against them and fix issues as they go.

4. **Knowledge Sharing**: Facilitate ongoing communication and knowledge sharing between blue team members.

5. **Lessons Learnt**: Capture lessons learnt from each engagement to improve defensive strategies and detection capabilities continuously.

**Example**: In a purple team exercise, they simulate a phishing campaign targeting employees, while blue teamers monitor email traffic and implement security controls to detect and block phishing attempts. The purple and blue team members collaborate closely throughout the exercise, sharing insights, tactics and lessons learnt to improve detection and response capabilities against real-world threats.

**Tabletop Exercises** – Tabletop exercises are discussion-based simulations that bring together key stakeholders to walk through various cyber incident scenarios and assess the organisation's preparedness and response capabilities. These exercises allow for testing incident response plans, communication protocols, and coordination among different departments. This typically includes the following five steps:

1. **Scenario Development**: Develop realistic cyber incident scenarios based on threats and organisational risks.

2. **Participant Selection**: Identify key stakeholders from across the organisation to participate in the tabletop exercise, ideally a combination of senior IT, business, product, and risk management personnel.

3. **Facilitation**: Facilitate tabletop exercises, guiding participants through the scenario and encouraging active participation.

4. **Discussion**: Encourage open dialogue and discussion among participants to explore potential responses to the scenario.

5. **Action Planning**: Capture action items and recommendations for improving incident response procedures and coordination.

**Example**: During a tabletop exercise, representatives from IT, legal, HR, public relations and senior management gather to simulate a data breach scenario. They discuss their roles and responsibilities, assess the potential impact of the breach and formulate a coordinated response plan. Through the exercise, the organisation identifies gaps in its incident response procedures and refines its strategies to effectively mitigate cyber threats.

**Security Control Effectiveness Testing (SCET)** – SCET involves conducting rigorous assessments to determine whether specific security controls operate as intended and provide adequate protection against potential threats. This type of testing typically includes the following five steps:

1. **Control Identification**: Identify the security controls implemented within the organisation's environment. This may include access controls, encryption mechanisms, intrusion detection systems, firewalls and other security measures.

2. **Test Planning**: A detailed test plan is developed to outline the objectives, scope and methodology of the testing process. This plan defines the specific scenarios and techniques that will be used to assess the effectiveness of each control.

3. **Control Execution**: During the execution phase, security testers simulate various attack scenarios to assess how well the controls withstand potential threats. This may involve attempting to bypass access controls, exploit vulnerabilities in the network infrastructure or circumvent encryption mechanisms.

4. **Data Collection and Analysis**: As the testing progresses, data is collected on the performance of each security control and any vulnerabilities or weaknesses identified. This data is then analysed to determine the controls' overall effectiveness and to identify areas for improvement.

5. **Reporting and Remediation**: A detailed report is prepared summarising the findings of the SCET process, including any vulnerabilities discovered and recommendations for remediation. This report serves as a road map for strengthening security controls and improving the organisation's overall security posture.

**Example**: Let's consider an organisation that has implemented access controls to restrict unauthorised users from accessing sensitive data stored on its servers. To assess the effectiveness of these controls, security testers may attempt to bypass the access controls using various techniques, such as password cracking, privilege escalation or exploiting misconfigurations. During the testing process, if the security testers successfully gain unauthorised access to the sensitive data despite the implemented controls, it indicates a weakness in the control effectiveness. Conversely, if the access controls successfully prevent unauthorised access, it demonstrates that the controls are functioning as intended and effectively protecting the organisation's data assets.

## Continuous Assurance

Continuous assurance involves ongoing assessments and validations of the organisation's cybersecurity controls and processes to ensure they remain effective against evolving threats. Unlike traditional periodic assessments, continuous assurance provides real-time insights into the organisation's security posture, allowing for timely detection and mitigation of vulnerabilities.

**Assurance Methodologies** – Several methodologies can be employed to facilitate continuous assurance and improve cybersecurity resilience:

- **Security Audits**: Regular audits help identify gaps and weaknesses in the organisation's security posture, enabling proactive remediation and improvement.

- **Vulnerability Scanning**: Automated vulnerability scanning tools can continuously monitor the organisation's network and systems for known vulnerabilities, allowing for prompt remediation.

- **Security Monitoring and Incident Response**: Continuous monitoring of network traffic and system logs, coupled with robust incident response procedures, ensures rapid detection and containment of security incidents.

- **Compliance Assessments**: Regular assessments against industry regulations and standards help ensure that the organisation's cybersecurity practices align with regulatory requirements and best practices.

By integrating continuous assurance practices into their cybersecurity strategies, organisations can effectively enhance their ability to detect, prevent and respond to cyber threats. Assurance methodologies provide valuable insights into the organisation's security posture, allowing for proactive risk management and continuous improvement of cybersecurity resilience.

## A Call to Action for Cybersecurity Leaders

Today's dynamic environment demands that cyber leaders depart from reactive cybersecurity measures to a more strategic, forward-looking approach that anticipates future threats and prepares their organisation to counter them effectively.

We encourage cyber leaders to create cultures of continuous improvement, to invest in developing and retaining top-tier cybersecurity talent, and to cultivate partnerships and collaborative networks that enhance collective cybersecurity defences. By doing so, they not only safeguard their organisations against the myriad cyber threats of today but also lay the groundwork for enduring cybersecurity resilience, operational delivery of excellence and sustainable risk reduction measures.

## CYBER LEADERS ON THE MOVE STORY 4

### Ashwin Ram – Cybersecurity Evangelist, Office of the Chief Technology Officer – Check Point and graduate of the Cyber Leadership Institute.

Ashwin is a distinguished cybersecurity advisor and thought leader, renowned for his ability to translate complex technical threats into clear business contexts. The incredible story of Ashwin, who spent part of his childhood growing up in Lakeba (pronounced Lakemba), a remote island in Fiji's Southern Lau Archipelago, comprised of six villages with only two vehicles in his time, is deeply inspiring, to say the least.

### How it all started

Ashwin Ram has been in the game for a while, boasting more than 15 years of experience helping several high-end enterprises fortify their defences against the menace of cybercrime. Like the majority of CLI graduates, Ashwin started in a technical support role. From there, he transitioned into various pre- and post-sales roles. He describes venturing into the world of cybersecurity as a natural evolution. Over the years, Ashwin deepened his technical knowledge, rising through the ranks into his current role as a cybersecurity evangelist within the Office of the CTO at Check Point, a global cybersecurity giant. In this role, he regularly gives media interviews, presents at cybersecurity conferences and advises CISOs and business executives.

### The quest to demystify cybersecurity

During his one and a half decades in the trenches, Ashwin has witnessed the rapid transition of cybersecurity, from a purely technical problem into a broader business risk with far-reaching strategic implications. As this transition unfolded, however, Ashwin noted with frustration that most cyber professionals were stuck in their technical world, struggling to translate complex matters into the language of the business. Ashwin is never the one to sit down and hope for matters to resolve themselves. After scouring the internet for relevant courses, Ashwin decided the CLP was best suited to advance his career ambitions.

Once Ashwin joined the CLP, he quickly immersed himself in the program, actively engaging in the weekly calls and developing new relationships with fellow CLI classmates. Ashwin sought a network of peers, and he describes completing our CLP with that and more beyond his expectations.

Throughout the intensive eight weeks, Ashwin learnt about vital challenges CISOs face, as well as practical steps to prioritise transformation initiatives, accelerate budget approvals and deliver unforgettable board presentations. Ashwin realised that a cyber resilience strategy must be rigorously tied to business goals, support digital transformation agenda and be understood by decision makers. His technical expertise still mattered, but the CLP helped him strike an excellent balance between technology and business acumen. Ashwin now engages with CISOs and executives at a deeper level, pitching cybersecurity as a growth advantage instead of a compliance-driven necessary evil. He helps businesses align their strategy to board-approved risk appetite and, from there, chunk complex programs into realistic milestones.

Ashwin is a man who has found his deepest *why*; he exudes a passion that is rare in the cyber world. In short, he loves his job. Ashwin describes being in his element when providing businesses with insights to develop their cyber strategies. Combining the insights he gets from the Check Point Incident Response team, research from the Check Point Research Team, and CLP leadership lessons has helped.

## Ashwin morphs into a well-rounded cyber leader

A large part of Ashwin's role involves presenting at and hosting events. It also requires a lot of media engagement. Ashwin says that the CLI has helped him develop talks that blend business and technical knowledge, and he can now articulate technical expertise in an easily consumable way. Throughout the CLP, participants get one-on-one mentorship from one of the course facilitators (seasoned CISOs). Ashwin says the active collaboration he had with Phil Zongo, CEO of CLI, helped during and beyond the program. Taking the knowledge, Ashwin says, and passing it on to others is an excellent benefit of the CLI community.

Ashwin has become a distinguished cybersecurity advisor and thought leader, renowned for his ability to translate complex technical threats into clear business contexts. In 2023, he was honoured as one of Australia's 'Top 100 Innovators' by KPMG and *The Australian*, standing out as one of only five cyber professionals on this prestigious list. This accolade celebrates the nation's leading next-generation leaders across various fields, including technology, cybersecurity, AI, finance, medicine and more.

Ashwin's journey in cybersecurity is marked by numerous accolades, including winning the 'Cyber Leadership Program' in 2020 and the 'Cyber Strategy and Transformation Program' in 2021 from the Cyber Leadership Institute. His dedication to advancing the industry earned him the Distinguished Evangelist Award from the Office of the CTO in 2022.

As a seasoned keynote speaker, Ashwin has captivated audiences at global cybersecurity events with compelling real-world stories and insightful security research. He is a trusted advisor to industry titans, start-ups and collectives, known for his expertise in cloud, threat intelligence, network, endpoint, mobile, IoT, and breach preparedness. His ability to switch effortlessly between 'tech talk' and 'business talk' makes him a go-to expert for organisations seeking to enhance their cyber resilience.

Ashwin attributes much of his success to the knowledge and practical experience gained through the Cyber Leadership Institute's programs, which helped him evolve from a deeply technical expert into a well-rounded cyber leader with the business acumen needed to make a significant impact in the industry. Additionally, Ashwin has hosted countless executive roundtables, fostering collaboration among industry peers on critical challenges such as stakeholder management and boardroom communication, supply chain risks, and breach preparedness.

Through his involvement with the Cyber Leadership Institute, Ashwin has provided thought leadership and support to the broader community. His passion lies in helping cyber executives understand emerging cyber threat trends and navigate cyber risk through ruthless prioritisation. With a unique blend of CISO consulting experience and technical know-how, Ashwin continues to make a profound impact on the cybersecurity landscape.

When describing the value the CLP has added to him, Ashwin sums it up nicely. He says, 'The missing link for a lot of CISOs is the business piece, and vice versa for business executives; it's the technical piece. I am now in a great position, and the CLP absolutely completes that piece.'

# Conclusion

As organisations seek to respond to increased regulatory pressures and rising expectations from various external stakeholders, the cyber leader is emerging as one of the most critical positions in the c-suite. Since founding CLI in 2018, our journey and the hundreds of cyber leaders we have collaborated with have given us unique insight into what works and what doesn't. The principles we share in this book go beyond the experiences of the three co-authors and represent an amalgamation of shared wisdom we have gained from our global community of cyber leaders.

Granted, there are several strategies cyber leaders can apply to distinguish themselves in today's hypercompetitive and interconnected global marketplace. But in our experience, nine strategies can disproportionately boost a cyber leader's effectiveness and organisational clout:

1. Nurturing a strong personal brand as a business-focused cyber security executive through consistent and compelling thought leadership and a track record of superior program delivery.

2. Developing deep self-awareness and crafting an effective strategy to close career-derailing leadership gaps and amplify critical strengths.

3. Designing and delivering high-impact cyber resilience strategies that doubly close critical business risks and advance top business goals, centred on the most vital digital assets.

4. Nurturing deep relationships with key decision makers,

turning detractors into supporters and creating a shared sense of purpose that motivates everyone to throw their total weight behind cyber transformation.

5.  Embedding a cyber-savvy culture deep into the bloodstream of the enterprise by motivating everyone to go beyond the call of duty to defend the organisation against cybercrime.

6.  Constantly rejecting the urge to get carried away by bleeding edge technologies and embedding operational excellence into the DNA of the IT enterprise by relentlessly focusing on mundane but essential cyber security controls (operational excellence).

7.  Communicating the cyber transformation agenda with clarity, persuasion and impact – equipping the board and executives with decisive and actionable insights to make risk-informed decisions.

8.  Preparing for inevitable high-impact cyber breaches and building a layered response framework to quickly recover critical business functions, provide solid assurance to external stakeholders, and minimise downstream impacts to customers, staff, and business partners.

9.  Having the board of directors and most senior business officers genuinely and actively engage in cyber transformation, exemplify expected behaviours and enforce strong cyber risk oversight.

But it's important to note that no cyber leadership journey is linear. To achieve your leadership potential, you must take bold steps, reject the myth of perfectionism and allow yourself to make mistakes. As James Thurber urged, 'You might as well fall flat on your face as lean over too far backwards.'

# Acknowledgements

Our gratitude to our global community of cyber leaders, whose steadfast belief in our vision to build a closely bonded community who actively support each other and lead their organisations towards cyber resilience, is boundless. Without our members, we could not have built CLI or written this book.

We extend our warm thanks to Andrea Penze, Paul Anderson and Emma Moylan, whose invaluable editorial guidance significantly elevated the quality of our book.

Our heartfelt thanks goes to the entire CLI team who work tirelessly behind the scenes to deliver exceptional service to our members.

Lastly, we are deeply grateful to our families and friends for their unconditional love and support, which has sustained our entrepreneurship journey.

# Author Profiles

## Phil Zongo

Phil is an international keynote speaker, multi-award winning virtual CISO and bestselling author of The Gift of Obstacles and The Five Anchors of Cyber Resilience (named one of the top five cyber security books in the UK in 2021). He is an official member of the Forbes Business Council, an Invitation-Only Global Community for Successful Business Owners and Leaders.

He was named one of 2020's Top 100 Most Influential People of African Descent (New York, USA) and the 2017 ISACA International's Best Article Award (Chicago, USA) winner. His opinions have been featured by Forbes, CISCO, NZ Business Herald, Financial Standard, SAP, etc. Among many global accolades, Phil was named one of the Top 7 Global Cyber Security Leaders (Security Magazine and ISACA) and among the Top 30 Australian cybersecurity executives in 2023 and 2024. At CLI, Phil teaches executive influencing, personal branding, board reporting and governance. In his personal life, Phil enjoys spending time with his two kids and playing golf.

## Darren Argle

Darren Argyle is a highly accomplished and internationally recognised executive in cybersecurity and technology. Darren has held Group CISO and executive cyber risk roles at prominent organisations, including Standard Chartered Bank, Qantas Airlines, and S&P Global (formerly Markit). His professional journey also includes roles at leading multinational technology vendors such as IBM, and showcases his entrepreneurial flair, bringing an innovative human risk management software cyber venture to market in 2015.

Darren's dedication to the cybersecurity profession has earned him several accolades. He graced the 2016 SC Magazine cover and was named one of the top 100 most influential global CISOs in 2017, 2018 and 2022. He was also awarded 'Innovator of the Year' by the SANS Institute in 2022 and the 'Outstanding Cyber Security Professional' award by Cyber OSPAs. In 2023, the CSO Magazine featured Darren in the top 30 cyber leaders for the third consecutive year.

At CLI, Darren teaches cultural transformation, senior stakeholder influencing, building high performance teams and is notable international speaker. Off the podium, he is an avid fitness enthusiast and meditation practitioner, promoting the balance between mental and physical wellness for peak professional performance.

## Jan Schreuder

Jan Schreuder is a cybersecurity industry veteran with a career spanning over 40 years. Named among the IFSEC Top 25 Most Influential Global Cyber Security Professionals in 2022, Jan is an independent consultant providing strategic advisory services in security strategy, governance, regulatory, and risk-related matters to boards and executives. He is a Boardroom Certified Qualified Technology Expert (QTE), certified to provide expert guidance on technology governance and cyber risk management at the board level. He is also a Chartered Accountant and Fellow of Chartered Accountants Australia and New Zealand (FCA).

With a 37-year career at PwC, including 27 years as a partner in South Africa, Australia, and Switzerland, Jan led the cybersecurity practices in Australia and Switzerland, providing strategy and transformation services to prominent multinational organisations, primarily in financial services. He remains actively involved in the payments industry as an advisor and investor in several fintech companies. As a passionate coach, Jan has helped several professionals break into executive roles and advised CISOs for large companies to sharpen their executive skills. He has lectured at the post-graduate level at several universities and served as Treasurer of the Abbotsleigh School for Girls Council for eight years. Jan actively promotes STEM education and the increased participation of women in IT and cyber.

At CLI, Jan teaches strategy design, cyber transformation, crisis management and risk management. In his personal life, Jan enjoys travelling, playing golf, and spending time with his children and grandchildren.

# Endnotes

1  Rothman, J. (2019). *What Is Leadership, Anyway?* [online] The New Yorker. https://www.newyorker.com/magazine/2016/02/29/our-dangerous-leadership-obsession

2  Panel®, E. (2023, May 29). *Council Post: 16 New And Potential IoT Developments Tech Leaders Are Excited About.* Forbes. https://www.forbes.com/sites/forbestechcouncil/2023/03/29/16-new-and-potential-iot-developments-tech-leaders-are-excited-about/?sh=436c19f31e16

3  Lockheed Martin. (2021). *F-35 Electro Optical Targeting System (EOTS).* Lockheed Martin. https://www.lockheedmartin.com/en-us/products/f-35-lightning-ii-eots.html.

4  Eyers, J. (2023, October 13). *How crypto is forcing banks, funds towards new digital asset markets.* Australian Financial Review. https://www.afr.com/companies/financial-services/how-crypto-is-forcing-banks-funds-towards-new-digital-asset-markets-20231013-p5ecoc

5  World Economic Forum. (2024, January 11). *Widening Disparities' and Growing Threats Cloud Global Cybersecurity Outlook for 2024.* https://www.weforum.org/press/2024/01/wef24-global-cybersecurity-outlook-2024/

6  Meacham, J. (2020). Great Leadership in a Time of Crisis. New York Times. https://www.nytimes.com/2020/03/24/books/review/great-leadership-in-a-time-of-crisis.html#:~:text=Still%2C%20as%20Winston%20Churchill%20once,%2C%20to%20broad%2C%20sunlit%20uplands

7  Frankl, V. (1946). *Man's search for meaning.* Beacon Press.

8  Cyber Leadership Institute. (n.d.). *Our Members.* https://cyberleadershipinstitute.com/our-members/

9  Takahashi, D. (2020, April 23). *Intel CEO: Bad companies are destroyed by crises ... great companies are improved by them.* VentureBeat. https://venturebeat.com/business/intel-ceo-bad-companies-are-destroyed-by-crises-great-companies-are-improved-by-them/

10  Maxwell, J. C. (2011). *The 360 [degree] leader: developing your influence from anywhere in the organization.* Thomas Nelson.

11  World Economic Forum. *Global Cybersecurity Outlook* (2023). https://initiatives.weforum.org/global-cyber-outlook/home

12  Zongo, P. (2018, June 15). *The Five Anchors of Cyber Resilience: Why some enterprises are hacked into bankruptcy, while others easily bounce back.* CISO Advisory.

13   IANS & Artico Search. (2023). *2023 CISO Compensation Benchmark Summary Report.* https://www.iansresearch.com/resources/infosec-content-downloads/research-reports/2023-ciso-compensation-benchmark-report

14   Argyle, D., Schreuder, J., & Zongo, P. (2020). *Cyber Leadership Program.* Cyber Leadership Institute. https://cyberleadershipinstitute.com/cyber-leadership-program-9/ .

15   Ruma, L. (Host). (2020, January 30). *Cybersecurity in 2020: The Rise of the CISO.* (No. 12) [Audio Podcast Episode]. In *Business Lab.* https://www.technologyreview.com/2020/02/24/276013/cybersecurity-in-2020-the-rise-of-the-ciso/

16   Porter, M. E. (1996, November–December). What Is Strategy? *The Magazine – Harvard Business Review. 74*(6), 61–78. https://hbr.org/1996/11/what-is-strategy

17   Bradford, M.E. (2018, December 14). *10 Top Executive Resume Tips For 2019.* Forbes. https://www.forbes.com/sites/forbescoachescouncil/2018/12/14/10-top-executive-resume-tips-for-2019/?sh=3dd2b0081a47

18   Pasteur Brewing. (2010, December 19). *Louis Pasteur: Chance Favors the Prepared Mind.* https://www.pasteurbrewing.com/louis-pasteur-chance-favors-the-prepared-mind/#:~:text=On%20December%207%2C%201854%2C%20as

19   Argyle, D. (2023). *CISO Playbook: First 100 Days.* Cyber Leadership Institute. https://cyberleadershipinstitute.com/ciso-playbook-first-100-days/

20   Bradt, G. (2016, July 27). *Want the Job? Bring a 100-Day Action Plan to the Interview.* LinkedIn. https://www.linkedin.com/pulse/want-job-bring-100-day-action-plan-interview-george-bradt/

21   Cyber Leadership Institute. (2022, January 14). *Saira Hassan – Beating the competition in interviews to land the CISO role.* [Video]. YouTube. https://www.youtube.com/watch?v=7nFH2k02AHw

22   Argyle, D. (2023). *CISO Playbook: First 100 Days.* Cyber Leadership Institute. https://cyberleadershipinstitute.com/ciso-playbook-first-100-days/

23   Scholtz, T. (2016). *A CISO's First 100 Days.* Bank Info Security. https://www.bankinfosecurity.com/interviews/interview-gartners-tom-scholtz-i-3325

24   Zongo, P., & Schreuder, J. (2023). *CISO Playbook: Compelling Board Cyber Risk Reporting.* Cyber Leadership Institute. https://cyberleadershipinstitute.com/ciso-playbook-compelling-board-cyber-risk-reporting/

25   Aguas, T., Kark, K., & François, M. (2016). The New CISO. Leading the strategic security organization. *Deloitte Review. 19.* 73–89. https://www2.deloitte.com/content/dam/insights/us/articles/ciso-next-generation-strategic-security-organization/DR19_TheNewCISO.pdf

26   Monty's Definition of Leadership. (1946, January 12). *The Advocate.* P6.

27   ISACA. (2022). *State of Cybersecurity 2022.* https://www.isaca.org/resources/reports/state-of-cybersecurity-2022

28   Goleman, D. (1995). *Emotional intelligence.* Bantam Books, Inc.

29    Goleman, D. (1995). *Emotional intelligence.* Bantam Books, Inc.

30    Goleman, D. (1998). *What Makes A Leader?* Harvard Business Review Classics. https://store.hbr.org/product/what-makes-a-leader-harvard-business-review-classics/10101

31    Cherniss, C. (2000) *Emotional Intelligence: What it is and Why it Matters.* Consortium for Research on Emotional Intelligence in Organizations. https://www.eiconsortium.org/reports/what_is_emotional_intelligence.html

32    Gregersen, H. (2018). *Questions Are the Answer: A Breakthrough Approach to Your Most Vexing Problems at Work and in Life.* HarperCollins.

33    Mazzola, C. (2024, January 1). *The Future of CISO: From Technical Expert to Business Leaders.* PECB Insights. https://insights.pecb.com/future-ciso-from-technicalexpert-business-leaders/

34    Lauricella, T., & Schaninger, B. (2020, May 28). *A data-backed approach to stakeholder engagement.* McKinsey & Company. https://www.mckinsey.com/capabilities/people-and-organizational-performance/our-insights/the-organization-blog/a-data-backed-approach-to-stakeholder-engagement

35    Cialdini, R. B. (2007). *Influence: The Psychology of Persuasion.* Collins.

36    Greene, R. (1998). *The 48 laws of power.* Profile.

37    Cialdini, R. B. (2007). *Influence: The Psychology of Persuasion.* Collins.

38    McDonald, R. and Bremner, R. (2020). *When It's Time to Pivot, What's Your Story?* Harvard Business Review. https://hbr.org/2020/09/when-its-time-to-pivot-whats-your-story.

39    Martin, S. (2015, May 28). *Get Your Message Across to a Skeptical Audience.* Harvard Business Review. https://hbr.org/2015/05/get-your-message-across-to-a-skeptical-audience.

40    Baldoni, J. (2008, November 19). *Leader's Credibility is Golden.* Harvard Business Review. https://hbr.org/2008/11/leaders-credibility-is-golden

41    Winnefeld Jr, J., Kirchhoff, C., & Upton, D. (2015). Cybersecurity's Human Factor: Lessons from the Pentagon. Harvard Business Review. https://hbr.org/2015/09/cybersecuritys-human-factor-lessons-from-the-pentagon

42    Security Magazine. (2023). Between 80 and 95% of cyberattacks begin with phishing. https://www.securitymagazine.com/articles/99696-between-80-and-95-of-cyberattacks-begin-with-phishing

43    The Editors of Encyclopaedia Britannica. (2024). *Anglo-Zulu War.* Britannica. https://www.britannica.com/place/Zululand

44    Maxwell, J. C. (2011). *The 360 [degree] leader: developing your influence from anywhere in the organization.* Thomas Nelson.

45    Collins, J. (2001). *Good to Great.* Random House.

46    KPMG. (2021, October). *PROTECT. TRANSFORM.* https://assets.kpmg.com/content/dam/kpmg/au/pdf/2021/powered-cyber-lead-factsheet.pdf

47    Okta. (2023). *Customer Identity Trends Report.* https://www.okta.com/sites/default/files/2023-05/CIT_Report_2023.pdf

48    Deloitte. (2016). *The Deloitte Consumer Review. Navigating Cyber Risks: Smooth Seas or Stormy Skies Ahead?* https://www.deloitte.com/content/dam/Deloitte/ie/Documents/ConsumerBusiness/IE_CB_ConsumerTrackerSurvey_0316_FINAL.pdf

49    Porter, M. E. (1996, November–December). What Is Strategy? *The Magazine – Harvard Business Review. 74*(6), 61–78. https://hbr.org/1996/11/what-is-strategy

50    Nieto-Rodriguez, A. (2016, December 13). *How to Prioritize Your Company's Projects.* Harvard Business Review. https://hbr.org/2016/12/how-to-prioritize-your-companys-projects

51    Gartner. (2023, September 28). *Gartner Forecasts Global Security and Risk Management Spending to Grow 14% in 2024. Public Cloud Services Growth to Bolster Cloud Security Spending.* [Press release]. https://www.gartner.com/en/newsroom/press-releases/2023-09-28-gartner-forecasts-global-security-and-risk-management-spending-to-grow-14-percent-in-2024

52    Ng, A. (2024, January 22). *The Overloaded Toolbox: Cybersecurity Tool Bloat and Why It Will Matter in 2024.* CDOTrends. https://www.cdotrends.com/story/3765/overloaded-toolbox-cybersecurity-tool-bloat-and-why-it-will-matter-2024

53    Ponemon Institute. (2020). *The 2020 Cyber Resilient Organization Study.* https://www.ibm.com/account/reg/us-en/signup?formid=urx-45839

54    SEEK. (2024, March). *Incident Manager Salary in AU.* https://www.seek.com.au/career-advice/role/incident-manager/salary

55    National Cybersecurity Alliance. (2022, July 1). *Identify Your 'Crown Jewels'.* https://staysafeonline.org/cybersecurity-for-business/identify-your-crown-jewels/

56    Permanent Subcommittee On Investigations. (2019, March 6). *How Equifax Neglected Cybersecurity And Suffered A Devastating Data Breach.* Committee on Homeland Security and Governmental Affairs. https://nsarchive.gwu.edu/document/18370-national-security-archive-u-s-senate-permanent

57    Bailey, T. (2022, August 23). *How to Combat Cybersecurity Burnout – and Keep Your Company Secure.* Mimecast. https://www.mimecast.com/blog/how-to-combat-cybersecurity-burnout--and-keep-your-company-secure/#_edn3

58    McKinsey & Company. (2019, March). *Perspectives on transforming cybersecurity.* https://www.mckinsey.com/~/media/McKinsey/McKinsey%20Solutions/Cyber%20Solutions/Perspectives%20on%20transforming%20cybersecurity/Transforming%20cybersecurity_March2019.ashx#:~:text=Companies'%20spending%20on%20cybersecurity%20does,correlate%20with%20level%20of%20protection.&text=Business%20leaders%20at%20all%20levels,responsibility%20of%20the%20IT%20department

59    Casey, T. (2018, May 28). *Survey: 27 Percent of IT professionals receive more than 1 million security alerts daily.* Imperva. https://www.imperva.com/blog/archive/27-percent-of-it-professionals-receive-more-than-1-million-security-alerts-daily/

60    CRI Group. (n.d.) *Intellectual Property: What do the statistics indicate?* https://crigroup.com/intellectual-property-what-do-the-statistics-indicate/

61    KPMG. (2016). Bangladesh hack indicates rising sophistication of attacks. https://assets.kpmg.com/content/dam/kpmg/xx/pdf/2016/08/swift-it.pdf

62    Mulvaney, M. (2018, October 25). *Fiscal Year 2018-2019 Guidance on Federal Information Security and Privacy Management Requirements.* https://trumpwhitehouse.archives.gov/omb/information-for-agencies/memoranda/#memoranda-2018

63    U.S. House of Representatives Committee on Oversight and Government Reform. (2018, December 10). *The Equifax Data Breach.* https://oversight.house.gov/report/committee-releases-report-revealing-new-information-on-equifax-data-breach/

64    Bibby, P. (2012, February 16). *ING takes a $30m hit in accountancy fraud case.* The Sydney Morning Herald. https://www.smh.com.au/business/ing-takes-a-30m-hit-in-accountancy-fraud-case-20120215-1t6ru.html

65    InfoSecurity Magazine. (2014, March 13). *Target May Have Ignored Pre-breach Intrusion Warning.* https://www.infosecurity-magazine.com/news/target-may-have-ignored-pre-breach-intrusion/

66    U.S. House of Representatives Committee on Oversight and Government Reform. (2018, December 10). *The Equifax Data Breach.* https://oversight.house.gov/report/committee-releases-report-revealing-new-information-on-equifax-data-breach/

67    WIPO (n.d.) *What is Intellectual Property?* https://www.wipo.int/about-ip/en/#:~:text=Intellectual%20property%20(IP)%20refers%20to,and%20images%20used%20in%20commerce.

68    The National Bureau of Asian Research. (2013). *Commission on the Theft of American Intellectual Property (IP Commission) Report.* https://www.loc.gov/item/lcwaN0009018/

69    The National Bureau of Asian Research. (2013). *Commission on the Theft of American Intellectual Property (IP Commission) Report.* https://www.loc.gov/item/lcwaN0009018/

70    Toren, P. (2012, September 21). *An Analysis of Economic Espionage Act Prosecutions: What Companies Can Learn From It and What the Government Should Be Doing About It!* https://news.bloomberglaw.com/ip-law/an-analysis-of-economic-espionage-act-prosecutions-what-companies-can-learn-from-it-and-what-the-government-should-be-doing-about-it

71    Wagner, J. (2017, June 1). *China's Cybersecurity Law: What You Need to Know.* The Diplomat. https://thediplomat.com/2017/06/chinas-cybersecurity-law-what-you-need-to-know/

72     The US-China Business Council. (2013). Recommendations for Strengthening Trade Secret Protection in China. https://www.uschina.org/sites/default/files/2013.09%20USCBC%20Recommendations%20for%20Strengthening%20Trade%20Secret%20Protection%20in%20China_0.pdf

73     Cybersecurity and Infrastructure Security Agency. (2021, July 8). *DarkSide Ransomware: Best Practices for Preventing Business Disruption from Ransomware Attacks.* https://www.cisa.gov/news-events/cybersecurity-advisories/aa21-131a

74     Cane, A. (2007). *Perspectives: Why do so many technology projects fail?* Financial Times. https://www.ft.com/content/c24b1248-9759-11dc-9e08-0000779fd2ac

75     Flyvbjerg, B., & Budzier, A. (2011, September). *Why Your IT Project May Be Riskier Than You Think.* Harvard Business Review. https://hbr.org/2011/09/why-your-it-project-may-be-riskier-than-you-think

76     Gaillard, J. C. (2018, November 18). *The 4 pillars of a lasting cyber security transformation.* The Digital Transformation People. https://www.thedigitaltransformationpeople.com/channels/cyber-security/the-4-pillars-of-a-lasting-cyber-security-transformation/

77     Morgan, S. (2019, June 10). *Global Cybersecurity Spending Predicted To Exceed $1 Trillion From 2017-2021.* Cybersecurity Ventures. https://cybersecurityventures.com/cybersecurity-market-report/

78     Mee, P., Matheis, M., Swette, K., & Brieger, D. (2019). *Cyber Spend Trends, Opportunities, and Implications for Procurement.* Oliver Wyman. https://www.oliverwyman.com/content/dam/oliver-wyman/v2/publications/2019/October/cyber-spend-trends-opportunities-and-implications-for-procurement.pdf

79     Ondov, Rhonda. (2001). *Managing software projects at AT&T: common risks and pitfalls.* Paper presented at Project Management Institute Annual Seminars & Symposium, Nashville, TN. Newtown Square, PA: Project Management Institute.

80     *The Financial Crisis Inquiry Report.* (2011). The Financial Crisis Inquiry Commission.

81     Tanium Staff. (2016). What Does Cybersecurity Awareness Mean to You? https://www.tanium.com/blog/what-does-cybersecurity-awareness-mean-to-you/

82     Heidrick & Struggles. (2023). *Board Monitor US.* https://www.heidrick.com/en/insights/boards-governance/board-monitor-us-2023

83     Australian Prudential Regulation Authority. (2021, November 23). *Improving cyber resilience: the role boards have to play.* https://www.apra.gov.au/news-and-publications/improving-cyber-resilience-role-boards-have-to-play

84    Daisley, M. & Nottingham, L. (2021, September 16). *Improve Your Board's Risk Visibility with One Critical Factor: Courage.* NACD. https://www.nacdonline.org/all-governance/governance-resources/directorship-magazine/online-exclusives/improve-your-boards-risk-visibility-with-one-critical-factor-courage2/

85    Casse, D. (2023, June 29). *3 Ways to Nail Your Presentation to the Board.* Harvard Business Review. https://hbr.org/2023/06/3-ways-to-nail-your-presentation-to-the-board

86    Milică, L. & Pearlson, K. (2023, May 2). *Boards Are Having the Wrong Conversations About Cybersecurity.* Harvard Business Review. https://hbr.org/2023/05/boards-are-having-the-wrong-conversations-about-cybersecurity

87    Badrick, C. (2018, April 17). *Trying To Get Boardroom Buy-In On Cybersecurity? Try A Material Risk Approach.* Turn-Key Technologies. https://www.turn-keytechnologies.com/blog/article/trying-to-get-boardroom-buy-in-on-cybersecurity-try-a-material-risk-approach

88    Milică, L. & Pearlson, K. (2023, May 2). *Boards Are Having the Wrong Conversations About Cybersecurity.* Harvard Business Review. https://hbr.org/2023/05/boards-are-having-the-wrong-conversations-about-cybersecurity

89    Chartered Governance Institute UK & Ireland. (2017, December 19). *Board packs are too long and backward looking to be properly effective.* https://www.cgi.org.uk/about-us/press-office/news-releases/board-packs-are-too-long-and-backward-looking-to-be-properly-effective

90    Walker, B. (2023, February 6). *90% Of Boards Are Not Ready For SEC Cyber Regulations.* Forbes. https://www.forbes.com/sites/forbestechcouncil/2023/02/06/90-of-boards-are-not-ready-for-sec-cyber-regulations/?sh=5ee936b088e7

91    Newman, C. A. (2019, January 23). *Lessons for Corporate Boardrooms From Yahoo's Cybersecurity Settlement.* The New York Times. https://www.nytimes.com/2019/01/23/business/dealbook/yahoo-cyber-security-settlement.html

92    NACD. (2017). *NACD Director's Handbook on Cyber-Risk Oversight.* https://boardleadership.nacdonline.org/Cyber-Risk-Handbook-GCNews.html

93    Daisley, M. & Nottingham, L. (2021, September 16). *Improve Your Board's Risk Visibility with One Critical Factor: Courage.* NACD. https://www.nacdonline.org/all-governance/governance-resources/directorship-magazine/online-exclusives/improve-your-boards-risk-visibility-with-one-critical-factor-courage2/

94    Patton, G, S. (1944, June 5). *Speech to the Third Army.* What So Proudly We Hail. https://www.whatsoproudlywehail.org/wp-content/uploads/2013/03/Patton_Speech-to-the-Third-Army.pdf

95    Zongo, P. (2018, June 15). *The Five Anchors of Cyber Resilience: Why some enterprises are hacked into bankruptcy, while others easily bounce back.* CISO Advisory.

96    Argyle, D. (2023). *Cyber Resilience Indices Template.* Cyber Leadership
      Institute. https://hub.cyberleadershipinstitute.com/posts/cyber-resilience-
      indices-template

97    Zinnsser, W. (2013, April 30). *Writing to Learn: How to Write – and Think –
      Clearly About Any Subject at All.* Harper Paperbacks.

98    The University of Oklahoma. (n.d). *Crisis Communication Strategies.* https://
      www.ou.edu/deptcomm/dodjcc/groups/02C2/Johnson%20&%20Johnson.
      htm

99    Brown, D. (2012, October 9). *Poisoning episode became case study in how to
      respond to crisis.* The Sydney Morning Herald. https://www.smh.com.au/
      national/poisoning-episode-became-case-study-in-how-to-respond-to-
      crisis-20121008-279at.html

100   Caesar-Gordon, A. (2022). Electric Airwaves. https://www.electricairwaves.
      com/40-anniversary-of-1982-johnson-and-johnson-tylenol-crisis/

101   Zongo, P. (2018, June 15). *The Five Anchors of Cyber Resilience: Why some
      enterprises are hacked into bankruptcy, while others easily bounce back.* CISO
      Advisory.

102   Ponemon Institute. (2023). *Cost of a Data Breach Report 2023.* IBM. https://
      www.ibm.com/reports/data-breach

103   European Union. (2016, April 27). *Art. 33 GDPR Notification of a personal
      data breach to the supervisory authority.* https://gdpr-info.eu/art-33-gdpr/

104   McGinn, D. (2017, November–December) Leading, Not Managing, in Crisis.
      *The Magazine – Harvard Business Review.* https://hbr.org/2017/11/leading-
      not-managing-in-crisis

105   Banerdh, W. (2019, April 30). *10 of the Best Open Source Threat Intelligence
      Feeds. D3 Security.* https://d3security.com/blog/10-of-the-best-open-source-
      threat-intelligence-feeds/

106   Venezia, P. (2014, 23 June). *Murder in the Amazon cloud. InfoWorld.* https://
      www.infoworld.com/article/2608076/data-center/%20murder-in-the-
      amazon-cloud.html

107   C-Net Systems. (n.d.). *Tape Backup Risks vs Online Backup. https://www.*
      cnetsys.com/offsite-data-backup/tape-backup-risks-vs-online-backup/

108   PCI Security Standards Council. (2020). *Responding to a Cardholder Data
      Breach.* https://www.pcisecuritystandards.org/documents/Responding_
      to_a_Cardholder_Data_Breach.pdf

109   Kral, P. (2012 February 21). *Incident Handler's Handbook.* SANS. https://
      www.sans.org/reading-room/whitepapers/incident/incident-handlers-
      handbook-33901

110   Ironbridge Legal. (2023, November 24). *Federal Court rejects Optus' legal
      privilege claim. When does privilege apply to forensic investigation reports?*
      https://ironbridgelegal.com.au/legal-professional-privilege-dominant-
      purpose/

111    Microsoft. Incident Response Reference Guide. (n.d). https://info.microsoft. com/rs/157-GQE-382/images/EN-US-CNTNT-emergency-doc-digital.pdf

112    Reik, T. (1965). Curiosities of the Self: Illusions We Have about Ourselvesby Theodor Reik, Essay 3: The Unreachables: The Repetition Compulsion in Jewish History, Quote Page 133. Farrar, Straus & Giroux.

113    Fiegerman, S. (2017, September 8). *Equifax Twitter account to followers: 'Happy Friday!'* CNN Business. https://money.cnn.com/2017/09/08/ technology/business/equifax-twitter-customer-service/index.html

114    Financial Times. (2014, December 1). *M&A cyber hackers target deal information*. https://www.ft.com/content/b4d6eab4-78e4-11e4-b518-00144feabdco

115    Forescout. (2019, June 24). *Forescout Study Reveals Cybersecurity Concerns on the Rise Amid M&A Activity*. https://www.forescout.com/press-releases/ forescout-study-reveals-cybersecurity-concerns-on-merger-and-acquisition-activity/

116    Australian Cyber Security Centre. (2022, June 10). *Mergers, Acquisitions and Machinery of Government Changes*. Australian Government Australian Signals Directorate. https://www.cyber.gov.au/resources-business-and-government/governance-and-user-education/governance/mergers-acquisitions-and-machinery-government-changes

117    Zongo, P. (2020, February 10). *Managing Cyber Security Risks in Mergers and Acquisitions: Ten Essentials*. Cyber Leadership Institute. https:// cyberleadershipinstitute.com/managing-cyber-security-risks-in-mergers-and-acquisitions-ten-essentials/

118    Beyond Trust. (2023, June 6). *What is Persistence in Cybersecurity and How Do You Stop an Advanced Persistent Threat (APT)?* https://www.beyondtrust. com/blog/entry/what-is-persistence-in-cybersecurity

119    IBM. (2014). *IBM Security Services 2014 Cyber Security Intelligence Index*. https://i.crn.com/sites/default/files/ckfinderimages/userfiles/images/crn/ custom/IBMSecurityServices2014.PDF

120    Freedberg, S.J., Jr. (2015, April 20). *Navy Rolls Out CYBERSAFE: 'Our Operational Network Is Under Fire'.* Breaking Defense. https:// breakingdefense.com/2015/04/navy-rolls-out-cybersafe/

121    Robinson, S. (2024, March). *General Data Protection Regulation (GDPR)*. TechTarget. https://www.techtarget.com/whatis/definition/General-Data-Protection-Regulation-GDPR

122    Macquad, M. (2010). *The Untold Story of NotPetya, the Most Devastating Cyberattack in History*. Wired Magazine. https://www.wired.com/story/ notpetya-cyberattack-ukraine-russia-code-crashed-the-world/